THE VIRTUAL REFERENCE EXPERIENCE

Integrating Theory Into Practice

Edited by

R. David Lankes   Joseph Janes

Linda C. Smith   Christina M. Finneran

The Virtual Reference Desk Series

Neal-Schuman Publishers, Inc.
New York   London

Published by Neal-Schuman Publishers, Inc.
100 William Street, Suite 2004
New York, NY 10038

Printed and bound in the United States of America.

The paper used in this publication meets the minimum requirements of American National Standard for Information Sciences—Permanence of Paper for Printed Library Materials, ANSI Z39.48–1992.

Manufactured in the United States of America.

Library of Congress Cataloging-in-Publication Data

The virtual reference experience : integrating theory into practice / edited by
    David R. Lankes . . . [et al.].
        p.   cm.
    Includes bibliographical references and index.
    ISBN 1-55570-512-X (alk. paper)
    1. Electronic reference services (Libraries). I. Title.

Z711.45 .V573 2004

2004053850

Contents

List of Tables

List of Figures

Preface

The impetus for *The Virtual Reference Experience: Integrating Theory into Practice* was the Fourth Annual Virtual Reference Desk (VRD) Conference held recently in San Antonio, Texas. The VRD Conference has become the premiere event for digital reference practitioners and researchers. The success of the conference demonstrates the synergy that results from the sharing of ideas and perspectives by researchers and practitioners. Select papers from the conference have been developed, updated, and refined for inclusion in this edited work. With the new material in this volume, we hope to extend that synergy beyond the conference to practitioners' real-world practices, researchers' studies, and students' thinking.

We have organized these topics according to scale, or roughly what researchers call units of analysis. The first two parts focus on individuals: patrons and librarians. The third examines digital reference services, which may exist either within a particular organization or as a shared effort between organizations. The final part looks at the broader context of digital library services: the societal, legal, and political environment in which these services operate.

We begin the book with a subject that has been much too neglected to date: patrons. *Part I: Patrons of Virtual Reference Services* looks at what four studies tell us about people who use digital reference services. Chapter 1 shows trends of AskERIC users over a four-year period. Chapter 2 reports on patron attitudes and usage of chat reference services, as well as chat applications in other aspects of their lives. Chapter 3 provides us with insight into what potential patrons of virtual reference report are their needs, and their suggestions regarding the marketing of such services. Chapter 4 discusses the quandary of patrons expecting services that exceed what digital reference service can reasonably deliver.

Part II: Virtual Reference Librarians shifts from users to experts by focusing on the training of practicing librarians and library science students. Chapter 5 addresses the lack of formal training; Chapter 6, utilizing a post-training survey, evaluates the effectiveness of an institution's training; Chapter 7 discusses effective computer-mediated communication techniques for building rapport with patrons.

In *Part III: Virtual Reference Services and Policies*, we return to the common service perspective, yet with a somewhat more critical view. Chapters 8 and 9 respectively study the policies as disseminated to the public and the guidelines shared among professionals. In Chapter 10 the boundaries of digital reference services are questioned, and arguments are made to extend them to instruction, readers' advisory, and roving reference.

We look beyond a particular digital reference service in *Part IV: Broader Context of Virtual Reference* and concentrate on the societal, political, and legal perspectives. Here we incorporate the keynote address of the VRD Conference by Robert S. Martin, Director of the Institute for Museum and Library Services, as Chapter 11. A national leader in museum and library policy, Dr. Martin's thoughtful essay links digital reference to the essential outcome to be strived for: increased learning. Chapter 12 presents a most disturbing examination of the part of USA Patriot Act which codifies the federal government's surveillance procedures. In this important chapter, the impact of such surveillance on digital reference transactions is analyzed. Finally, we close with a chapter discussing a proposed digital reference research agenda. This agenda presents the primary areas of inquiry within digital reference, and illustrates how they can be framed by different lenses or fields, such as policy, systems, behavior, or evaluation.

The Virtual Reference Experience: Integrating Theory into Practice is not necessarily intended to be read in order. For practitioners wanting to implement or improve their digital reference service, the more immediate relevance of a section may be dependent on the specific area of their project under study at a particular time. The book could also be used as a reader for a digital reference course that addresses current issues and challenges facing the digital reference practitioner of today.

The Virtual Reference Experience: Integrating Theory into Practice represents the latest thinking and frames the most important current issues in the digital reference arena and spans an array of digital reference topics. The digital age is upon us, and reference service is clearly undergoing a metamorphosis to accommodate the full potential of digital reference. Our challenge is to expedite that process by fostering the advancement and dissemination of innovative thinking and diversity of ideas. We hope that the VRD Conference in San Antonio and this resulting publication are significant steps in that direction, helping to define and achieve a digital reference universe that will fulfill its great potential.

Christina M. Finneran
Editor

Acknowledgments

The editors wish to thank the people who have contributed, directly and indirectly, to this book. Without the venue of the Fourth Annual Virtual Reference Desk (VRD) Conference, this book would not have come into being.

First and foremost, we want to express our gratitude to the Fourth Annual VRD Conference sponsors: U.S. Department of Education, OCLC Institute, Virtual Reference Desk at the Information Institute of Syracuse, American Library Association's Reference and User Services Association (RUSA), and Syracuse University School of Information Studies. The sponsors' foresight and generosity have enabled practitioners and researchers to come together to share their knowledge, understanding, and implementations within the digital reference domain.

Putting a successful conference together takes a tremendous amount of human creativity and effort. We are grateful to the following staff members from the Virtual Reference Desk and OCLC who played an essential role in planning and organizing the Fourth Annual VRD Conference: Blythe Bennett, Donna Gehring, Patricia Grimsley, Jane Janis, Nancy Lensenmayer, Steve Leonard, Scott Milewski, George Needham, Brian Quackenbush, Mary Ann Semigel, and Joann Wasik.

The authors are grateful to the speakers, panelists, and attendees at the Fourth Annual VRD Conference who enhanced the digital reference dialog. Further, we extend our utmost appreciation to the presenters who made the effort to put their thoughts and experiences to paper and, by disseminating their ideas more widely, have undoubtedly had an impact on future virtual reference efforts in a most constructive way.

In preparing this book, we received myriad assistance from

Blythe Bennett and the indexer Joann Wasik. Finally, we thank Neal-Schuman Publishers for their willingness to bring the products of the VRD Conference to a wider audience through print. We especially want to recognize Michael Kelley, development and production editor, and Charles Harmon, director of publishing.

Introduction

The Integration of Digital Reference

Joseph Janes

What we now think of as "digital reference" has been in existence for about a decade. Hesitantly, informally even and fitfully at first, people began answering questions that came in through the "back door," via e-mail; then we branched out to special-purpose e-mail addresses, to more increasingly sophisticated Web forms, to other synchronous technologies. Finally, software was developed that was specifically designed for the reference enterprises with many features unique to our domain.

It has been quite a decade, with so many librarians trying new things, experimenting, learning from things that worked (and from those that did not); thinking creatively about what is possible and desirable; designing, building, and maintaining services to meet the information needs of their communities; training themselves and their colleagues; creating new resources, then marketing and evaluating those services. The out-pouring of creativity and initiative and goodwill that we have seen over the last decade reinforces for me the dynamism and energy that librarianship has always drawn upon and that has always characterized our professional achievements.

Among the signal achievements of these last several exciting years has been the Virtual Reference Desk project, and, in particular, the annual Virtual Reference Desk (VRD) conference. The volume you now hold in your hands captures some of the

most important research presented at the Fourth VRD conference, held recently in San Antonio, Texas. The breadth of topics and approaches here illustrates how the field has continued
to evolve and grow and specialize.

Which is all to the good. Up to a point.

"Digital reference," as I have said, has been a term of art (under various guises: there's also "virtual reference," "electronic
reference," and a few other names flying around) for about ten
years. Arising, as it did, from a set of technologies both familiar and new, it is not surprising that the use of those technologies to extend traditional notions of reference created its own
way of thinking.

Thus, "digital reference" started out as something different
in some way from "reference" work of other types—and in
many quarters has remained so. This has been recognized and
commented upon broadly—and will be discussed in more detail shortly—and many people have talked about the need to
integrate "digital reference" into "reference."

But there are other important dimensions of integration to
be pondered, and I want to explore them here as well. In addition to the integration of all kinds of reference into a single service, it is also important to pay attention to the integration of
research into practice (and vice versa), and the integration of
all library-based information services into the lives of the people
those services are intended to serve. Finally, I want to think
more broadly yet, and contemplate what we want to achieve
through all this work.

INTEGRATION OF SERVICES

Although the definitive early history of digital reference has yet
to be written, I suspect many of the first services happened more
by accident than by design. I imagine a number of libraries had
rudimentary Web pages that included e-mail addresses, or perhaps they just publicized e-mail addresses through flyers, bookmarks and business cards. Those e-mail addresses got used for
all kinds of communication purposes, but were also used to ask
questions about policies, book renewals, holds, and the capital
of Bolivia. Other librarians, seeing the potential power in digi-

tal communications, launched explicit Internet- or Web-based services at roughly the same time.

Those Bronze Age efforts grew and developed into more fully formed services, based on a lot of sweat equity and, in many cases, not much else. A large proportion of early services were staffed and maintained by the early adopters and true believers, taking advantage of off-hours, slack time at the desk, information and technological resources already at hand, and the excitement and passion of doing something new. Larger and more widely known services such as AskERIC served as inspiration for people just starting out.

What distinguished almost all of those services, though, is that they were seen by just about everybody as separate and different. The librarians building and running them, their colleagues not yet taking part, administrators and supervisors, and I would imagine the people using them, all thought of them as something other than the ongoing, coexisting reference services. It was as though two trains were running on parallel tracks, headed for the same destination, taking effectively the same route but, yet, somehow not seen as the same.

This is only natural and, at least at the beginning, not problematic. Everything was bright, shiny, and new, and these services were finding their way, not getting hugely trafficked (since in many cases they were hidden or badly named and usually not publicized lest they become overwhelmed) and the people involved were learning how to do that work more effectively and efficiently. However, if there are two trains going to the same place, eventually somebody is going to ask why. Justifying a separate add-on service, potentially seen as duplicative or even wasteful, in tight budgetary times, is not easy.

This mercenary argument for integrating services is not even as compelling to me as the commonsense one. From a user perspective, surely it makes good sense to have a number of options for access to reference service (e-mail, Web form, phone, desk, live chat, whichever services are most appropriate for a given community and institution), publicize and describe them all in an integrated and meaningful way, and allow people to decide for themselves which they prefer, either in general or for a given query. We can use our professional judgment to suggest that, say, a person who initiates a chat session might in fact need more detailed assistance, and offer to e-mail them results of a search or suggest even that they come to the library to browse print works.

Thinking about what "reference" is and ought to be for a library's specific clientele and then developing *that* service seems much more reasonable, and straightforward, than duct taping a few very different things together.

INTEGRATION OF RESEARCH AND PRACTICE

I have been struck over the last couple of years at the dramatic growth of research in the digital reference world. Systematic examination and thinking about it has been going on since almost the beginning, of course, but up until fairly recently, there have been only a handful of researchers conducting investigations in this area, along with some descriptive works from practitioners. Lately, though, there has been a marked increase in the number of articles in the professional and scholarly press, the number of research presentations at conferences such as VRD and the American Library Association (ALA), and new doctoral students studying in this area. The work has become increasingly sophisticated and interesting.

One reads articles in the professional literature all the time about how important it would be to have research and practice inform each other. In many areas of librarianship, though, if we reflect honestly, the quality of that conversation is not as high as we might wish. All too often, the scholarly and practitioner communities seem to be pursuing quite different courses. That is unfortunate, and counterproductive, if perhaps not surprising.

I think the digital reference world has bucked that trend. If one looks at the kinds of research questions being asked, the domains in which research is being conducted, and the ways in which the results of that research are being disseminated, I think the digital reference research community has much to be proud of. In fact, we have even seen a major effort in the last two years to identify and articulate a research agenda for digital reference, drawing on experience and theory (Lankes et al., 2003).

I assume, and certainly hope, that that trend will continue, and that research results emerge that are meaningful and useful to the ongoing evolution of reference practice of all kinds. I also hope we begin to embark on more substantive research into the use and users of reference services. A great deal of fine work has examined services, libraries, librarians, their attitudes and practice, but substantially less that has looked at the user population and their experiences, or, for that matter, the people who have not been users of our services.

INTEGRATION INTO COMMUNITIES

One of the great joys of spending life in the groves of academe is being surrounded by youth and vitality. On a recent glorious day, I was walking across campus and was struck, as I so often am, by the range of ways in which I saw people interacting with each other and with technology. Cell phones beyond number, of course, and also personal digital assistants, at least one Blackberry, and other assorted wireless devices. (Mind you, I was observing all this while my trusty iPod was pumping away mp3 files as I walked—Duran Duran, if I am not mistaken.)

While campuses are unique in many ways, I don't think it is uncommon to see much of the same sort of display on the street almost anywhere these days. Add increasingly ubiquitous Internet access, bandwidth, and use, the explosion of text messaging and instant messaging especially among the young, and you get a complex picture of the ways in which people are communicating and dealing with information technology devices. For the record, along the way I also saw lots of people just talking to each other. Technologies tend to find their own niches and often add to, rather than replace or supplant, traditional forms.

There is also a growing body of evidence, from a number of surveys and studies, that the Internet is an ever more important source of information and advice for many people on issues both minor and substantial, including a large number of things that would have been "library" questions only a few years ago. A generation ago, people had far fewer options for getting information on demand. They could ask a friend, look something up, contact a library, maybe a few other possibilities.

Today, of course, it is an on-demand world. Music files can be downloaded, TiVo can record and store television programs to be viewed at leisure, pay-per-view services now allow movies to begin at almost any time. The information world that most people live in is far more fully featured and complex than ever before, with substantially more sources information more of the time, from almost anywhere. Without a doubt, reference services must be designed to operate in that kind of world.

Significantly, though, this describes the information world for most people, but not for all. Among the responsibilities of the library world is that we serve all the members of our clientele, including people who do not have lots of access, who live in much more impoverished information worlds.

Regardless of the technological sophistication of that information world, what is truly important is that the library and its reference service be central to it. When information needs arise, it is not important that people always contact or use the library; it is not important that they think of the library first. What is important is that the library is in the mix, that it is one of the sources and services that are in people's minds when they try to satisfy an information need.

That will happen if the services are designed around the clientele—their information needs and communities—and to fit in with how they want to get and use information.

THE PREFERRED OUTCOME

Where does this all leave us? Surely, if we are able to achieve all these forms of integration, we will have the right, best information service for all purposes. Except of course there is not one best service. There are as many flavors of information services as there are settings, communities, institutions, and clienteles. There will obviously be overlap and commonalities, but each setting will have its own idiosyncrasies and requirements and opportunities.

The preferred outcome is this: understand users and communities and their information needs, think hard and creatively about the nature of the information services that will help them to meet those needs, and then plan those services in such a way that they will succeed. The best reference services have always done precisely that.

Envisioning the best possible service for each environment, paying careful attention to making it seamless and easy to use, drawing on research in the context of practice, and working to achieve centrality in the information lives of its users are all integral to success. The papers here are steps in the right direction; enjoy.

REFERENCES

Lankes, R. David, Scott Nicholson, and Abby Goodrum, eds. 2003. *The Digital Reference Research Agenda*. Chicago: Association of College and Research Libraries.

PART I

Patrons of
Virtual Reference Services

OVERVIEW

How to best serve patrons is an especially important challenge in virtual reference. Patrons' prior experience with synchronous and asynchronous communication technologies can, needless to say, run a wide gamut. Further, their expectations of how virtual reference can serve them will often go beyond the service's capability.

The following four chapters not only increase our understanding of virtual reference patrons, but also demonstrate the variety of methods we can use to study such patrons. Jeffrey Pomerantz analyzes the results of multiple surveys over a four-year span to provide an interesting historical analysis of how characteristics of the patrons, such as their locations and roles, have changed. At their multicampus institution, Linda Frederiksen, Joel Cummings, and Lara Ursin conduct surveys on attitudes and use of chat in general, and more specifically on the satisfaction of the library's chat reference service. Rather than studying patrons who have used a virtual reference service, Beth Thomsett-Scott uses focus groups to learn from potential users how to better design and promote a virtual reference service. Finally, Joseph E. Straw analyzes the transcripts of chat reference interactions to identify the patrons' expectations and suggest how the librarians can meet or negotiate around them.

Together these authors have elicited input from a variety of patrons (potential users, first-time users, and regular users) and analyzed the data quantitatively and qualitatively to enhance our understanding of patrons' needs, and have together provided useful insights as to how best to meet those needs.

Chapter 1

A Repeated Survey Analysis of AskERIC User Survey Data, 1998–2002

Jeffrey Pomerantz

Four surveys of users of the AskERIC e-mail reference service were conducted during the years 1998, 2000, 2001, and 2002. Each survey presented a snapshot of the AskERIC user population and user satisfaction at a single point in time. This paper reanalyzes the findings from these surveys utilizing repeated survey techniques and presents the evolution of some of the demographics of AskERIC's user population over time, as well as the evolution of AskERIC user behavior. In examining what is perhaps the oldest AskA service, this analysis of AskERIC data sheds light on the evolution of all AskA services and of e-mail-based reference services in general.

INTRODUCTION

The Educational Resources Information Center (ERIC) (www.eric.ed.gov), funded by the U.S. Department of Education, has been providing access to literature on education research and practice since 1966. At the heart of ERIC is the largest education database in the world, containing more than a million bibliographic records. The mission of the ERIC system is to improve American education by increasing and facilitating the use of educational research and information to improve practice in learning, teaching, educational decision making, and research, wherever and whenever these activities take place (Educational Resources Information Center [ERIC] Annual Report, 2002). An excellent and thorough history of the ERIC system may be obtained by reading Burchinal (2000).

In January 2004, however, the Department of Education implemented a reengineering plan for ERIC. The ERIC database continues to exist, but the ERIC system is no longer the nationwide information network that it formerly was. The ERIC system was formerly composed of 16 subject-specific clearinghouses, associated adjunct clearinghouses, and support components, all of which have been closed. AskERIC, too, has been discontinued.

AskERIC was a personalized Internet-based reference service providing education information to teachers, librarians, counselors, administrators, parents, and anyone interested in education throughout the United States and also the world. It began in 1992 as a project of the ERIC Clearinghouse on Information and Technology and was, until its dissolution, one of several projects under the umbrella of the Information Institute of Syracuse (IIS) at Syracuse (N.Y.) University. While operational, AskERIC encompassed the resources of the entire ERIC system and beyond, and used the subject expertise of the 16 ERIC clearinghouses to respond to patrons' requests for education information. AskERIC served an average of 35,000 users a year.

BACKGROUND

Digital Reference

The term "digital reference" is used in this paper rather than the equally popular and nearly synonymous term "virtual reference." In her book *The Virtual Reference Librarian's Handbook*, Lipow (2002) acknowledges that there has been to date little agreement in the use of these terms. She defines the term digital reference broadly to indicate "a broad range of electronic ref-

erence activities that include creating and managing digital reference resources . . . *as well as* providing personalized reference
service *via* the Internet" (Lipow, 2002: xix), and the term virtual
reference more narrowly to indicate only reference service provided via synchronous technologies: chat, instant messaging,
voice over IP, etc. Lipow's distinction between these terms will
be maintained in this study, as the service formerly offered by
AskERIC with which this study is concerned was limited to
asynchronous interactions—digital reference conducted via e-
mail or Web forms. It should be noted that the AskERIC Live!
Service was offered from late 2001 until AskERIC's dissolution.
The AskERIC Live! Service was a chat-based service utilizing
the 24/7 Reference software (www.247ref.org). Thus, AskERIC
made inroads into the arena of *virtual* reference in addition to
its longer-standing *digital* reference services. The AskERIC Live!
Service was, however, not the object of any of the surveys reanalyzed for this paper and will not be discussed further.

The earliest digital reference services were offered via e-mail
as outgrowths of existing reference desk services in academic
and special libraries (Kittle, 1985; Howard and Jankowski, 1986;
Weise and Borgendale, 1986; Roysdon and Elliott, 1988; Hodges,
1989; Bristow, 1992; Still and Campbell, 1993). These digital reference services were developed both to extend the hours of
availability of the reference desk and to experiment with the
new technology provided by campuswide networks. Many
physical reference desks—in academic, special, and public libraries—continue to offer e-mail-based reference services. Almost as soon as the technology became available to create a Web
form, digital reference services began using Web forms for question submission (Lankes, 1998a; Lagace, 1999). Since that time,
the percentage of questions submitted to services via Web forms
has far outstripped the percentage submitted via e-mail (Carter
and Janes, 2000; Janes, Hill, and Rolfe, 2001).

In the early- to mid-1990s, reference services began to appear on the Internet that were not affiliated with a library, either physical or digital (Bushallow-Wilbur, DeVinney, and
Whitcomb, 1996; Philip, 1997). Lankes (1998a, 9) refers to services of this type of reference service as "AskA" services, "such
as Ask-A-Scientist," since most services of this type specialize

in a particular subject: for example, art (Ask Joan of Art, nmaa-ryder.si.edu/study/nav-joan.html), education (AskERIC), mathematics (Ask Dr. Math, mathforum.org), oceanography (Ask Shamu, www.seaworld.org/ask-shamu), etc. Having started in 1992, AskERIC was the first AskA service, followed by the Internet Public Library, started in 1995 (LeJeune, 1997).

AskA services arrived on the reference scene with little fanfare. Indeed, even innovators in the field took some time to recognize that there were unique aspects to AskAs that set them apart from digital reference services in general: Lankes and Kasowitz (1998, 8) wrote that "digital reference services are also referred to as AskA services." By the turn of the millennium, however, AskA services had been established as unique, so that Janes, Hill, and Rolfe (2001, 1106) could declare that AskA services "are human mediated, nonlibrary, commercial, or noncommercial information service projects that offer self-declared expert answers to user questions in innumerable subject areas, for free or for fee on the World Wide Web." By specifying that AskA services are unaffiliated with libraries, Janes, Hill, and Rolfe set them apart as a unique type of service, separate from the digital reference service offered by libraries.

As of this writing, AskA services have existed for just over ten years. In that time, there have been surprisingly few studies of AskA services as opposed to digital reference services affiliated with a library. Indeed, it was not until AskA services had been in existence for some years that anything was written about them at all. Much of the earliest literature on AskA services concerns the technical details involved in building and maintaining them (Lankes, 1998a, 1998b; Lankes and Kasowitz, 1998; Janes et al., 1999). To date, only two studies exist that specifically investigate AskA services rather than digital reference services affiliated with libraries. The first of these studies (Lankes, 1998a) deconstructs the processes employed by six AskA services to acquire questions, handle questions within the service, and output answers to the users. The second of these studies (Janes et al., 2001) investigates the types of services offered and offers a variety of performance measures for these services.

The fact that these two studies of AskA services focus on

the provision of the service itself is an indication that, even in these early days of the study of AskA services, there is already a trend towards measures for evaluating the quality of these services. In the past few years, a number of researchers and practitioners have begun to formulate measures for the evaluation of digital reference services. Kasowitz, Bennett, and Lankes (2000) present 12 characteristics that they suggest could be used to judge the quality of a digital reference service; these 12 characteristics form the basis of the Virtual Reference Desk Project's Facets of Quality (www.vrd.org/facets-06-03.shtml). White (2001) presents a framework for the analysis of a digital reference service, which includes 12 questions grouped into three categories concerning the quality of the service. McClure, Lankes, Gross, and Choltco-Devlin (2002) present 35 measures that can be used to assess various aspects of digital reference services. There is naturally some overlap among these various frameworks.

To date, however, there have been no studies published on the user population of digital reference services. When the users are even mentioned in digital reference service studies, they are equated with the questions they ask—that is, such studies proceed as if the only information that the service has about the patron is what is collected with the question. This is often true, since if the librarian sends a follow-up e-mail to the patron asking for clarification, the patron frequently does not reply. Further, there have been no longitudinal studies (at least none that has been published) of the changing face of this user population, or of the services themselves. All existing studies of digital reference services are snapshots of a service at a particular point in time, evaluating the services offered at that point in time. This reanalysis fills that gap in the literature by providing a longitudinal analysis of data collected both about the service and about the use made of that service by its patrons.

AskERIC Surveys

Four surveys of users of the AskERIC e-mail reference service were conducted: in 1998, 2000, 2001, and 2002. The 2000 and 2002 surveys were designed to study users' satisfaction with the

AskERIC e-mail service, while the 1998 and 2001 surveys were designed to study the composition of the AskERIC user population. These surveys were conducted primarily for internal use within AskERIC and the ERIC system: the results were used by the AskERIC service as a feedback mechanism for improving the service and were reported on at annual ERIC system meetings. Executive summaries of the 1998 and 2000 surveys were made publicly available and published on the AskERIC Web site.

These reports were designed to be stand-alone surveys, the data from which presented a snapshot of the AskERIC user population and user satisfaction at a single point in time. This paper reanalyzes the findings from these surveys utilizing repeated-survey techniques. Although these surveys were not designed with this purpose in mind, many questions on the surveys are repeated from one year to the next, making use of repeated-survey techniques possible. The purpose of this reanalysis is twofold: first, to gather data about digital reference user demographics and satisfaction, so that this data may be utilized by the many other digital reference and AskA services in existence to improve their service. Second, as perhaps the oldest AskA service in existence, AskERIC may be viewed as a revelatory case (Yin, 2003). Yin's definition of a revelatory case includes the element of being "previously inaccessible to scientific investigation" (42). While AskERIC has been in existence for a decade, this survey data has not been previously accessible for reanalysis. This reanalysis is not a case study, but it fulfills the other criteria for being a revelatory case: a study of the evolution of AskERIC is "worth conducting because the descriptive information alone will be revelatory" (Yin, 2003, 43) of the evolution of digital reference services.

METHODOLOGY

The findings from the four AskERIC surveys were reanalyzed utilizing repeated-survey techniques. Firebaugh (1997, 1) states that "repeated surveys ask the same questions to different samples of people." The AskERIC surveys were designed to be "one-off" surveys, to provide a snapshot of certain aspects of the state of the AskERIC service at a particular point in time. As a result, consistency of questions from one year to the next was not the primary concern in creating these surveys. Furthermore, these surveys were created by committee, and each committee had a different set of priorities regarding what questions should be asked and what questions from previous years should be redesigned or dropped. Nevertheless, several questions on the surveys were in fact consistent from year to year. It is the data from these repeated questions only that are reanalyzed in this paper.

In repeated surveys, the samples are generally non-overlapping; each sample is composed of entirely new individuals from the population. It is not possible to know whether the samples for the AskERIC surveys were entirely non-overlapping since personal information such as name and e-mail address was removed from the data before they were analyzed for the original reports; they could not be reconstructed for this reanalysis. It is, however, unlikely that there were individuals who responded to AskERIC surveys in more than one year. According to the 2002 *ERIC Annual Report* (ERIC, 2002), AskERIC received 34,181 e-mail requests in 2001. There is, of course, no way to know if these 34,181 requests were submitted by 34,181 different individuals or if—as seems likely—there were some repeat users.

AskERIC received equally large numbers of requests in the other years in which surveys were conducted: 43,405 in 1998; 38,157 in 2000; and 32,645 in 2002 (Jennifer Barth, personal communication). Even if approximately half of all AskERIC users are repeat users, as is indicated by the numbers in Table 1–3, there is still a very small chance that any individuals responded to AskERIC surveys in more than one year. Each of these surveys was administered during a narrow window of time, so only a small fraction of the population of individuals who submitted questions in any given year were solicited for the surveys. Surveys that were sent via e-mail were sent only once to any individual and repeat submissions by e-mail from any individual were deleted prior to the original analysis. Surveys that were administered as Web pages could be filled out more than once by any individual; however, any user who had already filled out a survey during the narrow window of time in which

Table 1–1
AskERIC Survey Response Rates

	# Surveys sent	# Surveys received	Response rate
1998	689	196	28%
2000	443	79	18%
2001	NA	547	NA
2002: round 1	1,151	970	84%
2002: round 2	752	143	19%

it was being administered would probably not be motivated to fill out another.

This reanalysis was therefore performed under the assumption that the samples of respondents were independent from year to year. The sample sizes for the four years in which the AskERIC survey was conducted are presented in Table 1–1.

The AskERIC service formerly maintained both a Web form and an e-mail address for question submission. The Web form asked the user for certain personal data, such as "You are asking this question in your role as a(n)," and "If you are in the United States, what US State are you in?" When a user submitted a question directly to the e-mail address, these data were not collected unless the user provided the information in his or her e-mail message.

The methodology for sampling AskERIC users for the 1998 and 2000 surveys was the same: an e-mail message was sent to every third user of the AskERIC service three days after the user received a response from the service, whether he or she had submitted a question via the Web form or the e-mail address. This e-mail message contained both a link to a Web form containing the survey and the text of the survey itself. The sampling methodology for the 2001 survey was different: for the span of a month, a link was conspicuously placed on most of the pages on the AskERIC Web site to a Web-form survey. Thus, the 2001 survey was "pulled" by AskERIC users rather than being "pushed" to them. The sampling methodology for the 2002 survey was different again; this survey was administered in two parts, over the span of two weeks. The first survey was sent to every user who submitted a question via the Web form; this first survey appeared as a Web form on the confirmation page that a user received when submitting a question to AskERIC via the question-submission Web form. For the second survey, an e-mail message was sent one day after the user received a response from the service; this e-mail message contained both a link to a Web-form survey and the text of the survey itself. A code was included in all survey responses so that the responses from both surveys could be paired for the same patron. For all of the surveys, respondents were instructed that they could fill out the survey electronically, or they could print it out and submit it by mail or fax; respondents did in fact submit surveys by all available methods. Thus, the 1998 and 2000 surveys were sent to a systematic sample from the user population (Fowler, 2002), the 2001 survey sample was self-selected, and the 2002 surveys were sent to all AskERIC users who submitted questions. Further, the 1998 and 2000 populations included users who submitted questions via both the Web and e-mail; the 2001 population included users who may or may not have submitted questions but were merely using the AskERIC Web site; the 2002 population included users who submitted questions only via the Web.

Because of these differences in sampling frames and usage of the AskERIC Web site, it is possible that the user populations sampled for the 1998 and 2000 surveys, the 2001 survey, and the 2002 surveys differ. There is, however, no reason to hypothesize that this is the case; though to be fair, there is no reason to hypothesize that this is *not* the case either. In fact, there is no evidence either way: no studies have been conducted to determine if there are differences between different segments of the populations of digital reference service users. While a self-selection bias exists when survey respondents are volunteers (as in the 2001 survey), it is not clear that these self-selected respondents—or any of the respondent pools for any of the surveys—are in any way unrepresentative of the population of AskERIC users as a whole.

A further limitation of the sampling methodology for all four surveys is the fact that the survey respondents were self-selected. Because the surveys were self-administered and voluntary, only those who selected to participate did so. As with most surveys, there was no way to force users to complete the AskERIC surveys. As Fowler (2002) recommends, the task of completing the surveys was made as simple as possible by creating them as Web forms, by utilizing checkboxes and pull-down menus wherever possible on these Web forms, and by providing links to the Web-form surveys in the e-mail solicitations. Nevertheless, it was beyond the control of the AskERIC service to determine which users would complete or not complete the surveys.

A final limitation of the sampling methodology for the 1998 and 2000 surveys is the fact that in those years surveys were sent only to users who received a response from AskERIC. AskERIC, like many digital reference services, has question-swapping agreements with other digital reference services. AskERIC is a member of the Virtual Reference Desk (VRD) Network, which is both a question-swapping consortium and a digital reference service in its own right. The VRD's description of themselves states that:

> When a subject specific service receives questions which are out of its stated scope area, it can forward those questions to the VRD Network for assistance. If a question cannot be addressed by another participating service, it will be handled by one of the VRD Network Information Specialists (www.vrd.org/network.shtml).

There are a number of other such consortia, both national and local: The QuestionPoint collaborative reference is managed by the Library of Congress and OCLC, while the Metropolitan Cooperative Library System (MCLS) is an association of libraries in the greater Los Angeles area. Of course, only those services that participate are allowed to swap questions within these consortia. As of this writing, the VRD has 30 participants (Blythe Bennett, personal communication), MCLS has 44 full and 26 associate members (www.mcls.org/webpublic/libraries/libraries.cfm), and "over 300 libraries are using QuestionPoint, including users in Australia, Canada, China, England, Germany, the Netherlands, Norway and Scotland" (Penka, 2003, QuestionPoint section, ¶ 3).

Because the 1998 and 2000 surveys were sent only to users who received a response from AskERIC, any users who submitted questions that were deemed out-of-scope and forwarded to the VRD would not have received these surveys. Thus, the user population sampled for these surveys was composed exclusively of users who asked questions within the scope of educational research and practice, parenting, and library science. The same is true of the second 2002 survey, which was also sent only to users who received a response from AskERIC. The first 2002 survey, on the other hand, was sent to all users who submitted questions via the Web form, whether those questions were later deemed out-of-scope or not. The population from which the 2001 survey respondents came was broader still, being all users who visited the AskERIC Web site during the month in which the survey link was displayed. Again, however, because no studies have been conducted to determine if there are differences among different segments of the populations of digital reference service users, there is no reason to hypothesize that the population of users who submitted questions to the AskERIC service is significantly different from the population of users of the AskERIC Web site.

RESULTS

The limitation of repeated-survey techniques is that in order to be applicable, a survey question must actually be repeated. While many questions on the AskERIC surveys were not consistent from one year to the next, many questions did in fact repeat from year to year. It is the data from these repeated questions that are reanalyzed here.

Geographic Location

The question "If you are outside the United States, what country are you in?" is asked on the AskERIC question submission Web form, yet data from this question were reported only for the 2000 and 2002 surveys. Additionally, although the AskERIC question-submission Web form provides the user with a pull-down list of the names of over 240 nations, the 2000 and 2002

Table 1–2
AskERIC User's Location

	Within the U.S.	Outside of the U.S.
2000	59	13
2002	291	160

reports collapsed the responses into two categories: Within the United States, and Outside of the United States. Although it would be interesting to know the specific breakdown of the percentage of users from various nations outside of the United States, those data were not preserved. Unfortunate though this may be, it is understandable given the fact that the mission of the ERIC system, as a project of the U.S. Department of Education, is to improve *American* education; the specific country in which a user is located, if it is not the United States, may therefore be seen to be irrelevant. Users' locations are presented in Table 1–2.

Because of the large value of N in the 2×2 table for this data, the data from this question were analyzed using χ^2 corrected for continuity. The value of χ^2 corrected for continuity = 7.74, which is significant at the 0.05 level. In other words, there was a significant change in the relative percentages of AskERIC users within and outside of the United States from 2000 to 2002.

This finding is particularly interesting since AskERIC's contract with the U.S. Department of Education does not provide funding to market the service. A distinction is made, however, in that dissemination of information in the form of publications, the AskERIC Web site, posters, brochures, bookmarks, and presentations at conferences is encouraged. This begs the question of how users come to know about the AskERIC service, but no data exist from the AskERIC surveys that can be used to answer this question. A further question is why an increasingly greater percentage of users outside of the United States were utilizing the AskERIC service while an increasingly smaller percentage of users within the United States were doing the same. No data collected by the AskERIC surveys can answer this question either; an interesting avenue for future research would be to determine if the use of digital reference services is decreasing within the United States and increasing internationally across all services, or if AskERIC was unique in this regard. Further, it would be interesting to identify the specific nations from which citizens are submitting increasing numbers of questions, since the state of network infrastructure around the world improved considerably in many nations between 2000 and 2002.

Knowing the geographic locations of the users of a digital reference service is interesting, but given the electronic nature of digital reference services, it is unclear how useful such information really is. After all, it might be as easy for users to lie about their locations as to tell the truth. On the AskERIC submission form, for example, there is no mechanism to determine the veracity of a patron's responses (short of, for example, the patron specifying the state as North Carolina and the country as Bolivia). One method of verifying the location of the patron is that utilized by the KnowItNow24x7 digital reference service of the Cleveland (Ohio) Public Library: users are required to enter their zip codes to use the service in an attempt to ensure that the patrons are actually residents of the Cleveland area. It would not, however, be difficult for a patron in North Carolina, or even Bolivia, to look up Cleveland-area zip codes. It is, therefore, impossible to know with certainty that the user of a digital reference service is telling the truth when providing his or her location. This is, however, no different for any respondent of a self-administered survey; one simply has to take it on faith that one's respondents are truthful.

Janes (2002; 2003) proposes a reexamination of the role of the reference transaction in digital reference. It is unlikely that reference could be performed in any media without a transaction between librarian and patron; it may, however, be that certain questions commonly asked in a desk reference transaction may prove to be unnecessary online. The patron's name, for example, is one piece of information that may not be necessary online and raises privacy concerns besides. Is the patron's geographic location similarly of limited usefulness, particularly for AskA services, which are by nature not tied to any specific geographic location?

The AskERIC service asks for a patron's location on their

Web submission form in order to determine what local resources are available to the patron. For example, if the patron's question is about educational standards, it is important for AskERIC to be able to direct the patron to resources from the appropriate state education department. Thus, AskERIC makes use of information about a patron's geographic location in formulating an appropriate answer. For digital reference services serving a patron community distributed geographically, knowing a patron's location may be crucial to formulating an answer.

Furthermore, AskA services do not stand alone: a consequence of existing entirely electronically is a necessarily heavy reliance on networking. One of the primary uses to which AskA services—and digital reference services in general—put networking technology is the routing and assignment of questions. This routing and assignment is referred to as triage (Virtual Reference Desk Project, 1998); a question is routed to a reference or subject expert "answerer" either within a service (when a question is received by a service, a "triager" assigns it to a specific reference or subject expert within that service) or between services (if a question is received by a service that for whatever reason it cannot or will not answer, the triager forwards that question to a different digital reference service). If a question is triaged outside of a service, the patron's geographic location may be quite important. For example, in a study of the triage process in digital reference services, Pomerantz (2003) found that the patron's geographic location was at times a critical element in the triage process.

> [A] respondent stated that his service will, whenever possible, forward questions about Texas to digital reference services in Texas, because libraries in Texas have state-wide access to databases about the state, and thus are able to provide more complete answers about Texas than any library outside of Texas would be able to do. (144)

Thus, the patron's geographic location dictates to the triager the preferred geographic location of an answerer and narrowed the range of possible triage recipients for that particular question. In this case, the patron's location is useful in both triaging a question to the appropriate answerer and in formulating an

Table 1–3
Previous Use of AskERIC

	First-time users	Returning users
1998	94	97
2000	41	34
2001	301	241
2002	665	282

appropriate answer. Information about the patron's location may not be useful for every question or for every patron, but for certain questions it may be crucial.

Repeat Users

The question "Have you used AskERIC more than once?" is one of the few questions that appears on all four AskERIC surveys that is not on the AskERIC question-submission Web form. While this question was asked in all four years, however, only the 1998 and 2002 surveys collected the number of previous uses, if greater than zero. This question was therefore analyzed first according to whether or not the user had previously used the AskERIC service. These data are presented in Table 1–3.

The data from this question were analyzed using the χ^2 statistic. The value of $\chi^2 = 51.75$ with df = 3, which is significant at the 0.05 level. By partitioning Table 1–3 into 2×2 tables, it was determined that the significant difference is between the combined values for the years 1998–2001 and the year 2002. In other words, between the years 1998–2001 the percentage of first-time and returning AskERIC users did not change significantly. Between 2001–2002, however, the relative percentages of first-time and returning AskERIC users changed significantly.

It is difficult to know how to interpret this finding. On the one hand, a single observation (the year 2002) is not enough on which to base a conclusion. The increase of first-time and decrease of returning users is not a significant trend over all four years; it could be that the 2002 values are a fluke, and that if the AskERIC survey were conducted again, the percentages would return to approximately 50/50.

Table 1–4
**Returning Users' Number of Previous Uses
of AskERIC during the Prior Year**

	1–3	4–6	7–10	10+
1998	70	24	11	5
2002	200	46	15	21

On the other hand, the interpretation that the increase of first-time and decrease of returning users is a trend is borne out by the following findings. As mentioned above, the 1998 and 2002 reports provide the number of previous uses a user had made of the AskERIC service. This follow-up question was as follows: "If yes [to 'Have you used AskERIC more than once?'], how many times have you used the service in the past year?" Unfortunately, the data from this question were collected in different units for these two surveys: the 1998 survey grouped numbers of previous uses, while the 2002 survey offered integer values. To compensate for this, the 2002 values were grouped according to the same categories as the 1998 survey data. These data are presented in Table 1–4.

It is evident from these values that the number of times that patrons had previously used the AskERIC service decreases rapidly. This bears out the interpretation that the increase of first-time and decrease of returning AskERIC users is a long-term trend. But this merely begs the question, why should this trend be occurring?

It is certainly desirable that AskERIC—or any digital reference service, for that matter—attract new users. It may not, however, be desirable that AskERIC users be predominantly new users. One well-known measure of satisfaction with a reference service is whether the patron would be willing to ask a question of that service or individual librarian again (Durrance, 1989; Dewdney and Ross, 1994). McClure and others (2002, 30) argue that the statistics on repeat users of a digital reference service "is one of the most important measures to collect" because it can be used as a stand-in for measures of user satisfaction. The use of this finding as a stand-in for user satisfaction, however, is extremely unreliable; a number of other interpretations are possible for the predominance of new users. McClure and others go on to suggest that, to aid in interpretation, this statistic be correlated with data on the patron's reasons for use of the digital reference service. In the absence of data that may be correlated with this, however, we must speculate.

One possibility is that an increasing percentage of AskERIC users had "one-time" information needs: their information needs do not frequently include educational research, but they had a single information need that AskERIC could fulfill. Another possibility is that over time AskERIC users become educated about the ERIC database, search techniques, and the subject area resources available on the various ERIC system Web sites. Indeed, AskERIC responses have always contained elements of bibliographic instruction: a response usually includes the search strategy that the subject or reference expert used to search the ERIC database, as well as annotations and explanations of the other resources provided. Thus, one would hope that over time AskERIC users would become increasingly self-reliant in their information seeking and have less need of the AskERIC service.

Use of AskERIC

Although the question about repeat use of AskERIC was asked on all four AskERIC surveys, a question about what patrons actually use AskERIC *for* was asked only on the 2000 and 2001 surveys. It is important to note that for the question "I use AskERIC for," respondents could check more than one checkbox, so the unit of analysis for this question is not the respondent, but the checkbox checked, that is, the uses of AskERIC. This data is presented in Table 1–5.

The data from this question was analyzed using the χ^2 statistic. The value of $\chi^2 = 49.78$ with df = 9, which is significant at the 0.05 level. By partitioning Table 1–5 into 2×2 tables, it was determined that the significant difference is between the use "Lesson plan ideas" and the combined values for all other uses. In other words, the use of the AskERIC service to locate lesson plans and ideas for lesson plans increased significantly between 2000 and 2001, relative to all other uses of the service.

Table 1–5
Use of AskERIC

	2000	2001
Current research articles and documents	59	297
Graduate research (master's or doctoral thesis)	34	140
Practical teaching tips and strategies	27	197
Obtain information for a third party	21	64
Parenting advice	19	49
Homework assignments	18	132
Lesson plan ideas	17	274
Other	8	38
School board decision making	7	29
My undergraduate education as a future teacher	4	81

This question was asked of all survey respondents, so these findings must be interpreted carefully. It seems likely that repeat and first-time users of a digital reference service will answer this question differently: repeat users may answer this question in terms of the use to which they put the service and the sorts of questions that they generally ask as a general rule, while it seems more likely that first-time users will answer this question in terms of the question at hand. It would therefore be useful to correlate the data from this question with data from the question about the patron's number of previous uses of the service. This is not possible here, however, as all data reported in the AskERIC survey reports were aggregated. Another way around this problem would be to collect data about a patron's use in terms of the question at hand. To elicit that data, the appropriate question might be the question that is frequently asked in reference transactions in desk reference services: "What is your planned use of the information?" This question is actually asked on the AskERIC question-submission Web form, but was not reported in the AskERIC surveys.

Role

The question "You are asking this question in your role as a(n)" appears on the AskERIC question-submission Web form, and

Table 1–6
Role in Which AskERIC
Patron Asked a Question

	1998	2000	2001	2002
K–12 teacher	30	19	198	249
Student	71	22	180	226
Other	27	9	39	90
Parent	18	13	21	53
College faculty	23	6	22	44
Administrator	8	6	15	67
Librarian	19	2	30	29
Preschool teacher	4	2	19	25

was reported in all four AskERIC surveys. It is important to note that respondents could check more than one checkbox in response to this question, so again, the unit of analysis for this question is the checkbox checked (that is, the role selected), and not the respondent. This data is presented in Table 1–6.

The data from this question was analyzed using the χ^2 statistic. The value of $\chi^2 = 101.31$ with df $= 21$, which is significant at the 0.05 level. By partitioning Table 1–6 into 2×2 tables, it was determined that there were several significant differences. The most highly significant difference, however, is between K–12 teacher and the combined values for all other roles. In other words, between the years 1998–2002 the relative percentage of K–12 teachers using the AskERIC service increased significantly, more than any other category.

It is not surprising that K–12 teachers have consistently been the greatest users of the AskERIC service, since that group is the primary audience for AskERIC's service, which is dedicated to educational research and practice. (It is rather unfortunate that educational administrators and college faculty are not greater users of AskERIC.) What is surprising, however, is the significant increase in the percentage of K–12 teachers making use of the AskERIC service. It begs the question of how users come to find out about a digital reference service in the first place; this question cannot, however, be answered from data reported in the AskERIC surveys. It would be a useful avenue for future research.

This finding is also consistent with the finding that the use of the AskERIC service to locate lesson plan ideas increased significantly between 2000 and 2001—the same interval that shows the greatest increase in the percentage of K–12 teachers using the AskERIC service. This is also unsurprising, as most of the lesson plans on AskERIC's Web site are written for use in K–12 classrooms.

Most Useful Resources

The subject and reference experts, called network information specialists, who replied to questions for the AskERIC service provided a variety of resources in their replies, including bibliographic records from the ERIC database, Internet sites, discussion groups, and print resource information. A sample of AskERIC's responses is available online at eduref.org/Virtual/Qa/archives. A question concerning the usefulness of these various resources was asked on the 2000 survey and on round 2 of the 2002 AskERIC surveys. This question had several variations: "If you received _____, please rate the following aspects of this portion of the response," where the blank was filled with one of three options: ERIC citations, Internet sites, discussion groups. One of the aspects that the patron was asked to rate was the relevance of the citation, site, or group to the question. The rating was a Likert scale, with 1=poor and 5=excellent. These data are presented in Table 1–7.

All three portions of AskERIC responses were rated very highly by users as being relevant to their question. This measure is problematic for two reasons. First, relevance can mean different things to different people: an information source may be judged relevant because it fully answers the patron's question, because it partially answers the question, because it points the patron to additional resources, or for other reasons. This question does not make that distinction, however, and treats all forms of relevance as equal. The second problem is that there is no way to determine what portions of AskERIC responses were rated highly by first-time or repeat users of AskERIC. Re-

Table 1–7
**Ratings Frequencies of the Relevance of Portions
of AskERIC Responses**

	2000			2002		
Rating	ERIC citations	Internet sites	Discussion groups	ERIC citations	Internet sites	Discussion groups
1	0	3	0	4	6	0
2	0	2	0	3	6	0
3	5	7	3	15	19	2
4	19	14	3	27	19	7
5	30	35	4	43	50	11

peat users are likely to have an idea of what to expect in an AskERIC response, and so may judge the relevance of the resources provided differently than a first-time user would, who might have no prior expectations about what to expect.

The portion of AskERIC responses that had the greatest percentage of 5 ratings, both in 2000 and 2002, was Internet sites, though interestingly, Internet sites also had the greatest percentage of 1 and 2 ratings. So, while Internet sites were frequently the most relevant portion of the response, occasionally they were the least relevant. After Internet sites, the portions of AskERIC responses that had the greatest percentages of 5 ratings were ERIC citations and then discussion groups. One might hope that ERIC citations would be the most highly rated portion of AskERIC responses, but there are a number of reasons why this might not be the case. Patrons might not have been interested in research articles, which many ERIC citations are; or patrons might simply have wanted to get access to the full text of materials immediately, which one can do with Internet sites but not ERIC citations. The accessibility of the full text of ERIC citations will be discussed further in the next section. Unfortunately, no follow-up question was asked to elicit why certain portions of the response were relevant or not; an interesting avenue for future research would be to investigate what types of resources are useful for answering certain types of questions or relevant in fulfilling certain types of information needs.

ERIC Citations and Full Text

The ERIC database, as discussed above, is the largest education database in the world, containing more than a million bibliographic records. The limitation, however, is that it contains *only* bibliographic records, and not the full text of any of these documents. The ERIC database contains two types of bibliographic records: ERIC documents (ED) and ERIC journal articles (EJ) (www.eric.ed.gov). EJs are articles that have been published in any of the journals indexed in the ERIC database and selected by human source-journal reviewers. EJs can be obtained from libraries or article reprint companies. EDs, on the other hand, are documents that have been submitted for inclusion in the ERIC database and which may not have been published elsewhere. Most EDs can be obtained from any of the more than 900 libraries that maintain an ERIC microfiche collection or from the ERIC Document Reproduction Service (EDRS) (www.edrs.com), though some EDs are only available from the publisher. Most EDs included in the ERIC database after 1992 are available in Adobe Acrobat format from EDRS. In order to obtain these EDs, however, one must have or be affiliated with an institution that has a subscription to EDRS' E*Subscribe service.

Thus, not all users of the ERIC database have easy access to the documents indexed therein. As mentioned above, AskERIC network information specialists provide bibliographic records from the ERIC database in their replies to users' questions; however, it may be that the questioner will not have easy access to the records cited in the answer. The question "If you received ERIC citations, were you able to obtain the full text of these journals/documents?" was therefore asked in the 1998 and 2002 surveys. Data from this question are presented in Table 1–8.

The data from this question were analyzed using the χ^2 statistic. The value of $\chi^2 = 0.78$ with df = 1, which is not significant at the 0.05 level. In other words, between the years 1998–2002 there was no significant change in the relative percentages of AskERIC users who were and who were not able to obtain the full text of the bibliographic records from the ERIC database provided in the reply to their question.

Table 1–8
Ability to Obtain Full Text
of AskERIC Documents

	1998	2002
Yes	80	52
No	52	43

Table 1–9
Source of Full Text for AskERIC Documents

	1998	2002
EDRS	21	15
Journal reprint provider	8	1
Public library	9	12
University library	65	41

Users who were able to obtain the full text of the bibliographic records from the ERIC database provided in the reply to their question were then asked, "How did you obtain the full text?" These data are presented in Table 1–9.

The data from this question were analyzed using the χ^2 statistic. The value of $\chi^2 = 5.81$ with df = 3, which is not significant at the 0.05 level. In other words, between the years 1998–2002 there was no significant change in the relative percentages of AskERIC users who obtained the full text of bibliographic records from the various sources available to them.

This finding is slightly disappointing, since between 1998–2002 EDRS has dramatically increased the number of ERIC documents available in Adobe Acrobat format, so that as of this writing, "approximately 92% of the documents abstracted in ERIC are available from EDRS" (edrs.com/Help/About.cfm). One would hope that the percentage of ERIC users who obtained the full text of documents from EDRS would have increased as EDRS made more of these documents available online. It may be, however, that many first-time users of AskERIC were unfamiliar with EDRS. It may also be that many AskERIC users were not affiliated with institutions that have subscriptions to the E*Subscribe service.

The final question on all four surveys was "What suggestions do you have for improving the service?" One of the most
common suggestions offered by survey respondents was "access to full-text," or any number of variations on that sentiment.
Of course the full text of most EDs *are* available through the
E*Subscribe service. This suggestion, therefore, indicates that
AskERIC users either were not aware that they could access the
full text of ERIC documents through E*Subscribe, or that they
were not affiliated with an institution that had a subscription
to E*Subscribe and were unable or unwilling to pay for access
themselves. Another factor that no doubt influenced responses
to this question is that EJs are *not* available from EDRS; EJs must
be obtained from a library that has the journal in its collection,
through interlibrary loan, or purchased from an article reproduction service.

This all raises an issue for librarianship in general, an issue
for which digital reference services are on the front line: the issue of electronic materials and copyright. Copyright laws are
complex and changing; patrons of digital reference services, and
of libraries in general, may not be fully aware of the copyright
restrictions on various types of materials, of what can and cannot
be made available electronically for free. Bibliographic instruction
is a task that has been performed by reference librarians for as
long as the profession has existed, and the need for instruction
in copyright for digital reference service patrons reaffirms the
need for bibliographic instruction in the online environment.

Discussion

The Methods section of this paper is full of explanations and
caveats concerning inconsistently collected data. This is unfortunately necessary because, as mentioned above, these surveys
were designed to present a snapshot of AskERIC at a single
point in time, and, at those points in time, little consideration
was given to longer-term concerns. This fact throws into sharp
relief the current difficulty of conducting rigorous research utilizing archival data from digital reference services: these data
are often inconsistent, if they exist at all.

There is a long tradition in librarianship of collecting statistics about the reference service provided in physical libraries. A great deal of this collection, however, is simple tick-marks: how many questions were answered by which librarian during his or her shift, and perhaps the topic of the question. Few desk reference data-collection instruments are much more detailed than this, and few desk reference services have conducted any sort of evaluation using these or any other data. Janes (2002, 552) reports that a mere 9% of reference librarians in public and academic libraries state that their libraries have performed "any kind of systematic user evaluation of their digital reference service." Of this small percentage of libraries that have performed evaluations, fewer still have published the results. Saxton (1997), in a meta-analysis of reference service evaluation, identifies 12 measures that have been utilized in multiple studies, including number of total volumes in the reference collection, number of service hours offered per week, and size of the service population. Saxton reviewed 59 research studies of reference service and identified 162 variables that had been used in these studies, but was able to make comparisons across studies for only 12 of these variables. This makes it eminently clear that, while there is work being done to evaluate reference services, most of this work is local, intended to evaluate a single service at a single point in time, with little or no thought to longitudinal studies or generalizability.

As mentioned above, some early work has been conducted to create standards and measures for the evaluation of the quality of digital reference services. Some work has also been conducted to create standardized data-collection instruments for digital reference evaluation; see, for example, the Patron Satisfaction Survey (PaSS)™ (www.vrtoolkit.net/PaSS.html), created by John Richardson and Matthew Schall in 2002. These standards and measures are, however, of very recent vintage, and not enough time has passed since their creation to know how widely they are being utilized in the digital reference community. A measure of success of these standards and measures will be if a meta-evaluation like Saxton's (1997) can be conducted in five or ten years and more than 12 measures are found to be comparable across many services, both nationally and internationally.

Stand-alone surveys, such as the AskERIC surveys, are useful for providing data about a service at a single point in time. Such data are useful for formative evaluation of that one service. In order to conduct research about a service over a longer period of time, or across multiple services, however, it is necessary to plan ahead, deciding what data will be collected by services and ensuring that it is collected consistently over time. It would, for example, have been interesting—as well as possibly useful to the AskERIC service—to know how users discovered the AskERIC service. Unfortunately, the question "How did you find out about the AskERIC service" was asked only on the 1998 survey (53% of users answered that they found out about the AskERIC service from the ERIC Web site, and 14% answered that they were referred by a professor or other individual). These data, aggregated across years, could have been useful to the AskERIC service for marketing purposes, as well as being interesting to other digital reference services looking to increase their "brand recognition."

One further point must be made concerning the difficulty of conducting rigorous scientific research utilizing data from digital reference services: in light of the current political climate and legitimate privacy concerns, any data collected by a digital reference service—indeed, by any library service at all—should be "anonymized" by removing any information that may serve to personally identify the patron or the librarian who participated in the transaction before storing the transaction in any sort of an archive. This is a simple enough matter where e-mail-based digital reference is concerned: deleting the To: and From: lines of the e-mail message, as well as the patron's and the librarian's signature blocks, will go far towards anonymizing an e-mail transaction. Some patrons put personally identifying information in the body of the e-mail message, however, and this requires a judgment call to determine what to delete from the message or whether to simply delete the entire message from the archive. Chat-based digital reference services face the same problem of anonymizing the transaction before storage.

Sadly, instead of taking the time to anonymize transactions before storing them, many libraries are opting for the admittedly easier, but short-sighted, course of simply deleting this rich source of data. Nicholson (2003) refers to this trend as "The Great Data-Wipe of Ought-Three," a potentially tragic loss of libraries' institutional memories. This policy of deleting all transaction data makes conducting rigorous research utilizing data from digital reference services difficult. Indeed, when no data at all exist because a service has decided to simply delete them, all research is impossible. Deleting all library data in order to prevent personal data from being misused, while understandable, is to lose an opportunity to study digital reference services both individually and collectively, and ultimately longitudinally. As Nicholson points out, if we delete our data-based library history, then it becomes impossible to discover patterns of use in library data. More than a hundred years of research exists on desk reference services. Because of the artifactual nature of the digital medium, however, this "shred first, ask questions later" policy precludes the building of any similar body of research on digital reference services, almost before that building process has broken ground.

CONCLUSION

Four surveys of users of the AskERIC e-mail reference service were conducted, during the years 1998, 2000, 2001, and 2002. This paper has reanalyzed the findings from these surveys utilizing repeated-survey techniques. There are several interesting and unexpected findings from this reanalysis, such as the increase of first-time and decrease of returning users of the AskERIC service, and the increases in K–12 teachers using the AskERIC service and the use of the AskERIC service to find lesson plan ideas. There are, however, also several ambiguous findings from this reanalysis, such as the findings that there were no significant changes in the percentages of AskERIC users who were able to obtain the full text of ERIC database citations, and the various sources from which users obtained full text.

As mentioned above, in January 2004, the Department of Education implemented a reengineering plan for ERIC, eliminating the ERIC system's 16 subject-specific clearinghouses and associated adjunct clearinghouses, as well as the AskERIC service. In response to this reengineering, many of the resources formerly available on AskERIC's Web site have been moved to a new Web site: www.eduref.org. While the resources created by the AskERIC service have survived the reengineering of the ERIC system, the AskERIC service itself sadly has not.

This paper is, therefore, AskERIC's eulogy. Like any eulogy, however, we hope it will serve to inspire those that remain. AskERIC was perhaps the oldest AskA service in existence, having been launched in 1992. This analysis of AskERIC data should serve as a point of comparison for others in digital reference services engaged in longitudinal analysis of their own data. The difficulties encountered in this analysis should also serve as a warning to others in digital reference services who wish to study and evaluate their own service and patron community: consistency of measures over time is critical, but more critical is the existence of data from these measures. Even if data are collected, they cannot be used for research or evaluation if they are not preserved. It is hoped that this paper has provided examples of the sorts of analyses that can be performed when the appropriate measures are collected. Different digital reference services may have different criteria for success: meeting the information needs of specific patron groups, providing access to specific types of resources, patron satisfaction, or any number of other possible measures. Evidence of success according to whatever criteria are important must be used to make the case to funding agencies that digital reference services are worth continued support and are an integral part of the future of reference and service to the patron community.

ACKNOWLEDGMENTS

The author wishes to thank the following people: Pauline Lynch Shostack, former AskERIC coordinator and creator of the surveys reanalyzed in this paper; Jennifer Barth, also former AskERIC coordinator, for giving the author access to the survey data; Lisa Pawlewicz, IIS computer consultant, whose CGI programming skills made the data collection for these surveys possible. Thanks also to Pauline and Jennifer for valuable feedback on early drafts of this paper.

REFERENCES

Bristow, Ann. 1992. "Academic Reference Service over Electronic Mail." *College and Research Libraries News* 53, no. 10: 631–637. Available: www.indiana.edu/~librcsd/reference/e-mail/01.html.

Burchinal, Lee G. 2000. "The Tale of Two ERICS: Factors Influencing the Development of the First ERIC and Its Transformation into a National System." *Journal of the American Society for Information Science* 51, no. 6: 567–575.

Bushallow-Wilber, Laura, Gemma DeVinney, and Fritz Whitcomb. 1996. "Electronic Mail Reference Service: A Study." *RQ* 35, no. 3: 359–369.

Carter, David S., and Joseph Janes. 2000. "Unobtrusive Data Analysis of Digital Reference Questions and Service at the Internet Public Library: An Exploratory Study." *Library Trends* 49, no. 2 (Fall): 251–265.

Dewdney, Patricia, and Catherine Sheldrick Ross. 1994. "Flying a Light Aircraft: Reference Service Evaluation from a User's Viewpoint." *RQ* 34, no. 2 (Winter): 217–229.

Durrance, Joan C. 1989. "Reference Success: Does the 55 Percent Rule Tell the Whole Story?" *Library Journal* 114, no. 7 (April 15): 31–36.

Educational Resources Information Center. 2002. *ERIC Annual Report 2002: Summarizing Recent Accomplishments of the Educational Resources Information Center.* Washington, DC: U.S. Department of Education.

Firebaugh, Glenn. 1997. *Analyzing Repeated Surveys.* Thousand Oaks, CA: Sage.

Fowler, Floyd J. Jr. 2002. *Survey Research Methods*, 3rd ed. Thousand Oaks, CA: Sage.

Hodges, Pauline R. 1989. "Reference in the Age of Automation: Changes in Reference Service at Chemical Abstracts Service Library." *Special Libraries* 80, no. 4 (Fall): 251–257.

Howard, Ellen H., and Terry Ann Jankowski. 1986. "Reference Services via Electronic Mail." *Bulletin of the Medical Library Association* 74, no. 1: 41–44.

Janes, Joseph. 2002. "Digital Reference: Reference Librarians' Experiences and Attitudes." *Journal of the American Society for Information Science and Technology* 53, no. 7 (May): 549–566.

Janes, Joseph. 2003. "Question Negotiation in an Electronic Age." In *The Digital Reference Research Agenda*, edited by R. D. Lankes, S. Nicholson, and A. Goodrum (pp. 48–60). Chicago: Association of College and Research Libraries.

Janes, Joseph, David Carter, Annette Lagace, Michael McClennen, Sara Ryan, and Schelle Simcox. 1999. *The Internet Public Library Handbook.* New York: Neal-Schuman.

Janes, Joseph, Chrystie Hill, and Alex Rolfe. 2001. "Ask-an-Expert Services Analysis." *Journal of the American Society for Information Science and Technology* 52, no. 13: 1106–1121.

Kasowitz, Abby, Blythe Bennett, and R. David Lankes. 2000. "Quality Standards for Digital Reference Consortia." *Reference and User Services Quarterly* 39, no. 4: 355–363.

Kittle, Paul W. 1985. "Putting the Medical Library Online: Electronic Bulletin Boards . . . and Beyond." *Online* 9, no. 3 (May): 25–30.

Lagace, Nettie. 1999. "Establishing Online Reference Services." In *The Internet Public Library Handbook*, edited by J. Janes, D. Carter, A. Lagace, M. McClennen, S. Ryan, and S. Simcox. New York: Neal-Schuman.

Lankes, R. David. 1998a. *Building and Maintaining Internet Information Services: K–12 Digital Reference Services*. Syracuse, N.Y.: ERIC Clearinghouse on Information & Technology.

Lankes, R. David. 1998b. *Building the Virtual Reference Desk*. Syracuse, NY: ERIC Clearinghouse for Information and Technology. Available: www.vrd.org/TelEd.shtml.

Lankes, R. David, and Abby S. Kasowitz. 1998. *AskA Starter Kit: How to Build and Maintain Digital Reference Services*. Syracuse, NY: ERIC Clearinghouse on Information and Technology.

LeJeune, Lorrie. 1997. "Before Its Time: The Internet Public Library." *The Journal of Electronic Publishing* 3, no. 2 (December). Available: www.press.umich.edu/jep/03-02/IPL.html.

Lipow, Anne Grodzins. 2002. *The Virtual Reference Librarian's Handbook*. New York: Neal-Schuman.

McClure, Charles R., R. David Lankes, Melissa Gross, and Beverly Choltco-Devlin. 2002. *Statistics, Measures and Quality Standards for Assessing Digital Reference Library Services: Guidelines and Procedures*. Syracuse, NY: Information Institute of Syracuse.

Nicholson, Scott. 2003. "On My Mind: Avoiding the Great Data-Wipe of Ought-Three." *American Libraries* 34, no. 9 (October): 36.

Penka, Jeffrey T. 2003. "The Technological Challenges of Digital Reference: An Overview." *D-Lib Magazine* 9, no. 2 (February). Available: www.dlib.org/dlib/february03/penka/02penka.html.

Philip, Brenda. 1997. "mayihelpyou@theelectronicreferencedesk?: An Examination of the Past, Present and Future of Electronic Mail Reference Service." Alberta, Canada: School of Library and Information Studies, University of Alberta. (March) Available: http://hollyhock.slis.ualberta.ca/598/brenda/e-mailref.htm.

Pomerantz, Jeffrey. 2003. *Question Taxonomies for Digital Reference*. Doctoral diss., School of Information Studies, Syracuse University, Syracuse, NY.

Roysdon, Christine M., and Laura Lee Elliott. 1988. "Electronic Integration of Library Services through a Campuswide Network." *RQ* 28, no. 1: 82–93.

Saxton, Matthew L. 1997. "Reference Service Evaluation and Meta-analysis: Findings and Methodological Issues." *Library Quarterly* 67, no. 3 (July): 267–288.

Still, Julie, and Frank Campbell. 1993. "Librarian in a Box: The Use of Electronic Mail for Reference." *Reference Services Review* 21, no. 1 (Spring): 15–18.

Virtual Reference Desk Project. 1998. "Virtual Reference Desk AskA Software:

Decision Points and Scenarios." Syracuse, NY: Virtual Reference Desk Project (September) Available: www.vrd.org/Tech/AskA-sw.PDF.

Weise, Frieda O., and Marilyn Borgendale. 1986. "EARS: Electronic Access to Reference Service." *Bulletin of the Medical Library Association* 74, no. 4 (October): 300–304.

White, Marilyn Domas. 2001. "Digital Reference Services: Framework for Analysis and Evaluation." *Library & Information Science Research* 23, no. 3 (Autumn): 211–231.

Yin, Robert K. 2003. *Case Study Research: Design and Methods.* Thousand Oaks, CA: Sage.

Chapter 2

User Perceptions and Virtual Reference Services

Linda Frederiksen, Joel Cummings, and Lara Ursin

As academic librarians embrace the Internet as an appropriate medium for information exchange, communication, and instruction, college and university students are also becoming more familiar and comfortable with emerging technologies, including both synchronous and asynchronous tools. Acceptance of Web-based products that provide speed, convenience, and anonymity cannot, however, be assumed, especially in a non-recreational context. Based on survey and interview responses, this paper discusses actual usage patterns and behaviors, what users in an academic setting expected to receive from an Ask a Librarian service, and the implications these findings might have on future virtual reference projects.

INTRODUCTION

Many technologists believe that advantageous innovations will sell themselves, that the obvious benefits of a new idea will be widely realized by potential adopters, and that the innovation will diffuse rapidly. Seldom is this the case.

Rogers, *Diffusion of Innovations* (2003)

The rapid inclusion of the Internet into daily life is a well-documented case study in technology diffusion. As more people have gone online, the development of Web-based products and services has also expanded to both meet and drive Internet-user expectations. While growing familiarity with all types of information technology theoretically increases the likelihood of more frequent use of other similar or more advanced technologies, it can also be said that the Internet is "a complex landscape of applications and purposes, and users" (Wellman and Haythornthwaite, 2002, 10) in which adoption of technological innovations cannot be predicted. For every "killer" application that because of its design and usefulness becomes indispensable to millions, there are many applications that, despite potential benefits to users, generate little interest. Understanding the reasons why new and available information applications are accepted or rejected may well turn out to be one of the major research questions to emerge from the digital revolution (Henderson and Divett, 2003).

Background

"Near synchronous" UNIX text-message systems have been in existence for more than 20 years (Grinter and Palen, 2002). Web-based, feature-rich synchronous communication applications, however, are relative newcomers to the online world. Early adopters of these new graphical and interactive tools included teenagers and young adults, who quickly took up instant messaging (IM) and chat features that the technology allowed (Lenhart, Lee, and Lewis, 2001; Jones, 2002). Recreational chat for this group is one of the Internet's killer applications, with nearly 2 billion instant messages sent on a daily basis (Edwards, 2003).

Many libraries are also taking advantage of synchronous tools that allow for online, real-time and interactive chat with users, and which also may include graphical co-browsing or "follow-me" features. For these libraries, the primary rationale for investing in commercial digital reference software is the desire to communicate with and support an ever-growing number of remote users who, by choice or necessity, access library resources and services via the Internet (Cooper et al., 1998). Despite the popularity of tools that allow chat, a recent declaration that "virtual reference in libraries is here to stay" (Helfer, 2003, 63) and the success of many e-reference initiatives (Tenopir and Ennis, 2002), it remains unclear whether library users expect, or will use, online help delivered by a library Web site. Librarians investing the time and money to establish digital Ask a Librarian services that respond to perceived user needs are often surprised by low initial traffic and the lack of repeat customers. Within this context, the authors examined a pilot virtual reference service project, looking for explanations of usage patterns and attitudes.

Washington State University is a multicampus, land grant university system, located in the Pacific Northwest. The main campus of the university, located in the southeast corner of the state in Pullman, Washington, serves approximately 16,000 undergraduate, graduate, doctoral, and professional students in a residential and rural environment. The Vancouver campus, situated in an urban setting near Portland, Oregon, serves an older adult, commuter population of 2,000 upper-division and graduate students. Synchronous-based virtual reference was implemented as a pilot project on both the Pullman and Vancouver campuses in the fall of 2002. During the course of the 2002–2003 academic year, a total of 141 nontest reference transactions were recorded, with only 15 return customers appearing in the activity logs of the software. While acknowledging the importance of marketing and promotion, scheduling, and instruction, librarians involved in the project felt that other variables, such as user demographics, attitudes, and perceptions, were also at work and may have significantly influenced actual use of the service. The research study reported here was grounded in the desire to understand the apparent gap between expected and actual outcomes for virtual reference. The authors also hoped to find indicators that might explain adoption patterns for virtual reference services by looking at perceptions about an existing interactive technology: synchronous communication, or chat.

Literature Review

The explosive growth of the Internet has generated an expanding body of research concerned with characteristics and effects of computer-mediated technologies in all disciplines. Given the high cost of under-utilization or non-use of technological innovations in the workplace, it is not surprising that theoretical models clustering around technology acceptance are fairly common in the literature (Ehrlich, 1987; Morris and Turner, 2001; Yi and Hwang, 2003). There are several studies that look at technology diffusion in general (Rogers, 2003) and adoption of instant messaging and online chat in particular (Grinter and Palen, 2002; Nardi, Whittaker, and Bradner, 2000; Herbsleb et al., 2002). As more organizations add synchronous tools to the suite of communication applications available to employees and customers alike, this area of research is expected to grow.

Librarians have a long tradition of providing user-centered services. The library literature is not lacking in examples of user needs and expectations assessment studies of traditional library services (Millson-Martula and Menon, 1995; Edwards and Browne, 1995). A great deal of current library literature also focuses on e-reference services in all types of libraries (Janes, 2002; Pomerantz et al., 2004; Francoeur, 2001), although much of this work is of a practical nature and does not look at the social psychology issues affecting perceptions of these services or applications. White (2001) and Gray (2000) have begun to research the diffusion of virtual reference service in academic libraries, and Penka (2003) has looked at the establishment of a research agenda for virtual reference. It is hoped that further investigation into the use, usefulness, and usability of digital reference will continue.

This study measured chat usage in a university population in an attempt to determine if perceptions of chat may have affected user behavior in terms of interest and trial use of virtual reference services.

METHODS

To reach a better understanding of synchronous-based virtual reference usage patterns and to determine the role and salience of virtual reference in an academic setting, the authors looked specifically at synchronous communication (or online chat). Two separate anonymous surveys and an informal usability study were designed. Usability-study interviews provided anecdotal evidence only and were not included in the quantitative data analysis.

A first survey ("Chat Survey") asked seven attitudinal questions pertaining to chat use in general, not limited to library chat service (see Appendix A at the end of this chapter). Participants were asked to designate their institutional status at Washington State University (i.e., undergraduate, graduate, faculty, staff, or other) and then respond to questions about frequency, purposes, and important aspects of their chat use. Participants who self-reported non-use of chat were given the opportunity to choose reasons why chat was not used. The final question asked whether the participant knew anything about Ask a Librarian services. This survey was distributed at several back-to-school events on the Washington State University (WSU) Pullman campus in the fall of 2003. The Chat Survey was also distributed on the WSU Vancouver campus and was made available at the library reference desk. A total of 178 surveys were completed, 113 from the Pullman campus, and 65 from the Vancouver campus.

A second survey ("Virtual Reference Survey") was distributed by e-mail to 62 patrons who used the Pullman Ask a Librarian service between August 2002 and October 2003. Patron e-mail addresses were collected from transaction logs available within the software. The number of responses to this survey was 18, a return rate of 29%.

Questions in the Virtual Reference Survey were reworded slightly but, as in the first survey, pertained to frequency and reasons for chat use or non-use (see Appendix B at the end of this chapter). This survey also asked participants where they had heard about the WSU Ask a Librarian service, if they had received the information they needed when using the service, and if they expected to chat with a real person or receive an automated response to their questions. Participants were asked if they were satisfied with the service they received, if it was helpful to follow a librarian through resources, and if the virtual reference service was more or less helpful than an in-person library-instruction session.

The third method used for data collection involved small and informal usability studies conducted on both campuses. Participants were asked to use the WSU Ask a Librarian service, complete the "Ask a Librarian Virtual Reference Survey," and take part in a short exit interview with one of the authors regarding their recent experiences with the virtual reference service. Participants were given the option of using individual research questions or choosing from a list of three hypothetical research scenarios. On the Pullman campus, participants were recruited from library-instruction classes, student groups across campus, and by signs placed around the library on the two nights that the usability study was conducted. In Vancouver, volunteers were solicited at the reference desk. Participants on both campuses received small incentives in return for involvement in the study. Exit-interview questions asked what the patron expected to receive from the Ask a Librarian service, if the service met those expectations, if the patron had any notion of whether answers were human or machine generated, and opinions on chat in general.

Ten students on the Pullman campus and two on the Vancouver campus completed activity scenarios and the virtual reference surveys. While several exit interviews were completed during this process on both campuses, the findings were mostly used for anecdotal evidence of attitudes towards virtual reference services and chatting in general.

RESULTS

The authors originally hypothesized that the reportedly widespread use of both synchronous communication and asynchronous tools (i.e., chat and e-mail) had already created a critical mass of users comfortable with these technologies. It was assumed that this familiarity would trigger expectations and use of similar or more advanced applications. Based on the array of potential items that might affect perception of virtual reference and to test the theories of diffusion and technology accep-

Table 2–1
Chat Usage on Two Campuses of Washington State University

	Both campuses	Pullman campus	Vancouver campus
Total Response	178	113	65
Chat Users	96 (54%)	68 (60%)	28 (43%)
Nonusers of Chat	82 (46%)	45 (40%)	37 (57%)

tance, it was determined that data collection would focus on the use of chat.

Chat Survey

There was a total of 178 respondents to the general Chat Survey from the two campuses (Table 2-1).

The sample included 10 faculty, 11 university staff, 63 graduate or professional student, 87 undergraduates, and 7 individuals choosing "other" as an institutional status. In terms of status, 32 (51%) of the graduate and professional students described themselves as chat users, and 55 (63%) of undergraduates reported using synchronous communication applications or tools. Three faculty, one staff member, and three of the "others" indicated chat usage, for a 25% use rate.

From a list of multiple categories, survey participants were asked to indicate purposes of their chat use. In response, 89 reported personal use, 24 used chat for school-related purposes, and eight marked work-related activities. The majority of respondents (93%) indicated that they used chat for recreational purposes. Survey participants who used chat were also asked how frequently they did so. There were 87 (78%) who responded to this question, and of these, 67 said they used chat at a minimum of a couple of times per week.

A question concerning the "likeability" of chat proved problematic. An error in wording resulted in respondents on the Pullman campus checking the choices that applied to them rather than ranking the seven choices on a scale of 1 to 7. In addition, 12 survey participants in Vancouver also checked rather

Table 2–2
Why Chat Users Liked Chat

| | Reasons respondents liked chat | | | |
Reason for using chat	Number of checked responses	Percentage of respondents who checked reason	Number of ranked responses	Average rank
Fast	68	86%	34	2.6
Free	55	70%	32	1.9
Easy	46	58%	34	3.6
Fun	36	46%	32	4
Anywhere	31	39%	32	3.7
Anonymous	9	11%	31	5.1
Other	4	5%	9	5.6

than ranked their responses to this question. A total of 79 respondents indicated applicable choices instead of ranking the responses. Responses from both ranked and unranked responses are examined in Table 2-2. The average rank in Table 2-2 is an arithmetical mean of all ordered responses for the category rounded to one decimal place. An additional problem with this question was that nonusers responded to the question by either checking or ranking reasons for chat use.

Eighty people provided answers to reasons why they did not use chat (see Table 2-3). Respondents were able to choose multiple reasons for nonuse. Six respondents reported both that they felt chat was a waste of time and that they were not interested in chat, while 39 individuals only listed one of these reasons for nonuse. With the majority of nonusers of chat indicating a negative attitude toward synchronous communication tools, it suggests that this type of tool would have low interest or trial priority. Nonetheless, when considering that nearly 60% of self-reported chat users indicated they used the technology because it was easy, the individuals in this category may still be potential virtual reference users.

To the question *Would you ever think of using chat to get help with research, homework, technical support, etc.?* 132 (74%) replied they would, 39 answered no, and 7 left the question blank. Thus,

Table 2–3
Reasons Nonusers of Chat Do Not Use Chat

Reasons for not using chat		
Reason for not using chat	Number of responses	Percentage of total number of respondents giving reason
E-mail is better than chat	39	49%
Not interested in chat	23	29%
Chat is a waste of time	22	28%
The telephone is better than chat	15	19%
Other	13	16%
Don't know how to use chat	9	11%
Do not know what chat is	5	6%
Chat is too difficult to use	2	3%

61% (50 out of 82) nonusers indicated they would use chat under the circumstances listed in the question.

In asking *Have you ever heard of an Ask a Librarian chat service?* the authors wanted to assess how well known this type of service is within academic populations. While 26 survey participants (17%) indicated they had heard of such a service, 123 participants (83%) indicated they had not.

Virtual Reference Survey

The Virtual Reference Survey was originally sent by e-mail to 62 individuals affiliated with the Pullman campus who had used the WSU Ask a Librarian service between August 2002 and October 2003. Eighteen people responded to this survey, a response rate of 29%. In addition, we administered the survey to a group of 12 students who were recruited to fill out the questionnaire and to take part in exit interviews. Although informative to the authors, the small sample size makes the results of the Virtual Reference Survey difficult to generalize beyond the local community.

The first question attempted to determine how prevalent

Table 2–4
Chat Usage Patterns Among Users of
the WSU Libraries Virtual Reference Service

Familiarity with chat	Number of respondents	Percentage of respondents
I have never used a chat program (1)	3	10%
2	13	43%
3	5	17%
4	3	10%
I chat more than five hours per week on average (5)	6	20%

chat usage was among previous users of the Ask a Librarian service. Respondents were asked to answer on a scale of one to five, with one signifying *I have never used a chat program* and five meaning *I chat more than five hours per week on average* (see Table 2-4).

Given the low amount of virtual reference traffic during the first year of service and the modest marketing efforts that went into promoting it, the authors included a question on this survey asking how users found out about the service. Of the 18 former users of the WSU Libraries Virtual Reference Service, 13 (72%) indicated that they found out about the service through the Libraries' Web site.

All 30 (100%) of the respondents indicated they did receive the information needed. The survey participants were asked about expectations for virtual reference services: 24 individuals indicated that they had expected to communicate with a human, while only 6 reported that they had expected to receive automated answers to their questions. This survey also attempted to discover how the WSU Libraries virtual reference service compared with other similar services. Participants were asked *How did your experience with Ask a Librarian compare with other chat or "ask-a-question" services?* Of the 28 responses to this question, only 16 attempted to make a comparison with other similar services. The responses that attempted to make comparisons suggest that participants did not have experience with any

Table 2–5
Expected Future Use of WSU Libraries Virtual Reference Service

Frequency	Number of respondents	Percentage
Never (1)	1	3%
2	14	47%
3	7	23%
4	6	20%
Several times a term (5)	2	7%

type of online synchronous reference service, although a few people did try to make a comparison with e-mail reference.

The survey participants were asked *Were you satisfied with the assistance you received compared to other services you have received via the Internet?* Nearly all respondents appear to have interpreted this question as *Were you satisfied with the assistance you received?* and did not attempt to make any comparisons, although they did respond both positively and negatively about the assistance received.

Participants were also asked *Was it helpful to have a librarian guide you through library databases, the catalog, other Web sites, etc.?* Twenty-three respondents reported in their comments that it was helpful, while five others claimed that the question did not apply to their reference transaction.

To the question *Was using this service more helpful than attending a library instruction session or visiting the reference desk in person?* 12 respondents indicated that it was and 12 others indicated that it was not. Five individuals gave mixed or noncommittal replies. Ten respondents to this question made comments citing the convenience of the WSU Librarian Virtual Reference Service. Participants were asked to rate the frequency with which they expected to use the WSU Libraries Virtual Reference Service in the future on a scale of one to five, with value one described on the questionnaire as *Never* and value five described as *Several times a term* (see Table 2-5).

The survey participants were asked to suggest improvements for the WSU Libraries Virtual Reference Service. The most prevalent response concerned increasing the speed of the connection, indicating a possible problem with the graphical interface and co-browsing functions of the digital reference software used.

DISCUSSION

The findings should not be generalized because the sample size was so small and factors regarding individual differences—such as overall experience with the Internet, other information technologies, and library services—were excluded. Further, specific characteristics of the Ask a Librarian product and service, such as its ease of use and usefulness, were left out of survey questions. Although the findings may be consistent across user groups of varying experience levels, to gain a better understanding of users' perceptions and attitudes about virtual reference products and services, future research should include these applicable factors. Finally, the behaviors in our study are self-reported rather than observed. Although these measures are widely used and are easy to administer, there may be problems with accuracy and bias.

Despite these shortcomings, the findings do provide some interesting insights into the study of college students' Internet habits. It was evident from this study that chat usage is a local phenomenon and highly variable. Based on the data gathered, older college students, as represented by Vancouver campus survey respondents, appear to be satisfied with asynchronous means of communicating, for example, and as a result may not expect or be ready to adopt synchronous tools that provide reference assistance. At the same time, younger students, as represented by those on the Pullman campus, may have a higher expectation that an online help service will be available. It remains to be seen if teenagers, as the heaviest users of chat services, will have even higher expectations for real-time online help when they enter the college environment. While a popular method of communication, chat is by no means the only one by which students might interact remotely with a library system. Chat usage, therefore, should not be seen as the only predictor for use or non-use of virtual reference service at Washington State University.

This preliminary research suggests a number of questions for future investigation. Are potential e-reference users likely to be drawn from the general population of chat users or non-users of chat, or is prior chat experience an irrelevant factor in predicting who will or will not use virtual reference services? It would appear from this research that within the academic environment, current users and non-users of chat are both reasonably, although not predictably, likely to employ virtual reference services. Similarly, frequency of chat usage does not appear to be a determining factor in future virtual reference use. Another area to explore is whether the prevalence of chat usage for personal or recreational purposes leads to a perception, in the academic community at least, that synchronous communication is frivolous or a waste of time, and, therefore, not entirely appropriate for scholarly or professional activity, thus making adoption unlikely.

Further research and controlled data-gathering studies are needed to investigate how perceptual variables relate to e-reference usage, usefulness, and usability. The conclusions suggest that librarians must continue analyzing the expectations and needs for these services.

REFERENCES

Cooper, Rosemarie, Paula Dempsey, Vanaja Menon, and Christopher Millson-Martula. 1998. "Remote Library Users—Needs and Expectations." *Library Trends* 47, no. 1 (Summer): 42–64.

Edwards, Ellen. 2003. "Middle Schoolers, Letting Their Fingers Do the Talking." *The Washington Post* (May 14). Style Section: C01.

Edwards, Susan, and Mairead Browne. 1995. "Quality in Information Services: Do Users and Librarians Differ in Their Expectations?" *Library and Information Science Research* 17: 163–182.

Ehrlich, Susan. 1987. "Strategies for Encouraging Successful Adoption of Office Communication Systems." *ACM Transactions on Office Information Systems* 5, no. 4: 340–357.

Francoeur, Stephen. 2001. "An Analytical Survey of Chat Reference Services." *Reference Services Review* 29, no. 3: 189–203.

Gray, Suzanne. 2000. "Virtual Reference Services: Directions and Agendas." *Reference & User Services Quarterly* 39, no. 4 (Summer): 365–375.

Grinter, Rebecca, and Leysia Palen. 2002. "Instant Messaging in Teen Life." In *CSCW [Computer Supported Cooperative Work] '02: Proceedings of the Con-*

ference in New Orleans, Louisiana, November 16–20, 2002, by the ACM, 21–30. New York: ACM Press.

Helfer, Doris. 2003. "Virtual Reference in Libraries: Status and Issues." *Searcher* 11, no. 2 (February): 63–65.

Henderson, Ron, and Megan Divett. 2003. "Perceived Usefulness, Ease of Use and Electronic Supermarket Use." *International Journal of Human-Computer Studies* 59: 383–395.

Herbsleb, James, David Atkins, David Boyer, Mark Handel, and Thomas Finholt. 2002. "I Think, Therefore IM: Introducing Instant Messaging and Chat in the Workplace." In *CHI 2002: Proceedings of the Conference in Minneapolis, MN, April 20–25, 2002*, by the ACM, 171–178. New York: ACM Press.

Janes, Joseph. 2002. "Digital Reference: Reference Librarians' Experiences and Attitudes." *Journal of the American Society for Information Science and Technology* 53, no. 7: 549–566.

Jones, Steve. 2002. "The Internet Goes to College: How Students Are Living in the Future with Today's Technology. Available: www.pewinternet.org/reports/pdfs/PIP_College_Report.pdf

Lenhart, Amanda, Lee Rainie, and Oliver Lewis. 2001. "Teenage Life Online: The Rise of the Instant Messaging Generation and the Internet's Impact on Friendships and Family Relations." Available: www.pewinternet.org/reports/pdfs/PIP_Teens_Report.pdf

Millson-Martula, Christopher Menon, and Vanaja Menon. 1995. "Customer Expectations: Concepts and Reality for Academic Library Services." *College & Research Libraries* 56, no. 1: 33–47.

Morris, Michael, and Jason Turner. 2001. "Assessing Users' Subjective Quality of Experience with the World Wide Web: An Exploratory Examination of Temporal Changes in Technology Acceptance." *International Journal of Human-Computer Studies* 54: 877–901.

Nardi, Bonnie, Steve Whittaker, and Erin Bradner. 2000. "Interaction and Outeraction: Instant Messaging in Action." In *CSCW [Computer Supported Cooperative Work] '00: Proceedings of the Conference in Philadelphia, Pennsylvania, December 2–6 2000*, by the ACM, 79–88. New York: ACM Press.

Penka, Jeffrey. 2003. "The Technological Challenges of Digital Reference." *D-Lib Magazine* 9, no. 2. Available: www.dlib.org/dlib/february03/02penka.html

Pomerantz, Jeffrey, Scott Nicholson, Yvonne Belander, and R. David Lankes. 2004. "The Current State of Digital Reference: Validation of a General Digital Reference Model through a Survey of Digital Reference Services." *Information Processing and Management* 40, no. 2:347–363.

Rogers, Everett. 2003. *Diffusion of Innovations.* New York: The Free Press.

Tenopir, Carol, and Lisa Ennis. 2002. "A Decade of Digital Reference: 1991–2001." *Reference & User Services Quarterly* 41, no. 3 (Spring): 264–273.

Wellman, Barry, and Caroline Haythornthwaite, eds. 2002. *The Internet in Everyday Life.* Malden, MA: Blackwell.

White, Marilyn Domas. 2001. "Diffusion of an Innovation: Digital Reference

Service in Carnegie Foundation Master's (Comprehensive) Academic Institution Libraries." *Journal of Academic Librarianship* 27, no. 3: 173–187.

Yi, Mun, and Yujong Hwang. 2003. "Predicting the Use of Web-Based Information Systems: Self-Efficacy, Enjoyment, Learning Goal Orientation, and the Technology Acceptance Model." *International Journal of Human-Computer Studies* 59: 431–449.

APPENDIX A

WSU Libraries Chat Survey Questions—Fall 2003

The WSU Libraries want to test the effectiveness of our services. The purpose of this survey is to learn if and how people use online chat and if the Libraries' chat reference service might be useful to the campus community. To do this we are conducting a study to discover how people use online chat.

1. How would you classify your status at WSU?

    a. Undergraduate student
    b. Graduate student
    c. Post-doctoral student
    d. WSU Staff
    e. WSU Faculty
    f. Other—please explain

2. Do you use online chat, such as AOL Instant Messenger, Yahoo Chat, or MSN Chat?

    a. Yes
    b. No (if no, skip to Question #4)
       If Yes, how often do you use online chat?
    a. Several times a day
    b. Once a day
    c. A couple of times a week
    d. Very infrequently

3. Why do you use chat (check all that apply)?

    a. For school purposes (part of an assignment, get help, etc.)
    b. For work purposes (chat with co-workers, fulfill projects, etc.)
    c. For personal use (have fun, chat with friends, etc.)
    d. Other (explain)

4. In your opinion, what are the most important aspects of online chat? Please rank the following options by typing

a number (1 through 7) in the box next to each option with "1" being most important and "7" being least important.

a. It is free
b. It is fast
c. It is anonymous
d. I can be anywhere
e. It is fun
f. It is easy
g. Other (explain)

5. If you have never used chat services, what are some reasons why you have not used it?

a. I do not know what chat is
b. I am not interested in chat
c. I do not know how to use chat
d. It is difficult to use
e. Chat is a waste of time
f. The phone is a better way to communicate
g. Email works just fine for me
h. Other (explain)

6. Would you ever think of using chat to get help with research, homework, technical support, etc.?

a. Yes
b. No

7. Have you ever heard of an Ask a Librarian chat service?

a. Yes
b. No

Thank you for your time!

APPENDIX B

Ask a Librarian (Virtual Reference)
Survey Questions—Fall 2003

1. On a scale of 1 to 5 (with 1 being "I have never used a chat program" and 5 being "I chat more than 5 hours per week on average"), how familiar are you with Internet-based chat programs, such as ICG, AOL Instant Messenger, Yahoo Chat, or others?

2. If you have *never used* a chat program, please select the most likely reason for not using one:

   a. I have never heard of chat programs.
   b. I have heard of chat programs, but do not know how to use them.
   c. My Internet connection is too slow.
   d. I have never had a reason to use a chat program.
   e. Chat programs are a waste of time.

3. If you *frequently use* chat programs, please select the most likely reason for using them:

   a. Leisure/Entertainment
   b. Getting my questions answered
   c. Doing research
   d. As a communication tool
   e. Getting technical support
   f. Other (please describe)

4. If you are an *infrequent user* of chat services, select the most likely reason for not using these services more:

   a. Slow Internet connection or other technical problems
   b. Easier to use the phone
   c. Dissatisfied with service as it was presented
   d. I don't have enough time to use
   e. I didn't get the answer/service/support I expected

5. How did you find out about the Ask a Librarian service? (Check all that apply):

a. Read about it in the student newspaper
b. Noticed a link to it on the library Web site
c. Heard about it in a class
d. Saw it on a bookmark or other handout
e. Other (please describe)

6. When you used the Ask a Librarian chat reference service, did you receive the information you needed?

a. Yes
b. No

7. Choose one of the following options based on when you used the Ask a Librarian service:

a. I expected to chat with a real person
b. I expected to receive an automated answer

8. How did your experience with Ask a Librarian compare with other chat or "ask-a-question" services?

9. Were you satisfied with the assistance you received compared to other services you have received via the Internet?

10. Was it helpful to have a librarian guide you through library databases, the catalog, other Web sites, etc.?

11. Was using the service more helpful than attending a library instruction session or visiting the reference desk in person?

12. On a scale of 1 to 5, with 1 being never and 5 being several times a term, how often do you think you might use an Ask a Librarian service?

13. What would you like to see improved about library chat services? About chat services in general?

Submit your Survey.
Thank you for your time!

Chapter 3

If You Ask, I Will Tell You: Future Users of Virtual Reference Share Their Thoughts on the Design, Operation, and Marketing of Virtual Reference

Beth Thomsett-Scott

Twenty-seven students, a mixture of undergraduates, graduates, and online learners, at the University of North Texas were asked to brainstorm on what they expect from virtual reference and how they want virtual reference services to be marketed. Since only one student had used any form of virtual reference, the comments are highly useful when considering the implementation of a virtual reference service or determining why a current service is not attracting the expected number of users. The information on marketing and promoting a virtual reference service, or any other library service, is especially pertinent as it comes directly from the users' mouths, providing librarians with insight into what strategies may work and which ones may not.

INTRODUCTION

With the advent of virtual reference, from its humblest beginnings as telephone reference, through the early e-mail and chat years, to its current advanced state of page pushing, many studies have been done on the reactions of users to the various systems. These studies tend to focus on reactions to specific virtual reference products or services. In fact, several presenters at the Virtual Reference Desk 2003 Conference discussed the evaluation of their virtual reference services.

Relatively low use of their virtual reference systems has plagued most libraries. The literature is now discussing how best to market virtual reference, again with little input from current or future users of the products.

The idea of "if we build it, they will come" thus appears to be guiding the creation of virtual reference products and services, yet this may not be the most effective approach. Libraries need to aggressively market their products and actively seek and respond to patron satisfaction (Balas, 2003). Bruseberg and McDonagh-Philp (2002) state that effective products rely on input from the future users of the product. In a recent column, Janes (2003) suggests that it is more important than ever to gather input from users as the tendency towards "fast and easy" may be taking over the need for quality, especially among teens and young adults, making it even more important to know and understand your users' needs and wants.

A series of focus groups involving 27 students took place at the University of North Texas (UNT) Libraries to ask students about their views on virtual reference and virtual reference services. Students brainstormed on four questions centered on virtual reference products. The results provide valuable information into what student users expect from virtual reference and offer some insightful ideas on marketing and promoting a virtual reference product. The purpose of this paper is to provide opinions directly from students concerning what they want to see in a virtual reference product and how they suggest marketing it. Comments on design issues are also provided.

LITERATURE REVIEW

Focus groups are used in the study as they are well suited to exploring participants' behaviors, concerns, needs, and desires and for determining how users will react to new services, products, or ideas (Crowley et al., 2002). Cavill (2002) notes that focus groups are a powerful research tool as they explore participants' feelings about various issues. There is an array of literature on the use of focus groups. For the reader looking for background information, David Morgan (1997) provides an excellent comprehensive introduction to the methodology and uses of focus groups, and Beryl Glitz (1998) offers a highly informative summary on the use of focus groups in libraries. Originally used primarily for user satisfaction, focus groups have more recently been used to evaluate library services. Examples of the use of focus groups for evaluative purposes are Widdows, Hensler, and Wyncott (1991); Connaway, Johnson, and Searing (1997); and Massey-Burzio (1998).

Focus groups are also an effective way of evaluating the design of products and Web pages (Crowley et al., 2002). Bruseberg and McDonagh-Philp (2002) write that the qualitative information garnered from focus groups is particularly useful to product designers at the decision-making stage. Burns and Evans (2000) and Jordan (2000) note that focus groups are beneficial for product designers as they effectively provide information on participants' satisfiers—the tangibles and intangibles that make the product enjoyable and satisfying. Product designers want input from users early in the design process (Bruseberg and McDonagh-Philp).

The focus group technique was chosen specifically as it provides for the synergistic flow of ideas as a result of the group interaction (Perry, 2002), which was deemed especially important for this part of the study as we were asking participants about something that few of them had used before. Large, Beheshti, and Rahman (2002) note that focus groups utilize group interactions to solicit a wide range of ideas.

METHODS

As part of a Web-site usability study, 30 students were hired at a rate of $10/hour. After the task-based testing of the UNT Libraries Ask a Librarian Web site, students participated in focus groups. The 30 participants were equally divided among the three academic status categories: undergraduates, graduates, and those with online learning experience. Gender, race, first language (ESL), and discipline were also considered during participant selection. Twenty-seven students returned for the focus groups. Table 3-1 shows the breakdown of the participants in the six focus groups.

There were six focus groups established—two for each of the three categories of students. One OU student had to attend a G group because of scheduling issues. Cavill (2002) and Crowley et al. (2002) note that focus groups are more effective when the participants have commonalities, such as level of education. However, the addition of an undergraduate to the graduate group or the mixing up of graduate and undergraduate online learners did not inhibit the synergy of the groups. In fact, it may have helped the discussion as the differences enhanced the range of ideas discussed. It is possible that this effect was a result of the relative closeness in age of all the participants, as the majority of the participants were under 25 years old.

Dividing the participants as above provided for an average number of five in each group, which is smaller than the traditional eight to twelve. Perry (2002) notes that smaller groups are becoming more common as they tend to promote more discussion because of the increased comfort level of the participants. Norlin (2000) used focus groups that had between three and five participants and obtained satisfactory results.

The author served as the moderator for all sessions, and two other librarians alternated in the observer role. Sessions were audio-taped once agreement among all participants had been reached. The tape recorder was set out of the view of the participants to prevent participants' focusing on being recorded and becoming more nervous. Both the moderator and observer took notes as well. The librarians would respond to quick, factual questions or explanations, such as "Why don't you have an online form to renew books?" Although this differs from the traditional approach of the moderator's and recorder's remaining out of the discussion (Crowley et al., 2002), our method appeared to encourage participation as the students knew that we were truly interested in them, rather than merely seeing them as "data."

A large conference room in the main library was selected for the focus groups. Participants were given glasses of water and

Table 3–1
Gender, First Language Learned,* and Status**
of Participants Arranged by Focus Group Number

Focus Group	Gender	ESL	Status
FG1	F	N	OG
FG1	F	Y	OU
FG1	F	Y	OU
FG1	M	N	OG
FG1	M	Y	OG
FG2	F	N	OU
FG2	F	Y	G
FG2	M	Y	G
FG2	M	Y	G
FG2	M	Y	G
FG3	F	N	G
FG3	M	N	G
FG3	M	N	G
FG3	M	Y	G
FG3	M	Y	G
FG4	F	Y	OG
FG4	F	Y	OG
FG4	F	Y	OU
FG4	M	N	OU
FG5	F	N	UG
FG5	F	N	UG
FG5	M	N	UG
FG5	M	Y	UG
FG6	F	N	UG
FG6	F	Y	UG
FG6	M	N	UG
FG6	M	Y	UG
NA	F	N	UG
NA	M	N	G
NA	M	N	UG

* referred to as *English as a second language* (ESL), where Y means the student's first language was one other than English
** Status is defined as undergraduate student (UG), graduate student (G), online learner undergraduate student (OU), or online learner graduate student (OG)
NA = student did not attend the focus group but participated in the usability study

cookies. A relaxed and inviting atmosphere was established and maintained. Hernon and Altman (1998) emphasize that a friendly, informal setting is essential. Large, Beheshti, and Rahman (2002) add that the focus groups perform better if they are held away from the usual work place. Although the groups worked out well, it may have been helpful, in retrospect, to hold the focus groups in a less formal-looking room, perhaps outside of the library, although that would have required additional funds.

The first four questions dealt specifically with the Ask a Librarian Web site at UNT. The other four questions allowed participants to brainstorm on virtual reference and provided the basis for the content of this paper. For purposes of the discussion, virtual reference was described as "any online communication between you and a librarian."

The questions were:

1. What would you expect from virtual reference?
2. What would make virtual reference attractive to you?
3. How should the libraries market and promote a virtual reference product?
4. What would you find difficult or uncomfortable about using a virtual reference product?

The groups began with introductions, assurances of confidentiality, and a comment on respecting the opinions of other participants. Initially, participants answered each question in a round-robin process, and then commented freely. This method was beneficial in ensuring that all participants had a chance to vocalize at least one point to reduce any initial hesitation. As most participants participated at about the same level, this technique worked well.

For purposes of this paper, comments are linked to particular focus groups rather than individuals, except to differentiate among graduate and undergraduate learners and the one online learner in the graduate focus group. Complete data analysis included the individual participant information to provide for examination of trends among genders, language, and categories.

The moderator was responsible for compiling and analyzing the data. Krueger and Casey (2000) recommend that the analysis be performed by someone who was present at the focus groups to allow for the unspoken comments gained from body language and behaviors of the participants. Data were compiled into a Microsoft Word table and included the number of the participant(s) to whom the comment could be attributed, as well as the focus group and question number. Tracking the focus-group number and question number allowed the researchers to go back and look for trends within questions and focus groups. The comments were then broken up by sentence or phrase so that they each represented one idea. During this action, major themes emerged: general comments, design issues, terminology, use of virtual reference, service issues such as hours and timeliness of answers, information sought and desired responses, and the need to market the product in a variety of ways in order to reach as many potential users as possible. This was all performed with a series of Word tables, cutting and pasting the comments into the appropriate table according to the major theme. Crowley et al. (2002) utilized index cards with the comments typed on them and then sorted and coded the cards. The themes are presented here as smaller units to facilitate easier identification of issues.

RESULTS FOR VIRTUAL REFERENCE QUESTIONS

Virtual Reference in General

All but one of the 27 focus group participants liked the idea of some form of virtual reference. They mentioned that it would be "useful," "good," and "helpful." The sole participant who preferred a "live body" was a very library-experienced graduate student. It is possible that she has built a relationship with the library and preferred this relationship over the anonymity of a virtual experience. However, it is important not to lose sight of the idea that not everyone will prefer virtual over in-person reference service.

FG5 participants agreed that virtual reference provided an additional way to get help and appreciated the alternatives that UNT offered. One participant stated, "UNT is great! My previous school did not have chat!" The undergraduate student in

FG2 noted that virtual reference would be helpful when she was busy working on the computers in the library so she would not have to leave the terminal to seek out reference assistance. A graduate student in FG4 stated, "Chat is attractive when you are busy working, you can just go and chat." The other participants agreed. FG1 students agreed that in-person reference desk staff should suggest the use of virtual reference when there were line-ups at the desks. "I would not have to speak to a librarian face to face, so I would be able to ask more honest questions," stated a participant in FG6. Another student in FG6 noted, "Once the librarian helps you in the library and the librarian mentions virtual reference, it isn't impersonal any more." "Online is self-gratification," noted a participant in FG3.

There was a discussion in FG2 concerning when it would be appropriate to use virtual reference over a face-to-face interaction, specifically whether there should be a face-to-face interaction prior to the virtual reference visit or if virtual reference was acceptable for first contact. There was no consensus on the issue, but there was overall agreement that it depended on the student and his or her comfort level with using library resources.

When asked if there was anything they would find difficult or uncomfortable about using a virtual reference product, participants had some interesting ideas. The student who had previously noted a strong preference for face-to-face interactions stated that she would prefer to rely on coming into the library rather than talking with someone through virtual reference and then having to go to the libraries anyway and wasting her time. Several participants across the groups indicated the obvious— if the product was difficult to use, they would use it less. It was interesting that they said they would use it less, but they would still use it. Participants in various groups also pointed out that difficulty is subjective.

Participants in FG1 raised the issue of what questions were appropriate to ask. After a good laugh by the group, they agreed that any library-related questions would be acceptable. FG6 participants noted that some people do not like computers at all and that others may be afraid of chat rooms. One participant added, "Get them to use the product. They'll learn that you are friendly and get over the 'scary computer.'" "The computer is impersonal. You need to make it seem like a friendly interface with a friendly librarian operating it," noted another student. He added that his previous poor experience with a library staff member would make trying a new service uncomfortable. Participants in the undergraduate groups, FG5 and FG6, expressed a concern over how to end the session.

Participants in FG2 were concerned with the waiting time of e-mail and chat. One student expressed a dislike of potentially waiting for answers, and the others agreed with this. If the virtual reference staff member had to "leave" while answering a question, it was important to the group that they be told how long before the virtual reference staff would reply again and that the staff person keep in reasonably continual contact with the patron.

Design and Appearance of Virtual Reference Products

The majority of the comments for this section came from issues that participants had with our chat room and that they had noticed during the task-based testing; however, they can be applied to other systems. Many virtual reference systems are "out of the box," with little customizability, and these comments may be useful to exhort virtual reference providers to modify their products. Readers may also be able to extrapolate from the comments to increase the usability of their Web pages as well.

Participants had a number of comments on the design and appearance of the virtual reference product. A participant in FG1 stated, "There should be a good look and feel in the window we use, as it makes us use the tool more often." There was general agreement with this comment. FG3 participants expressed unanimous concerns that the virtual reference product should have an attractive interface, such as that of Yahoo Chat, and use graphics. FG4 students mentioned the need for graphical icons, such as a magnifying glass for the search symbol. A graduate participant in FG1 stated, "I haven't used UNT's virtual reference product, but I figured out that it has got not so good a look and feel. Most people get attracted by how it looks and how easy it is to use." The other participants agreed. In all cases, the discussions were initiated by an ESL student.

General comments included ensuring that the main things are easily seen through a good distribution and organization, using an adequate font size, avoiding clutter, making it easy to find the right links, offering an easy-to-read layout, and reducing "jumbling." Other comments were "Need a good and comfortable look with good color and spacing" and "Things need to be clear, especially options." An FG6 participant stated that it "must have a user-friendly appearance that appeals to even the computer non-literate." "I feel that improving the look and feel of a site makes a person surf the site longer," noted another person in FG6. "It needs to be in an order, make it easy so I can find things easily," added a participant in FG3. A respondent in FG4 reminded us to "Watch for providing too much information without drawing attention to specifics," noting that users of the virtual reference product want to see what they need to do quickly without having to read too much. This concept was also brought out in FG1, FG3, FG5, and FG6.

Bolding was recommended by participants in FG1, FG4, and FG5 as being useful to highlight important things, and was usually suggested by ESL students. The use of graphics was suggested by students in FG1 and FG4. Participants in FG1, FG2, and FG6 mentioned icons specifically and agreed that the icons need to be related to what they are describing. "I like the WebCT page. It has good graphics—I know what the pictures stand for," stated an undergraduate in FG1.

Bullets and stepwise instructions were suggested by all groups. "New things need to have more detail. All others should have short descriptions and use bullets," stated a student in FG2. A participant in FG6 added, "Differentiate things so we don't miss anything because it all looks the same." Providing a design suitable for scanning to find information was emphasized in the other groups as well. "Don't want to read—keep it short!" noted the undergraduate student in FG2. An FG4 undergraduate participant stated, "Information has to be easily accessible."

Color was a common issue for the participants in FG2, FG3,

and FG5. A student in FG3 mentioned, "Color coding for related pages or services would be useful, so that we will always know which section of the site we are on." One participant in FG5 talked about the "power of color"; putting different items in different colors enabled them to stand out. "Using different color options helps to make things more noticeable," stated a graduate participant in FG2, and the undergraduate student in the same group noted, "Different colored pictures or boxes would really help."

There were many comments about links. Participants in FG3, FG4, FG5, and FG6 desired links that are easily recognizable as being links, such as being in blue font and underlined, and FG1, FG2, FG5, and FG6 students emphasized that the links should be clearly labeled. A participant in FG3 emphasized that the links must be well organized. Students in FG3, FG4, and FG6 mentioned concerns about having too many repetitive links. One participant in FG6 noted, "Repetition can be helpful, but can also be too much."

Other design issues included: "Start at a general level, even if you have to go another page" (FG3); "Have clear objectives so navigation makes sense" (FG3); "Be as specific as possible" (graduate FG2); and "Be clear what each option will or can do" (graduate FG4). Any help or tutorials should be "interesting and short" noted an undergraduate student in FG4, and the rest of the group agreed. The undergraduate student in FG2 thought animation would be a helpful addition to virtual reference products.

Terminology

Terminology was another issue for the participants. "It must be understandable to us" was a common sentiment from participants in FG1, FG3, FG4, and FG5. "Terminology needs to be consistent" reminded students in FG3 and FG4. A student in FG3 stated, "Prevent phrasing and terminology that is confusing; just give me the simple stuff," and added, "Where logically I expected information to be, it wasn't. Make it easy for me to find what I need," and the rest of the group concurred.

Information Desired

During the discussion, participants indicated what types of information or questions they would ask through virtual reference. Online participants mentioned the desire to retrieve interlibrary loan information through virtual reference, possibly because at the time of this study we did not have an online method to do this. Other participants indicated "information" (FG1) and "information about other libraries, both part of UNT or nearby locations" (FG5). An FG5 respondent suggested, "Help with what areas or online programs would be right for finding the information I was looking for." "Information on the libraries and the services offered," added an undergraduate participant in FG4. A graduate participant in FG1 suggested virtual reference as a tool for asking where books are if they are not where they are supposed to be. Participants in FG2 and FG3 suggested offering alternatives when what they wanted was not available.

Expectation of Answer

Participants had a variety of expectations for the answers received through virtual reference. All participants in FG3, FG4, FG5, and FG6 stressed that the virtual reference staff should be "basically knowledgeable." They allowed that referring the patron to another person or the in-person methods was sufficient but at least wanted the virtual reference staff to get them started on an answer. An FG1 graduate participant noted that the virtual reference staff should guide the questions, but not ask invasive questions. This expanded to a consensual thought that there should be some sample questions available prior to entering the virtual reference product. Participants in FG6 thought that virtual reference staff should ask for helpful information, such as the course number, at the beginning of the transaction. One undergraduate student in FG1 noted, "I need an exact solution to my problem," and "I want to have a good and prompt answer for any of my problems any time of day." FG6 participants noted that librarians answering questions and giving out links was what they wanted. Participants in FG1 expected a more extensive answer than they would receive in the library and that the virtual reference staff would provide links to reliable Web sites. While FG6 participants agreed that hot links were good, they noted that they wanted a conversation, not just librarians throwing out links. All FG5 participants agreed that virtual reference should be personal and desired elaboration to their original question so they would not have to come back. An undergraduate student in FG4 raised the issue that virtual reference staff should give maximum help without giving too much, and other participants agreed.

Hours of Operation

Participants had comments on when and how long a virtual reference service should be open. As anyone familiar with library patrons would expect, the most common comment was that virtual reference should be available 24/7. After some discussion among the participants in groups FG1, FG2, and FG6, they reached consensus that longer hours should be available, quoting at least as long as regular reference desk hours (FG6) or as long as the library was open (FG1 and FG2). The undergraduate participant in FG2 suggested that both virtual reference and the reference desks should be open from 11 p.m.–2 a.m.

Response Time of Virtual Reference

The most common thoughts on the desired response time were "quick," "immediate," "rapid reply," "timely," and "fast." All participants felt the same way regardless of demographics. One person in FG6 added, "I have lots of things to do; I don't want to wait. There should be lots of people to answer right away." An FG1 graduate student stated, "I feel that a good/prompt response is the most attractive one if someone is using virtual reference." "It's a time issue; I want the information in the time that I think it should come through or I won't use it again," responded a student in FG3. The undergraduate participant in FG2 stated, "I want to know immediately, and not wait."

Several students noted that the initial response via virtual reference must also be timely and not just be a canned answer or directions to an answer. An FG4 graduate student noted, "There must be a quick response, even if I'm asked to hold," and an undergraduate student in the same group stated, "I want an immediate reaction, even it is 'Can you wait a minute.'" A respondent in FG6 added that the virtual reference product must be easy to find and fast loading.

After-Hours Alternatives

Participants also had comments concerning the need for communication and options when virtual reference was closed. Students in FG2, FG4, FG5, and FG6 noted that any directions to other options or another system, such as e-mail or another virtual reference system, need to be obvious and highlighted. Participants in FG2 were especially concerned that there be clear communication, whether virtual reference is open or not. One graduate student expressed it as "There needs to be something that says 'I am online, ask me for help' or 'I'm offline, send me a message.'" An FG6 student emphasized that he expected a live person during open hours, and when virtual reference was closed there needed to be a clear statement of what other options were available.

Staffing Issues

Already mentioned by a participant in FG6 is the desire to have a live person staffing virtual reference. Participants in FG2, FG4, and FG6 also noted this preference. "The virtual reference staff also need to be properly trained," added student in FG3.

FG5 participants unanimously desired a picture of the virtual reference staff member they were chatting with. They also noted the desire to have the name of the librarian. Participants in FG2 wanted the first name of the librarian, and, as one person stated, "A first name is more comfortable." The others concurred. However, an FG4 graduate student noted that there was "no uncomfortable feeling of a nameless or faceless person." A student in FG5 also wanted to know where the virtual reference librarian was located, and the rest of the group agreed.

Participants in FG1, FG5, and FG6 mentioned the need for

"friendly" and "pleasant" librarians. One student in FG6 noted that it must be "friendly service by first experience" or she would not use it again. An FG2 participant stated, "Anything is OK as long as we get help." "Whatever works is the best path," noted a student in FG3. Another person added, "I might rely more on coming here." All participants in FG6 agreed that there must be many librarians available to answer questions to avoid waiting times. The participants in FG3 noted that any virtual reference system needs to avoid too much "we'll get back to you soon" and must be reliable.

RESULTS FOR MARKETING AND PROMOTION QUESTIONS

Slogans

Participants suggested a variety of slogans for the virtual reference products. Building on an initial comment by a graduate student, FG1 decided that "virtual help" is a better term, since "reference" sounds like the "old reference." UNT's system is currently called "online reference help desk," and the participants in FG1 noted that this term does not indicate any form of interactivity, which is an important feature of virtual reference. An undergraduate participant in FG1 added that she "thought 'online help desk' was a search engine." FG5 participants emphasized that advertising for virtual reference requires positive slogans, such as "We want to help you." FG4 participants suggested, "To get help, click here," or similar slogans, and FG2 students added "Contact us."

Need for Marketing and Advertising

There was general agreement that the virtual reference product needs advertising and marketing. A participant in FG6 noted that UNT needs to be more successful at "getting the idea out there—many don't know." "People should know that there is a virtual reference service," stated the FG2 undergraduate. A graduate participant in FG1 added that it is important to advertise the benefits of virtual reference and what a user can expect. This comment received strong support from the rest of the group. In addition, all FG1 participants agreed that there should be a list of frequently asked questions (FAQ) and possibly sample questions. An FG1 undergraduate student noted, "I feel that every student should be aware of that product. I didn't know about the chat room until last week even though I connect to the libraries' site at least once a week." FG2 participants agreed that we need to advertise and that "students would be happy with it." FG3 participants suggested that increased access to the product would encourage students to use it. One participant in FG3 noted that word of mouth is the best marketing tool of all. "I hope that these steps will automatically market and promote the virtual reference product," stated an undergraduate participant in FG1.

Participants also had comments about marketing any new products or services. Students in FG6 implored us to "make the advertising obvious." FG2 participants agreed: "If you are advertising new things, better put in more information so we know how it benefits us," and "Highlight points you want students to remember." FG4 participants added that if we are advertising new things, we need to provide more detail and make it easy to scan when reading. A participant in FG3 suggested, "Start at a more general level—simplify things, especially terminology," and the rest of the group agreed and added that libraries need to write Web pages designed specifically for when students have specific objectives, such as "I need three articles on xyz topic."

Computer-Based Marketing Ideas

Participants offered numerous ideas for marketing with computers. FG2, FG4, FG5, and FG6 respondents suggested having a link on the libraries' home page. The FG2 undergraduate student suggested a "big, big link on home page" and added that "New services should be promoted on the libraries' home page for one month." A graduate student in FG2 stated, "Put something on the Web site that explains what virtual reference is and make it easily accessible, rather than just a link." FG5 participants agreed that there should be a new service advertised every day on the home page. An FG6 student noted, "The main home page needs to have a link to chat. It is all about fast, being fast," suggesting that a direct connection is needed, not just a link to another page. Another undergraduate student in FG6 disagreed and stated, "Advertising virtual reference on the home page would make it too busy. Everyone would use it." A student in FG2 added, "Advertise on more than the Web site."

Participants suggested the use of other Web pages for marketing virtual reference. The home page for the university was suggested by FG1, FG2, FG3, and FG4 students. FG2 participants agreed to a suggestion by a graduate student to put a link to the libraries on the main university page. An undergraduate student in FG4 expanded the suggestion to putting scrolling information about the library on the university home page. The student-services home page was mentioned by FG1, FG3, and FG4 participants as being a place to advertise virtual reference. Pages relating to online learners, such as the WebCT home page and the Libraries' Services to Off-Campus Users page, were suggested by F1, F2, and FG4.

Various forms of electronic communication were also discussed. An FG3 student suggested an electronic bulletin board for library information. Two students in FG6 and one FG4 graduate student suggested using e-mail, although participants in FG5 were united in their dislike of advertising through e-mail. An FG1 graduate student suggested using the Hotmail messenger system as a marketing tool.

There were several comments about using pop-up windows. A graduate participant in FG1 suggested using pop-ups, but only while the home page was loading, and the others agreed as long as it was a quick pop-up. FG4 and FG5 respondents also mentioned a very quick pop-up box that remains just long enough to be read and then disappears. An FG5 student suggested using a pop-up screen to provide a tip of the day as well. "I feel that a pop-up banner should appear on the front page when a new feature is added or modified," added a participant in FG1. In FG5 and FG6, participants suggested the use of screen savers or desktops for marketing virtual reference. FG5 participants favored screen savers, while FG6 students focused more on desktops.

Scrolling advertisements were suggested by participants in FG2 and FG4. A student in FG2 thought the advertisement should be at the bottom of the screen, and the others agreed. Participants in FG4 did not have strong feelings about where the ad should be located when it was raised by an online-learning graduate student.

An undergraduate respondent in FG1 suggested a flashing light or icon when users signed onto the computers. A flashing link to catch the user's attention was also suggested in FG5.

Posters, Pamphlets, and Flyers

An important aspect of marketing with flyers was expressed by a student in FG6, who stated, "If we can't get over there to see the pamphlets, make it easy for us and put them beyond the libraries." Specific in-library suggestions were putting placards on tables (FG1, FG6); leaving pamphlets or having banners at the Cyber Café (the libraries' coffee shop) (FG6); hanging them in advertising cases in high-traffic areas (FG4); or posting them in the washrooms (FG4). An undergraduate student in FG1 added, "I also feel that slips should be given to people who come to libraries about the virtual reference product and ways of using it."

Public computer labs on campus were suggested by participants in FG1, FG4, and FG5 as areas where flyers should be placed. The student union was mentioned by FG3 and FG5 students, specifically near the food court (FG3) and near the common seating areas (FG5). Banners were also suggested by FG5 participants as a way to advertise in the union.

Other areas on campus were also mentioned. A graduate participant in FG1 noted that "Slips should be kept on all the UNT notice boards about this product." FG3, FG4, and FG6 participants suggested well-designed banners around high traffic areas on campus. FG6 students agreed that the university newspapers would be a good place to advertise. A participant in FG6 suggested delivering postcards to students in residences. Another student in FG5 suggested advertising in residences. FG4, FG5, and FG6 participants mentioned advertising on the data-feed TVs located in various buildings.

Adding advertising materials for the libraries, and virtual reference specifically, in orientation brochures was suggested by students in FG3, FG4, and FG6. A participant in FG3 also advised that marketing materials should be included in admission packages. The course catalog (FG4), student calendar (FG3), and schedule of classes (FG5, FG6) were also suggested as places to advertise. A student in FG6 noted, "My boyfriend didn't have a pamphlet about the library and he is a transfer student."

There were suggestions to include flyers in student mailboxes; however, there was no consensus on the issue. Participants in FG5 did not agree with mass mailings to students, although several thought postcards would be acceptable as long as they had useful information on them. One student in the group emphasized, "Only important information should be included on the flyers, don't clutter them up with extraneous stuff." FG4 participants thought mass mailings would be alright, while FG6 students only agreed to postcards rather than traditional flyers. FG4 participants suggested distributing the flyers to organizations on campus and asking them to pass out the information in their offices and at meetings. International students' associations were specifically mentioned by both ESL and non-ESL participants.

The participants had a number of comments on the design and campaign of a visual presentation. A participant in FG5 noted the importance of changing the poster every month or so to keep it new, and the other participants agreed. Ensuring that print communications are colorful was emphasized by a student in FG2. The importance of ensuring that the communications are visually interesting and short was noted by an undergraduate participant in FG4 and readily agreed to by the other participants. Students in FG2, FG3, FG5, and FG6 emphasized the importance of clearly delineating the purpose of the virtual reference product and its benefits to the users when advertising. Participants in FG1, FG2, FG4, and FG5 mentioned that the brochures should explain what virtual reference is and how to use it. A student in FG6 reminded us that positive and easy-to-remember slogans are necessary when marketing.

In-Person Marketing Ideas

Participants suggested a variety of in-person ideas. A number of these focused on librarians' emphasizing new things, especially virtual reference, during training sessions, classes, and tours. A graduate student in FG2 noted that training sessions need more advertising. FG2 participants agreed that there should be an orientation to the libraries' Web site and services at the beginning of the semester. A student in FG3 mentioned the need for special emphasis on international students, and this idea was popular with the other participants. "The university tours were not enough. I was here on a university-arranged tour, and it was too fast. We walked into the library and walked out. Make orientations mandatory for students and include the library. It would help grades go up," stated a participant in FG6. A respondent in FG5 noted that we need to make the sessions fun for students. "Campus tours should be mandatory and include the libraries," suggested a student in FG5, and the other members agreed. FG4 participants emphasized the necessity of marketing our services beyond the libraries and suggested having courses somewhere in the student union and advertising these on both the TVs and the university's Web site.

Participants also suggested that the libraries use university activities to advertise and market the virtual reference product. Employment fairs (FG3), freshmen orientation (FG5), student club day (FG6), and international student orientations (FG4) were mentioned as potential marketing opportunities. Having "freebies," such as highlighters, bookmarks, pens, candy, etc., and food were noted as being especially important for any in-person sessions by students in FG4, FG5, and FG6. A suggestion by participants in FG5 was to have a computer at events or to take one to residences and cafeterias to let people try out the virtual reference product. One student said, "Go to the residence hall and have a hook-up for a computer and also have librarians to help. Have food." "Market it to someone who doesn't know how to use it," was a comment from another participant in FG5. "Go where the crowds are," stated participants in FG3 and FG5. Students in FG6 suggested that librarians participate in the marketing opportunities so students get to know them.

Involving the academic departments in the marketing of virtual reference services was a popular idea. Encouraging the academic departments to advertise the virtual reference system was suggested by participants in FG1, FG2, and FG4. "Ask the professors to tell the students about library services, especially virtual reference," was proposed by an FG1 undergraduate student and an FG4 graduate respondent. Participants in FG1 and FG4 agreed that the libraries should have special services, such as virtual reference, put on the syllabus. A graduate student in FG4 suggested asking the various departments and schools to promote the virtual reference service. "Instructors should be asked to pass out library information at the beginning of the semester," stated an undergraduate student in FG4. Participants in FG1 and FG4 unanimously agreed that the departments should put a link to the libraries on their home pages. "Advertising information for virtual reference could also be put on the departmental bulletin boards," suggested a student in FG2. An undergraduate participant in FG4 suggested that the departmental Web pages should have a link to library subject guides that list books and journals for the department or discipline.

SUMMARY

There was no clear variance in the comments between those of different academic status or gender. While not particularly strong, there was a trend towards a greater willingness to wait for an answer for those older than 25 years of age. Undergraduates, regardless of ESL status, wanted an immediate reply but were willing to wait once the first response came through. ESL students tended to be more vocal about wanting designs that included icons, bulleting, stepwise instructions, and highlighting to enhance the readability and usability of the product. However, all students wanted the ability to scan without reading. Use of colors was also raised as being an important component of an effective virtual reference system by many participants.

Several groups suggested providing a FAQ and sample questions. A number of participants wanted to know how the virtual reference worked and what they could expect from it.

Participants expected a live person during their virtual reference transaction. They were concerned that there be sufficient staff available to answer the questions and that the staff be able to get them started on the answer. Many students wanted to have the name, at least the first name, of the staff member, and several wanted to know where the staff member was located. The desire for a friendly, pleasant experience was a definite trend, and they felt virtual reference staff should work hard to put some personality into their interactions with users.

Although the most common response for open hours was 24/7, participants decided that virtual reference should be open at least as long as the library itself. There was concern that any form of after-hours support, such as e-mail or another virtual reference service, be clearly noted.

Participants had numerous ideas about marketing and advertising. Many of the comments focused on marketing beyond the library buildings. Attending university events and going to residences with a computer to allow students to try out the service were suggested. Marketing materials need to be colorful, scannable, and informative. Academic departments, student organizations, and Web pages were brought up a number of times as places to advertise. Including information on the libraries' services in student materials, such as admission packages, course schedules, and course syllabi was also suggested. Students suggested using computer technology, such as desktops, screen savers, and Web pages, as avenues for marketing virtual reference. Advertising through e-mail or mass mailings of flyers were not popular ideas. Sending postcards with the bare essentials received support from the majority of the students. Participants also noted that the marketing and advertising need to include information on how the product will benefit the users. The library should not expect users to automatically know what the virtual reference service can do for them or why they should use it.

CONCLUSIONS

Although only one of the participants had used any form of virtual reference, most students were interested in it and seemed willing to use it. The major concerns were open hours, timeliness of the first response, knowing the name of the virtual reference staff person, substance of the answer, being referred rather than helped, and wondering what types of questions could be asked. Developing a FAQ page and sample questions for the virtual reference service was a popular idea. Participants emphasized that marketing of the service needs to be outside of the library and done in several different ways. They suggested that virtual reference staff should assist with the in-person marketing in order to put a friendly face on virtual reference. The participants are looking forward to using a virtual reference service, and they appreciated being asked for their thoughts.

AUTHOR'S NOTE

While attending the Virtual Reference Desk Conference where this paper and the others in this book were presented, I was struck by how similar some of the comments were from my group of those with no virtual-reference experience compared with comments of those who had used a virtual reference service and were responding to a survey or some other method of evaluation. I would like to thank Gayla Byerly and Frances May from UNT Libraries for their assistance in gathering the data, and for their support and guidance while I was writing this paper.

REFERENCES

Balas, Janet L. 2003. "How to Make Your Library's Web Site Your Patrons' Favorite." *Computers in Libraries* 23, no. 1: 55–57.

Bruseberg, Anne, and Deana McDonagh-Philp. 2002. "Focus Groups to Support the Industrial/Product Designer: A Review Based on Current Literature and Designers' Feedback." *Applied Ergonomics: Human Factors in Technology and Society* 33, no. 1: 27–38.

Burns, Andrew D., and Stephen Evans. 2000. "Insights into Customer Delight." In *Collaborative Design: Proceedings of Co-Designing 2000*, UK, 11–13 September, edited by Stephen A.R. Scrivener, Linden J. Ball, and Andree Woodcock (pp. 195–203). London: Springer-Verlag.

Cavill, Patricia. 2002. "The Power of Focus Groups." *PNLA Quarterly* 66, no. 2: 4–6.

Connaway, Lynn Silipigni, Debra Wilcox Johnson, and Susan E. Searing. 1997. "Online Catalogs from the Users' Perspective: The Use of Focus Group Interviews." *College and Research Libraries* 58: 403–420.

Crowley, Gwenneth H., Rob Leffel, Diana Ramirez, Judith L. Hart, and Tommy S. Armstrong II. 2002. "User Perceptions of the Library's Web Pages: A Focus Group Study at Texas A&M University." *Journal of Academic Librarianship* 28, no. 4: 205–210.

Glitz, Beryl. 1998. *Focus Groups for Libraries and Librarians*. Chicago: Medical Library Association.

Hernon, Peter, and Ellen Altman. 1998. "Listening to Customers through Focus Group Interviews." In *Assessing Service Quality: Satisfying Expectations of Library Customers*, by Peter Hernon and Ellen Altman (pp. 137–146). Chicago: American Library Association.

Janes, Joseph. 2003. "Wrestling with Teens and Technology." *Voice of Youth Advocates* 26, no. 3: 201.

Jordan, Patrick W. 2000. *Designing of Pleasurable Products: An Introduction to the New Human Factors*. London: Taylor and Francis.

Krueger, Richard A., and Mary Anne Casey. 2000. *Focus Groups: A Practical Guide for Applied Research*, 3rd ed. Thousand Oaks, CA: Sage.

Large, Andrew, Jamshid Beheshti, and Tarjin Rahman. 2002. "Design Criteria for Children's Web Portals: The Users Speak Out." *Journal of the American Society for Information Science and Technology* 53, no. 2: 79–94.

Massey-Burzio, Virginia. 1998. "From the Other Side of the Reference Desk: A Focus Group Study." *The Journal of Academic Librarianship* 24: 208–215.

Morgan, David L. 1997. *Focus Groups as Qualitative Research*, 2nd ed. Thousand Oaks, CA: Sage.

Norlin, Elaina. 2000. "Reference Evaluation: A Three-Step Approach—Surveys, Unobtrusive Observations, and Focus Groups." *College and Research Libraries* 61, no. 6: 546–553.

Perry, Valerie E. 2002. "Putting Knowledge to Work Effectively: Assessing Information Needs through Focus Groups." *INSPEL* 36, no. 4: 254–265.

Widdows, Richard, Tia A. Hensler, and Marlaya H. Wyncott. 1991. "The Focus Group Interview: A Method for Assessing Users' Evaluation of Library Services." *College and Research Libraries* 52: 352–359.

Chapter 4

Expecting the Stars but Getting the Moon: Negotiating around Patron Expectations in the Digital Reference Environment

Joseph E. Straw

The emergence of digitally based reference services is changing the way people use libraries. The introduction of real-time, or chat, reference is having a dynamic influence on the way reference service is conducted. Increasingly the real-time option is becoming the medium of choice for virtual reference. Added to the electronic resources that libraries already have, chat reference services may be creating another level of expectations for librarians to ponder. An exploratory study of chat reference in an academic library will be examined to see how user expectations are playing out in this new environment. Suggestions and techniques for handling chat encounters will also be offered.

INTRODUCTION

In recent years, the nature of reference services has been transformed. The emergence of real-time technologies has made it possible to provide services in ways that could hardly be imagined a few years ago. Virtual reference services like real-time chat are allowing users to ask questions at the point of need, diminishing their dependence on the physical library. Reference librarians working on the front lines of these changes can hardly fail to notice that the expectations of their users may be rising with the technology. The library at the University of Illinois at Urbana-Champaign is a good example of a large research library that has integrated real-time reference into its service offerings. This paper will present an exploratory case study of chat reference transactions at Illinois to sketch out the expectations that users are bringing to these encounters and look at the possible disconnects between the expectations of users and what they are getting from the library. Practical suggestions for using the reference interview for negotiating through user expectations will also be pointed out and emphasized.

REVIEW OF THE LITERATURE

The literature in library and information science strongly endorses the idea of thoughtful consideration of user expectations. In the 1980s, many researchers began to focus on the new electronic technologies being introduced to libraries. Developments such as online catalogs and the conversion of print indexing and abstracting tools to usable electronic formats would inevitably change the way reference services were conceived (Cline and Sinnott, 1983). The very real possibilities presented by electronic resources could only lead some to feel that the desires of users would be conditioned by online technology (Fayen, 1982).

A more user-centered approach to user needs began to emerge in the years that followed. A study by Edwards and Brown (1995) of the expectations of faculty for library service found that academics and librarians differ on the emphasis that each places on aspects of service. A similar study by Xia (2003) found that a gap exists between users and librarians related to perceptions of digital service. Hanson (1999) speaks of a broader gap between the users' needs and the service capacity of the library. Fountain (2000) contends that this gap is best closed by libraries' providing the widest array of digital service offerings. Clearly, discerning user expectations is seen as playing a central role in setting up and evaluating future reference service.

The current literature does not provide a sense of user expectations as they happen in a dynamic reference setting. However, unlike a desk encounter or a user survey, real-time transactions leave a record of the actual question and the librarian's response, and so the type of expectations that users bring to virtual encounters can now be examined as they occur. Looking at records of chat transactions can provide a sense of what users expect from digital reference services. Examining virtual reference in this setting could provide an interesting mirror into the way that real-time service is actually working.

THE UNIVERSITY OF ILLINOIS

A logical starting place for looking at the dynamics of real-time reference would be a large research setting like the University of Illinois. The University of Illinois is one of the original land-grant institutions, opening in 1867. The campus is the largest in Illinois, covering almost 1,500 acres in the twin cities of Urbana and Champaign. A student body of 38,291 consists of 28,271 undergraduates and 10,020 graduate and professional students. Students come from all 50 states and over 100 countries, and over 90% of the undergraduates are Illinois residents. At the undergraduate level, eight colleges offer over 150 programs, and graduates can choose from 100 programs, including professional degrees in business, law, library and information science, and veterinary medicine. The University of Illinois [UIUC] is a Carnegie I research institution that ranks in the top five in the number of doctorates earned annually (UIUC, Campus Overview).

THE UNIVERSITY LIBRARY

The educational and research efforts of the university are supported by an extensive library system. The university library is one of the largest academic collections in the United States, with over 10 million volumes. More than 40 departmental libraries make up a system that serves students, faculty, and the general public. At the heart of the library system is the main library, which houses over 20 departmental libraries and the central stacks, which themselves contain two-thirds of the library's print collection. The remaining departmental libraries are spread across campus or situated near the academic units that they serve (UIUC, Library Help).

General reference service is provided by the reference and undergraduate libraries. The reference library is located in the main library and serves as a gateway to the library system as a whole. A collection of nearly 25,000 items supports the research needs of the university community and the general public. The reference library also provides assistance with identifying and using print and digital resources (UIUC, About Central Reference).

The undergraduate library primarily serves the undergraduate student population. Located across from the main library, the undergraduate library is the largest departmental library with over 200,000 items. Resources and assistance are provided for students doing class assignments for their core undergraduate courses. This library also plays an active role in promoting instruction and teaching with the ultimate objective of making students independent learners (UIUC, Undergraduate Library Tour).

VIRTUAL REFERENCE AT ILLINOIS

Both the undergraduate and reference libraries offer e-mail and real-time services. E-mail is, of course, the oldest virtual service, going back more than a decade. Many of the departmental libraries offer an e-mail option for their users. At the present time, only the reference and undergraduate libraries offer a real-time chat option, which has been in operation since 2001. The service is powered by the HumanClick software, which allows for very basic question-and-answer interaction. Currently, Human-Click does not provide for co-browsing or other more advanced interactive capabilities. Users can enter the service by clicking on the "Ask a Librarian" link from the library's gateway page. They will be welcomed into the system and they can pose questions when they are ready. Both the reference and undergraduate libraries have chat reference integrated into their regular reference desk service, and all staff pick up real-time questions as they occur.

THE PROJECT

Chat transactions were chosen as the best way to examine the operation of virtual reference services. The volume of transactions and the synchronous nature of chat services allow for an interesting view of how real-time reference is actually working. A dynamic record of a live librarian-user interaction can provide a sense of what questions are being asked in chat and what kind of expectations users might be bringing to these encounters.

The goal of this exploratory project was to see the expectations that users bring into the chat encounter and to see the extent of the gap between the expectations of chat users and what they get from the library. Expectations were found to be answers, advice, directions, or instruction that users seek from librarians in working through information problems. It was found that users could be grouped into two different categories of very general expectations: users seeking general reference assistance and those seeking information about known resources or services. Those looking for general reference assistance were asking what could be labeled traditional reference desk questions. These questions could be for locating books or articles on a particular subject, finding general information for a project, or just help about doing something in the library. The users in this category had no predisposition about the type of resource the librarian could use to solve their particular problems.

Users looking for a known resource or service were asking for things that they have some acquaintance with or experience in using. A basic level of research has already been completed and more specific assistance is being sought to negotiate a particular tool or service. This particular user may also be seeking an embedded answer based on the knowledge or perception that such content might be available.

Chat transaction logs in both the reference and undergraduate libraries for two weeks of interactions were chosen for examination. Two weeks from different "busy" periods were identified. The months of October in the fall and April in the spring are traditionally the months of heaviest activity at Illinois. The weeks of October 1–7 2002 and April 1–7 2003 were picked for the project. The questions were further analyzed and subjected to a rubric in which users were either directed to or asked for

- full-text online embedded answers,
- online indexing and abstracting tools,
- online catalogs,
- print resources, and
- directional or general library questions.

It should be noted that the transaction logs in Human-Click do not provide any personal information about users or library staff. When users enter the chat service, no name or contact information is solicited. Users of the system are advised that logs are being generated that could be used for management or statistical purposes. Unless users volunteer specific information, privacy of identity and security of place are largely secured in the HumanClick software.

LIMITATIONS OF THE PROJECT

Only two weeks of transactions were examined, so the activity of other weeks and months is not included. Since this examination is only looking at one institution, the chat experiences of other institutions, large and small, are also not included. The limitations of the Human-Click software might also affect how chats were worked through. Lack of co-browsing and other capabilities must be seen as affecting the answers to many of the chat questions. Given these limitations, the applicability of any general statement about the way real-time reference works will clearly be limited.

RESULTS OF THE PROJECT

Overview

In the two-week period, 594 chats were examined. Of these 594 transactions, 361 (61%) were completed to conclusion and 233 (39%) were not finished. The chats that were not completed include those that were never started and those that were worked on until they were terminated for some reason. Of the 233 chats that were not completed, only 21 (9%) were ended during the chat, and 212 (91%) were scratches that never got off the ground. Clearly, the percentage of chats not completed raises questions about the operation of the service. Users are obviously entering the system mistakenly or out of curiosity and not initiating chats. Queuing and the movement of questions through the system must also be seen as a concern that must be looked at in refining the chat service for the future.

When the chat operator responds to a live chat, a canned greeting is presented that asks the user to identify his or her affiliation as a student, faculty/staff, or general public. Of the 594 chats that were examined, in 342 (58%) the users' affiliation could be discerned. In these 342 transactions, 293 (86%) called themselves students and 22 (6%) were faculty and staff. Another small group of 27 (8%) were the unaffiliated general public, who can use the system but the service offered is generally restricted to specific questions about library holdings or services. Some of the students were able to identify themselves as either undergraduate or graduate students, but most just used the designation "student," which made it difficult to get a sense of the breakdown between different classes of students. Despite these problems, students clearly made up the bulk of chat users during the period examined.

General Reference Questions

Of the 594 chats examined, 382 could be classified as either general reference questions or questions about a known resource or service. Of these 382 transactions, 181 (47%) could be seen as general reference questions. These questions would be recognized by librarians working in a traditional desk setting where the expectation of the user is to solve an information problem. From actual chats, examples of this type of question would include the following:

> "Could you help me find information on how child abuse affects how kids do in school?"

"How can I research the ethics of genetic engineering?"
"I need to find information about campaign finance re-
form."
"I need help finding books, articles, or anything about
television violence."
"What is the current school population of Illinois?"
"I am a UIUC student doing research on the advertis-
ing industry from 1965–1979."

The user comes into this encounter without any knowledge
about a process or a resource that could help answer or work
out a given problem. Clearly, the librarian has the control in directing the user towards an answer or process that may help
tackle a particular question.

A very small percentage of these 181 chats directed users
towards an online full-text embedded answer. These solutions
involve delivering to the user a full-text article, document, reference resource, Web site, or something that delivers content
directly through the chat line. Of the 181 general questions, only
7 (4%) transactions directed users toward embedded answers
of any type. This low percentage reflects the librarians' understanding that full-text answers may not always be available or
have serious limitations in addressing general reference questions.

A far greater number of users were directed toward online
indexing and abstracting tools. Of the 181 general reference
questions, 78 (43%) were directed to this type of resource. Part
of a chat illustrates this type of encounter:

> User: I need to find recent information on ethnic mascots
> on sports teams.
> Librarian: Are you interested in college or pro sports?
> Would books, newspapers, or articles help you?
> User: It could be either. I would like to look at some recent
> articles.
> Librarian: Sure, you might be able to find some recent ar-
> ticles by using our InfoTrac or EBSCO databases.
> These can be good general places to look for informa-
> tion on a number of topics. If you have a few min-
> utes, I can tell you how to get on to these databases.

All of these 78 chats involved introducing the user to some kind of process. The process could be describing how to get into, navigate, or search through a particular database. These numbers certainly reflect an understanding by librarians of the importance of research articles in academic research and the need for instructing users about the complex workings of these resources.

Library catalogs were also suggested to a significant number of users. Of the 181 general reference questions, 33 (18%) dealt with library catalogs of some type. This would include directing users to the library OPAC, statewide union catalog, or a larger union catalog like OCLC, or RLIN. Part of an encounter of this type would include a discussion like this one:

> User: I need help getting information about Langston Hughes.
> Librarian: Do you need something in an article, book, or a short overview?
> User: I need something in more detail.
> Librarian: Would a formal biography or treatment of his work be OK?
> User: Yes, that would be fine.
> Librarian: Great, you may want to start by searching the libraries' book collection.
> Librarian: You can do this by searching the libraries' online catalog. You can get there by going to the library gateway page at: http://www.library.uiuc.edu and selecting the "UIUC Library Online Catalog" link. If you would like I can give you some tips on searching the catalog?
> Librarian: When you click on the catalog select "Quick Search" and you can start with a subject search under Hughes, Langston, and this will call up biographies and other things about Hughes, and might be a good starting point.

All of these encounters involved describing a process or instructing users on access or use. While these encounters directed many users to available print collections, a very small number of chats actually directed users to specific print resources. Only 5 chats (3%) directed users to a print resource, clearly placing print options outside of consideration as a resource of first re-sort for this group of users.

A surprising number of questions dealt with directional or general library issues. Users with no experience of services or policies were put into this general reference category. Of the 181 general reference questions, 58 (32%) were directing users to in-formation about locations, service offerings, and library policies. Examples of questions of this type would include:

> "Can I get a book from another university sent here?"
> "Does the library have a Web page?"
> "Can undergraduates check-out things from the Main Li-brary?"
> "I have not been to the library can you tell me where the English library is?"

Clearly users still want to find out about what the library has to offer, and librarians are ready to provide this kind of infor-mation through the real-time medium.

Users expect that real-time chat can provide for them very standard and conventional reference service. Librarians are di-recting users to online databases, library catalogs, and other re-sources that have long resided in the library. The approach to answering the majority of these questions is process oriented rather than answer oriented. In tackling questions from this group of users, the librarian recognizes that instructing users about a resource is connected to the library's ultimate utility in solving a particular problem.

Known Resource or Service

Of the 382 chats that could be classified, 201 (53%) were ques-tions about a known resource or service. These encounters seek focused assistance on things about which the user has knowl-edge or experience. From actual chats, examples of these types of questions would include:

> "I need to use the Contemporary Women's Issues database; how can I access it?"
> "Can I sort by sponsoring institution in Compendex?"

> "Can I just call up full-text articles when I search Periodical Abstracts?"
> "The gateway is confusing; how can I get to ERIC?"
> "I used to be able to get JSTOR from home and now I can't."
> "How can I mark and save documents in Psycinfo?"
> "I am a graduate student looking for the full-text of an article called "New Imperialism."

The user brings into this encounter some experience and is looking for additional help in working through a particular resource. The users clearly have more initial control in presenting their expectation of service in this type of encounter.

A large percentage of these 201 encounters were users asking for delivery of online full-text embedded answers. Users wanting specific documents, articles, and Web sites are asking the library to provide real content through the chat mechanism. Of the 201 chats of this type, 65 (32%) were asking for this type of assistance. Of these 65 users, only 15 (23%) were actually provided with some type of embedded answer while 50 (77%) were directed to some other resource. Part of an actual encounter illustrates how most of these were worked through:

> User: I am looking for a link to the full-text of the August 2002 Journal of Strength and Conditioning Research volume 16 page 343."
> Librarian: Hold on while I check.
> Librarian: The library does not subscribe to an electronic version of this journal and we only carry the journal for 1993 (Vol. 7) in print. Can you look at any other journals?
> User: They said that this would be a good article. I need to find articles about conditioning for football.
> Librarian: OK. Something like Sport Discus will help you find other articles about conditioning.
> User: How do I get in?
> Librarian: Begin at the Web page: http://www.library.uiuc.edu.
> Click the link "Article Indexes & Abstracts Full Alphabetical List."
> Click the letter "S."
> Scroll to "Sport Discus."

All of the users not getting embedded answers were redirected to some kind of indexing or abstracting tool and given instructions either for access or searching. This is an interesting disconnect between users who see the real-time mechanism as a delivery tool for content and the librarian who looks at real-time as a communications technology that can clarify and work through questions but is limited in providing answers to the desktop. This group of users is bringing a very high expectation into the chat encounter and perhaps getting a very practical lesson in the limitations of digital technology.

Another large group of users were seeking help with online indexing and abstracting tools. All of these users were looking at a specific database and wanting instruction on accessing, navigating, searching, or reading citations. Of the 201 chats about a known resource or service, 47 (23%) were of this type. Of these 47 encounters, 32 (68%) were able to work through the question within the confines of the resource that the user specified. Another 15 (32%) could not be worked through with the specified resource and the user had to be redirected to the library OPAC, Web site, or print resource. Here is part of an encounter of this type:

> Patron: I am using ERIC to find some sources about John Dewey.
> Patron: I am getting lots of information most of it on using theory in classrooms.
> Librarian: Are you looking for something more general?
> Patron: Yes.
> Librarian: You could try to look up something biographical in the library catalog.
> Patron: That would work.
> Librarian: Have you used the online catalog?
> User: Yes I have. Can I search under Dewey?
> Librarian: Yes, search under subject for Dewey, John.

In some of these cases a disconnect is evident, with the user expecting good things from a particular resource, and the librarian having to temper the expectation based on more appropriate options that may exist inside or outside the library.

A few users requested help in using library catalogs. Of the

201 encounters about a known resource, 25 (12%) were related to issues of accessing, searching, or troubleshooting library catalogs. Examples of some of these questions would include

> "Does the library catalog find videos?"
> "Will my catalog search cover things in the commerce library?"
> "Can I limit my search to books after 2000?"

All of these encounters were worked through within the confines of the specified catalog, which in all cases was the library OPAC. With users being directed to available print collections through the OPAC, still only a small number of users were asking about specific print resources. Of the 201 chats dealing with known resources, only 11 (6%) were asking for help about specific print resources.

The number of chats dealing with directional or general library questions was again surprisingly high. Users that had some experience with locations or general library services were put into this category. Of the 201 encounters in this category, 53 (26%) were asking about known library locations, policies, or services. Questions of this type would include

> "I am faculty using the 'my account' feature trying to remember how to renew books."
> "I remember using an hours page on the Web; can you tell how to access it?"
> "I was in the reference room and no one was at the desk. Have the hours changed?"

All of these chats were worked through and involved some kind of instruction in helping the user better understand what library services are available.

Chat users are asking more questions about things in which they have some knowledge or experience. In most cases, the librarian can work through the question within the parameters set up by the user. In other cases, however, a gap exists between what the user expects and what the librarian can provide. The gap is greatest for users who expect delivery of full-text content on their desktops. Clearly not everything is available full-text, and librarians must be prepared to honestly grapple with technological limitations and be able to suggest viable alternatives. For those using online indexing and abstracting tools, an awareness of a specific resource may not guarantee that it will be appropriate or suited to the actual information need.

WORKING THROUGH EXPECTATIONS

User expectations are an important consideration when thinking about the form of real-time reference options. Some expectations for services in the virtual world have been identified in the virtual reference transactions of a large academic library. It has also been found that most of these encounters involve working out a process or a resource to help the user. Clearly, techniques for working through real-time encounters must be given serious consideration when thinking about this kind of service. Changing technology has not changed the central role that negotiation and the reference interview play for both librarians and the user.

GENERAL REFERENCE QUESTIONS: CONTINUITY OF THE REFERENCE INTERVIEW

In this sample of real-time chat just under half the users (47%) were asking for general reference assistance. These questions are more open-ended and are not tied to a particular source. These are some more examples of this type of question:

> "I am a UIUC student looking for literary criticism on a poem by Emily Dickinson."
> "I wanted to know how to research for a biology project."
> "I am looking for information about Puerto Rican health issues."

These users are looking for information on a topic and are ready and willing to accept information as directed by a librarian. This situation is not all that different from what librarians face at the traditional reference desk. In this environment, the reference interview can proceed quite logically from the question to an answer. With some modification for the chat medium, the basic pattern of the reference interview can work well in this type of situation. The principal steps of greeting/introduction, questioning, finding information, and presenting information can remain basically the same.

Greeting/Introduction

The initial introductory communication is as important in the real-time world as it is at the reference desk. At the University of Illinois a canned message provides the initial greeting that welcomes the user and asks for affiliation as a student, faculty, staff, or general public. Canned messages can sometimes provide the first contact from the librarian's point of view, but if the user offers an initial greeting the librarian should respond with another greeting. Establishing some kind of informal rapport can often provide a strong start to a chat encounter. A "hello" or some kind of greeting establishes the user as a human being and sets the tone that the encounter will take to the end. An informal conversation sets up the working relationship that will establish the level of trust the user will surrender to the librarian. In the chat world, an initial conversation creates a steady flow that can help keep the chat running smoothly.

Questioning

Questioning is at the heart of the reference interview. A large group of users in this sample want solutions to broad problems, and good questions can establish the context in which the users' needs can be discerned. The mix of closed- and open-ended questions can help the librarian sort out what will work in solving a particular information problem. Questions should always come before answers, and librarians should avoid rushing into a quick solution. Part of an actual chat is a good illustration of what librarians might want to avoid:

> User: I am a student looking for information on ethics in business.
> Librarian: Use InfoTrac to find articles on this topic. You

> can get a lot of article information that's current and
> print out many of the references' full text.

Jumping into this answer may provide a helpful resource, but
the user may not want or need articles for this project. A series
of initial questions can give a more accurate sense of what a user
might actually want or prefer. Questioning can give the user a
chance to reflect on the question and better help the librarian
to provide the ultimate answer.

The chat medium can also complicate the communication
process during questioning. The reference librarian and the user
are physically separate and have no access to each other's nonverbal or visual cues. Sometimes typed responses can give clues
to the emotional level of the encounter, but the reference librarian has the responsibility to clarify the direction of the chat to
ensure that both parties understand each other (Bowman, 2002).

Finding Information

After the user's need has been discovered, finding the information is the next stage in the process. Searching for the information is the application of the librarian's skill in connecting the
user with the right information. In chat reference, the librarian
and user are separated from the physical library, and this conventional boundary can pose problems. To find the information,
the librarian may need to break abruptly from the encounter to
verify a fact or sketch out a strategy for a database. This situation can prove to be stressful because the user is put on hold
and can't see what the librarian is doing. The librarian must be
prepared to tell the user what he or she plans to do, and advise
the user to hold the line while the librarian works through the
question (Straw, 2000).

Presenting Information

Presenting some kind of information closes the reference interview. Communication in a chat mode requires typing out questions and responses, which can prove to be problematic. In the
haste to provide quick answers, committing typos and spelling

errors can be very common. Sometimes responses can also come out jumbled or incoherent, and the intended meaning can be altered or changed. To assure that the correct information gets through, librarians should consider breaking up longer answers and sending out shorter messages. Long composition periods should be avoided, and a conversational tone should be maintained as the chat encounter is concluded (Ross, Nilsen, and Dewdney, 2002).

KNOWN RESOURCE OR SERVICE: ADAPTABILITY TO FIT THE SITUATION

A very traditional type of reference interview can be effective in working through the large number of users who are asking general reference questions in this sample, but is the reference interview different in addressing questions about known resources or services? In this examination of chat transactions, more than half of the users (53%) were asking for a resource that they had some acquaintance with. Many of these questions show users needing resources that the librarian can't provide, creating some additional challenges. Clearly, the reference interview is much more answer driven in this type of encounter and does not proceed seamlessly from a question to an answer. Librarians must be ready to provide an initial answer and hope to move the encounter to more generalized questioning that might clarify a hidden user need. Librarians must also be prepared to negotiate through the answer they provide because they may be different from the users' initial expectations.

Initial Answer

Many users in this sample are specifying the search engine, full-text resource, or database that they think will solve an information problem. At home, in the library, or at work users have done some foundational research and are seeking further advice. The reference interview is starting from a different point and may not conform to the tidy steps that librarians have been taught. Librarians are clearly obligated to answer the user's question, but they also have a responsibility to discern the context of the user's question. An example of a chat illustrates this well:

> User: I am a UIUC graduate student looking for the online full-text of Feminist and ethnic literary theories in Asian American literature by Shirley Lim in Feminist Studies, fall 1993 V.19 n3 p.571.?
>
> Librarian: Let me check that for you.
>
> The library does not have an online version of this journal but we do have the whole run of this journal in print from 1972–present under call# 396.05FE in our Main Stacks.
>
> Are you researching theories about Asian American literature?
>
> User: Yes, I am trying to find research articles dealing with sexual and racial identity.
>
> Librarian: Have you looked anywhere or found anything?
>
> User: Really, just getting started. I have some books but I have just the reference to the one article.
>
> Librarian: You might want to consider trying the MLA bibliography, which is a database of literary criticism and analysis. You can get there from the library Web (http://www.library.uiuc.edu) and select the "Online Research Resources" link. At the next screen type in MLA in the box labeled "Words in description," and a link for the MLA database will come up at the next page.
>
> User: Thank you I will give it a try.
>
> Librarian: Given your subject you may want to visit and run this question by the librarians in the Women and Gender Studies library (http://www.library.uiuc.edu/wst/) and the Asian Library (http://www.library.uiuc.edu/asx/). These libraries have collections and knowledge in these areas that may give you some more ideas.
>
> User: Thanks for your help.

The reference librarian must be prepared to turn an answer into a question and create an opportunity for discovering if anything deeper might lie beneath the surface. This can be done by posing a question with the answer and looking to see if a user might supply more information for further questioning. If users are coming to chat after having done searching on their own, the librarian can also ask about their search strategies, suggesting ways that they could be modified to produce better results. These things can help the librarian clarify a hidden agenda and provide more focused and useful help.

Negotiating through Questions

When users come into chat asking about a specific resource or service, the librarian must face the possibility that they may be asking for something that might be unavailable or inappropriate. Those who have a sense of what they want, particularly for digital information, are forcing librarians to adapt to a new kind of user. Users today are computer savvy and are accustomed to speedy information gratification. Many have been seduced by the ease of browsing the Web and bring into the real-time encounter heightened expectations for quick and easy answers. Librarians have an educational responsibility to help the user better understand the difference between their own computer skills and the research skills they need to be developing. Being able to explain the workings and limitations of the available electronic technology is an important first step in redirecting the user. The librarian has to be prepared to negotiate the user down and suggest a source that has its own value in answering the question. Having real alternatives is clearly a key in working through this kind of encounter. These encounters are great opportunities to redirect the user into the library, where the librarian's knowledge of the collection is central to providing alternatives and value-added service to the user.

CONCLUSION

Real-time reference options are perhaps the fastest growing virtual reference service offered by libraries today. Expectations for this type of service were examined by looking at chat transactions from a large academic library. This project found that users expect answers to general reference questions, and they are increasingly looking for known resources or services. Users and librarians differ in their expectations for full-text delivery, and to some extent with online indexing and abstracting tools. Librarians must be ready to negotiate through all types of expectations using both traditional and modified reference interview techniques. The efforts to work through chat questions must be seen as real opportunities to educate the user and market the services of the library.

REFERENCES

Bowman, Vibiana. 2002. "The Virtual Librarian and the Electronic Reference Interview." *Internet Reference Services Quarterly*, 7 no. 3: 3–14.

Cline, Hugh F., and Lorraine T. Sinnott. 1983. *The Electronic Library*. Toronto: Lexington Books.

Edwards, Susan, and Mairead Brown. 1995. "Quality in Information Services: Do Users and Librarians Differ in Their Expectations?" *Library & Information Science Research*, 17 (Spring): 163–182.

Fayen, Emily Gallup. 1982. "The Electronic Library in an Academic Setting." In *Managing the Electronic Library: Papers of the 1982 Conference of the Library Management Division of the Special Libraries Association*, edited by Michael Koenig (pp. 9–13). New York: Special Libraries Association.

Fountain, Lynn M. 2000. "Trends in Web-Based Services in Academic Libraries." In *World Libraries on the Information Superhighway: Preparing for the Challenges of the New Millennium*, edited by Patricia Diamond Fletcher and John Carlo Bertot (pp. 80–93). Hershey PA: Idea Group Publishing.

Hanson, Terry. 1999. "Managing Reference and Information Services." In *Managing the Electronic Library: A Practical Guide for Information Professionals*, edited by Terry Hanson and Joan Day (pp. 335–336). New Princeton, NJ: Bowker-Saur.

Ross, Catherine, Kirsti Nilsen, and Patricia Dewdney. 2002. *Conducting the Reference Interview*. New York: Neal-Schuman.

Straw, Joseph. 2000. "A Virtual Understanding: The Reference Interview and Question Negotiation in the Digital Age." *Reference and User Services Quarterly*, 39 (Summer): 376–379.

University of Illinois at Urbana-Champaign. 2003. Campus Overview (4 October 2003). Available: www.uiuc.edu/overview/facts.html.

University of Illinois Libraries. 2003. Library Help (21 October 2003). Available: http://door.library.uiuc.edu/libraryhelp.html.

University of Illinois Reference Library. 2003. About Central Reference (3 September 2003). Available: http://door.library.uiuc.edu/rex/about.html.

University of Illinois Undergraduate Library. 1999. Undergraduate Library Tour: Frequently Asked Questions about the Undergraduate Library (19 February 1999). Available: http://door.library.uiuc.edu/ugl/BI/Tour/uglfaq.htm.

Xia, Wei. 2003. "Digital Library Services: Perceptions and Expectations of User Communities and Librarians in a New Zealand Academic Library." *Australian Academic & Research Libraries* 34, no. 1 (March): 56–70.

PART II

Virtual Reference Librarians

OVERVIEW

As with traditional reference, the service ethic is of critical importance in the universe of virtual reference. Yet computer-mediated communication is clearly presenting unique and difficult challenges to librarians. The importance of properly preparing librarians for their new role within the virtual reference domain is apparently taking time to ripple through established educational and training programs. For training, many librarians heretofore have had to rely on vendors, who naturally focus on the nuances of their particular software.

In this section, Lydia Eato Harris argues that training digital reference librarians, in both graduate courses and continuing professional education, must encompass computer-mediated communication and multitasking skills along with software skills. Joseph A. Salem, Leela E. Balraj, and Erica B. Lilly surveyed virtual reference staff members several months after their training to identify the importance and proficiency of the following skill sets: technical, communication, instructional, database-searching, and Web-searching skills. Jessica Bell and April Levy offer constructive advice on how digital reference librarians can better incorporate approachability and friendliness in their language and Web design.

These three chapters demonstrate that virtual reference has moved from being merely a software tool to a distinct way librarians can assist patrons. While its full potential is yet far from being realized, it is critically important that we continue to work on how to best prepare librarians for this public service medium.

Chapter 5

Software Is Not Enough: Teaching and Training Digital Reference Librarians

Lydia Eato Harris[1]

For three years, the question of whether software training is enough to prepare digital reference librarians has been researched. The first study involved library and information science (LIS) students as well as current digital reference practitioners. The second study focused on digital reference librarians and their experiences. The results of both studies suggest the need for additional training and practice in order to conduct asynchronous and synchronous digital reference. An introductory digital reference course was designed at the University of Washington that focused on practice. Student evaluation indicated software training was not enough. Further examination of digital reference education as developed by other universities has led the author to consider the need for developing three key components in the area of digital reference education.

INTRODUCTION

"[Real-time virtual reference] replicates the intimacy of one-to-one reference interviews and requires little retraining on the part of the reference professional (other than technical training)" (Lankes, 2000, 7). This quotation from the organizer of the Virtual Reference Desk Conference triggered a series of studies designed to investigate the validity of the premise that librarians need "little" other training than training in software applications to adequately handle the virtual reference environment. Specifically, the first research project (Smith and Harris, 2001) asked if there are differences in the knowledge, communication skills, and environmental elements utilized in a traditional reference situation versus a virtual reference situation. If so, what are they? Are the necessary skills for successful virtual reference librarianship being taught in the traditional reference class? The second research project (Harris and Smith, 2002) focused on the specifics of computer-mediated communications in a synchronous virtual environment from the librarian's perspective.

The results of these studies led to the development of an introductory course in digital reference. Based upon the students' feedback, a cursory study was conducted that examined how other library and information science (LIS) programs incorporate digital reference into their curricula. Finally, the digital reference course was redesigned and a set of considerations for the training and education of digital reference librarians was developed.

REAL-TIME VIRTUAL REFERENCE REQUIRES REAL-TIME VIRTUAL REFERENCE SKILLS

In order to assess any differences in the knowledge, communication skills, or environmental elements in the traditional versus virtual reference experience, two exploratory studies were conducted to gain insight into librarians' experience (Smith and Harris, 2001). The first study focused on asynchronous virtual reference, otherwise known as electronic mail (e-mail) reference services. Using e-mail, information seekers submit their questions to an online service. Librarians receive the questions, may try to obtain clarification through an additional e-mail interaction, research the questions, and send return messages within the specified period of time set by guidelines. The second study surveyed virtual reference librarians working in synchronous, also known as chat, or real-time, virtual reference services. For this study, synchronous virtual reference involved the information seeker's querying the librarian in real-time through a computer connection. The librarian researched the information while maintaining written (text) contact with the information seeker, eventually providing direction or information as requested.

Students enrolled in the University of Illinois at Urbana-Champaign distance option for LIS education (LEEP) who had taken a reference class (LIS 404) were recruited via their bulletin boards. The course, taught by Smith (2003), is offered online to students utilizing both synchronous (live) class sessions and asynchronous instructional media. One of the assignments involved volunteering as a digital librarian for the Internet Public Library (IPL) and answering at least five questions.

Eighteen students, all of whom had completed the required IPL course requirement, responded to an 11-question survey distributed via e-mail. The survey contained open-ended questions regarding prior reference experience, other reference courses taken, feelings of preparedness, the challenges of and the sources of satisfaction with the experience, continuing education needs, and if involvement in the LEEP program made a difference.

Eleven of the students had no prior reference experience. Of the remaining seven, prior experience ranged from students with 12 years' experience to one student who had just acquired a reference librarian position during the class. Six of the students had completed or were taking other reference courses, such as science and technology, business, social science, medical, government documents, and online retrieval. Therefore, this self-selected sample had a number of students with a vested interest in reference work and a distinct desire to develop their reference skills.

All but one of the students indicated they felt prepared for the IPL assignment as a result of their LEEP experience. Many of the responses discussed the similarities between the LEEP and the IPL virtual environments. When asked about the skills they found they needed to develop or modify for the IPL experience, the majority identified four:

- knowledge of online resources,
- written communication skills,

- research strategies, and
- online searching skills.

Three predominant themes were mentioned as challenges in the IPL environment. One was the lack of "face time," being unable to obtain clarification from information seekers as is naturally facilitated in the traditional reference desk interview. Since IPL policy restricted the students to providing freely accessible resources on the World Wide Web, this was an additional challenge. Last, librarian students were unsure how to cope with the lack of feedback from users, not knowing if the answers they provided were sufficient.

The student librarians found a number of sources of satisfaction with the asynchronous virtual reference experience. They enjoyed the freedom in self-scheduling the work; the ability to take the time to search for a good answer without the information seeker being present; the problem-solving; being able to select questions; exploring different resources and expanding their abilities through the process; receiving positive responses from users; a feeling of a lack of pressure; and receiving interesting questions from interesting users.

Fifteen of the respondents described continuing education needs for asynchronous reference work. Five areas were identified:

1. to be regularly updated on freely available, authoritative resources;
2. improving search strategies, i.e., identify best practices and tips;
3. writing skills;
4. new technology;
5. feedback from other researchers.

One of the additional benefits the LEEP students were able to enjoy was posting their answers to a private class bulletin board, and sharing questions and answers. There were several features of the LEEP experience the student librarians mentioned that they felt contributed to the successful completion and positive reaction to the IPL assignment. Online research was developed as a pattern of behavior for them in the LEEP environment, a normal part of their regular school work. Students mentioned feeling a "personal connection" to the information seekers, drawing similarities with their daily class requirements of posting to bulletin boards. As one student stated, she felt "accustomed to considering the real person behind the virtual message, and treating them with respect for their intelligence and their need." Others mentioned that in the LEEP experience one learned the nuances of creating an electronic answer, learning to write concisely and clearly. Finally, one student stated that "LEEP fosters a commitment to cooperation and mutual assistance, so it seems perfectly natural to attempt to help someone who has requested it online."

In the second study, a ten-question survey instrument (containing all but the LEEP question) was distributed via e-mail to librarians who were recruited through listservs and currently working for a synchronous reference service. Of the 43 respondents, 18 were public librarians, 24 were academic librarians, and for 1 the type of library was unknown. Thirty-two of the respondents had obtained their master's degrees between 1980 and 2001; 34 had less than 20 years of reference experience. All but two of the respondents had been involved with synchronous reference for two years or less. The question regarding the amount of time spent each week involved in synchronous reference produced ambiguous answers.

All but four of the respondents indicated they had received software training, primarily offered by vendors. The other four were self-taught. When asked what knowledge and skills were needed to conduct synchronous reference interactions, the respondents gave several varied responses:

- Multitasking
- Learning the mechanics and idiosyncrasies of the software
- Written communication skills
- Learning to "compact" the reference interview
- Interacting effectively in the chat environment
- Compensating for the lack of nonverbal cues
- Speed typing
- Quick thinking
- Knowledge of Web resources and efficient search techniques

- Rapid evaluation of the quality of Web resources
- Learning to maintain an online presence in the virtual environment
- Evaluating the software to support the service

Synchronous reference librarians also mentioned a number of challenges. Similar to the asynchronous library students, they discussed the lack of face-to-face contact and nonverbal cues. However, they also discussed the technology as not being "there" yet, difficulty in providing instruction, slow communication, time pressures, and the lack of patience expressed by users.

There were certain similarities in the sources of satisfaction between the synchronous and asynchronous virtual reference experiences: interesting questions from interesting users, receiving appreciative responses from users, and doing something new. Synchronous librarians also mentioned being able to answer questions in real-time and serving remote users from other states and countries as sources of satisfaction. The continuing education needs were also similar between the two sets of respondents, although the synchronous librarians specifically mentioned learning the best use of co-browsing technology.

TOMORROW'S VIRTUAL REFERENCE LIBRARIANS: AN ANALYSIS OF COMPUTER-MEDIATED COMMUNICATIONS (CMC)

A follow-up study, using open-ended questions, was conducted via an e-mail survey of degreed and experienced synchronous reference librarians. Only 15 responses were received: 4 from public librarians, 6 from academic librarians, and 5 from an unexpected third group, synchronous librarians working in a specialized environment.

Public librarians mentioned conducting synchronous reference while at the reference desk, while academic librarians were in specific office space. Public librarians stated that most of their interactions involved ready reference, and they experienced a real "fast food" feel to the answers. Questions involving source-related responses were to be referred to another service. Some questions were not amenable to synchronous reference for the public librarians, such as genealogical or mathematical questions. For the public librarians, the challenges mentioned involved resisting the impulse to give an answer, "any answer because you're live online"; handling interruptions, since virtual reference was being conducted simultaneously with regular desk service; having consortia users who did not realize they were not contacting their home libraries; and trying to establish relationships with the users. All of the public librarians mentioned the need for more practice with synchronous reference.

Academic librarians reported conducting synchronous reference from an office environment in which two-hour shifts were the maximum. They reported having a minimal amount of training or prior experience before working in a virtual chat environment. Academic librarians made use of print resources and expert assistance, e.g., subject specialists, on a regular basis. All reported receiving many thanks for their work. An interesting point made by one of the respondents was "Training . . . is needed in order to maintain the highest standard of reference service. Sometimes the virtual world can seem more informal, and it shouldn't be considered so by librarians." Another felt, ". . . if you have a decent education in librarianship, you can apply service concepts to digital reference as well as physical services." Still another admitted, ". . . at first I was nervous and would forget to conduct the traditional reference interview. I was just happy to zap a Web page with the information. Now I'm asking more questions and do more instruction and guiding so that they will become independent researchers."

Of the specialized-environment librarians, all were part-time or full-time synchronous reference librarians who were not based in a library environment. These librarians reported they had received software training, but little else. They seemed to be an almost distinctive group, reporting very high satisfaction levels with their work, discussing the adjustment to conducting reference interviews "via the keyboard," and realizing that some of the reference transactions would have been much faster in person or over the telephone. Their answers regarding the challenges were varied. One mentioned the high stress level of trying to handle multiple calls simultaneously. Others mentioned the need to be professional. Another stated there was less "burnout" in virtual reference than in traditional face-to-face.

AN INTRODUCTION TO DIGITAL REFERENCE

An essential element mentioned by students and practitioners of digital reference was the need for practice. In spring 2003, in conjunction with Dr. Joseph Janes, I developed a course at the Information School at the University of Washington, "An Introduction to Digital Reference." Among the objectives of this course were the following:

- To review the reference interaction with attention on search models and conducting reference in a digital medium
- To read scholarly articles on digital reference
- To familiarize students with online sources and conducting online searches
- To practice reference in an asynchronous environment
- To practice reference in a synchronous environment

In summer 2003, a two-credit course was taught with 20 MLIS students for three hours each day for nine consecutive days. The regular reference course was a prerequisite for taking the course. Students were instructed in models of searching, reference-interview techniques and considerations, as well as a brief review of online sources. QuestionPoint was used for conducting both asynchronous and synchronous reference, with the students having an opportunity to be both librarians and users of the system.

Of the 20 students, 19 completed evaluations of the course. Ninety-five percent rated the course as excellent or very good, with 79% rating the opportunity for practicing what was learned as excellent or very good. Fifty-nine percent of the students felt the intellectual challenge of the course was higher than average when compared to other college courses taken. Students reported they spent a median of 12.5 hours per week on the course and reported they felt the 12.5 hours were valuable.

Written feedback from the students centered on the need for even more time for practice. Most students requested the course be offered for four credits. Some of the students felt they did not have adequate time to absorb the concepts and skills required for digital reference and they depended too heavily on using search engines, specifically Google. During the synchronous sessions, students felt intimidated by the immediacy of the digital environment, often forgetting to conduct a complete reference interview. They also wanted additional time to evaluate the adequacy and sufficiency of their answers.

WHAT ARE OTHER SCHOOLS DOING?

During discussions on whether the digital reference course should be offered again or as part of the reference curriculum for the Information School, the University of Washington, Lorri Mon (personal communication, 2003) mentioned an informal review she had conducted of LIS programs. The question was how many of the programs included some form of digital reference as part of their curriculum. Mon reviewed the curricula for 24 LIS programs. A total of 33 "digital reference courses" was offered; however only 8 required "hands-on" digital reference practice. The majority of the courses included readings on digital reference or discussion of the traditional reference interview in the digital medium. In addition, Mon noticed "digital library" courses tended to focus on collections rather than services. Courses that stated they included "online services" or "digital reference" were referring to online searching and search negotiation rather than the virtual interview process. She also noted that courses with sections on "computer-mediated communication," "Internet communication technology," or "Internet" were not studying digital reference.

I attempted to replicate this review and was unable to verify any of the eight "hands-on" courses. I reviewed the syllabi for 16 reference courses offered by LIS programs in the United States and Canada. All made mention of digital reference and included readings; however, only three included a "hands-on" digital reference assignment.

While it was clear a course in digital reference practice has value to the students, it also became clear that such a course should not be conducted without consideration of theoretical context. In conjunction with Mon, the summer course is being redesigned, incorporating theoretically applicable information along with practice. During summer 2004, a two-section course will be offered for a total of four credits. The first half of the course will focus on the theory of digital reference, including information behavior in the online environment with discussion of social presence theory (Short, Williams, and Christie, 1976) and media richness theory (Daft and Lengel, 1984) from the CMC literature. Students will be required to read key articles from the digital reference literature focusing on the synchronous and asynchronous digital reference interview as well as research literature on digital reference users and online services, including current development, such as the rise of chat reference library consortia and automated disintermediation. The second half of the course will then focus on the practice of digital reference, including active learning in asynchronous and synchronous reference via the use of e-mail and chat software. Students will be encouraged to develop expertise in online intermediation interactions while maintaining appropriate attention to professionalism and quality of answers.

Developing the course raised more questions regarding the education and training of digital reference librarians, resulting in a broader vision of key issues for the field.

A FUTURE VISION OF LIBRARY AND INFORMATION SCIENCE DIGITAL REFERENCE EDUCATION

The research and teaching efforts described in this paper have led to a future vision of LIS digital reference education composed of three components. The first component is LIS education as taught at the master's level in accredited institutions. Should digital reference be incorporated into the structure of the traditional reference course or designed as a separate course? Are LIS educators who have taught traditional reference equipped to teach digital reference? Perhaps it is time to re-evaluate the traditional segmentation of reference coursework in its entirety. As Mon's (2003) study indicated, there are inconsistencies in terminology for educational purposes. Standardization of terms around core competencies would facilitate understanding between and among institutions and professionals. A research agenda in digital reference education is called for and should be answered through the Digital Reference Education Initiative (2003). However, this re-evaluation should not be interpreted to imply that traditional reference education should be eliminated. As Smith (2003) indicates, the traditional reference course serves multiple purposes in educating all LIS professionals whether they engage in the practice of reference or not. The studying of core reference materials, the emphasis on research strategies, and evaluation have value for all practitioners of LIS.

A second component of this future vision centers on supporting current practitioners. Continued life-long learning and education for librarians must be placed in the hands of LIS professionals and not left to vendors. The previous research supports the notion that software training is not enough. It is not sufficient, however, to provide practice, evaluation, and on-the-job training for practitioners. It is incumbent upon the profession to ensure institutional support for independent learning and education of librarians. Getting institutional support means developing institutional understanding, which requires educating institutional stakeholders to the value of continued education. In addition, the development of a framework of feedback and interaction for digital reference professionals would support both students and practitioners alike. A professional-to-professional network could be a source of continued learning for all members of the profession.

The last component is one that has been addressed in a number of venues: research. There are questions regarding context, such as can we educate for contextual differences and similarities? User analyses must continue to be conducted to answer questions such as how do asynchronous and synchronous reference services fit into the information-seeking behavior patterns of information service users? Education can be enhanced by the study of techniques: What computer-mediated communication techniques are effective in a reference service context? Lankes, Nicholson, and Goodrum (2003) have provided an outline for considering the digital reference research agenda.

NOTES

1. Special acknowledgment must be made to Dr. R. David Lankes for providing the inspiration for the initial research question; Dr. Linda C. Smith for collaborating and supporting the research; Dr. Joseph Janes, and Lorri Mon for encouraging discourse that aided in the development of this work.

REFERENCES

Daft, Richard L., and Robert H. Lengel. 1984. "Information Richness: A New Approach to Managerial Behavior and Organization Design." *Research in Organizational Behavior* 6: 191–233.

Digital Reference Education Initiative. (2003). Available: http://drei.vrd.org/about.cfm.

Harris, Lydia E., and Linda C. Smith. 2002. "Tomorrow's Virtual Reference Librarians: An Analysis of Computer-Mediated Communications (CMC)." Presentation at the Virtual Reference Desk Fourth Annual Digital Reference Conference, "Charting the Course for Reference: Toward a Preferred Future," Chicago, November, 2002.

Lankes, R. David. 2000. "Introduction: The Foundations of Digital Reference." In *Digital Reference Service in the New Millennium: Planning, Management, and Evaluation*, edited by R. D. Lankes, J. W. Collins III, and A. S. Kasowitz. New York: Neal-Schuman.

Lankes, R. David, Scott Nicholson, and Abby Goodrum, eds. 2003. *The Digital Reference Research Agenda*. Chicago: Association of College and Research Libraries.

Short, John, Ederyn Williams, and Bruce Christie. 1976. *The Social Psychology of Telecommunications*. London: John Wiley & Sons.

Smith, Linda C. 2003. "Education for Digital Reference Services." In *The Digital Reference Research Agenda*, edited by R. David Lankes, Scott Nicholson, and Abby Goodrum. Chicago: Association for College and Research Libraries.

Smith, Linda C., and Lydia E. Harris. 2001. "Real-Time Virtual Reference Requires Real-Time Virtual Reference Skills." Presentation at the Virtual Reference Desk Third Annual Digital Reference Conference, "Setting Standards and Making It Real," Orlando, FL, November 2001. Available: www.vrd.org/conferences/VRD2001/proceedings/smithharris.shtml

Chapter 6

Real-Time Training
for Virtual Reference

Joseph A. Salem, Jr., Leela E. Balraj,
and Erica B. Lilly

This paper examines training methods for virtual reference in general, focusing particularly on those employed at Kent (Ohio) State University in preparing to staff the "Chat with a Librarian" service through OhioLINK, a statewide library consortium. To better understand the needs that were met during training as well as the areas of focus for further training, the investigators surveyed staff after they had had the experience of working in the virtual environment. This paper reports the results of that survey as well as the training program that it measured and the steps taken to create a virtual reference culture among librarians at Kent State University.

INTRODUCTION

It should come as no surprise that staff training and development are considered to be essential to the success of any reference service; however, they are particularly important when implementing a virtual reference service. Even experienced members of a reference staff will need additional training before feeling competent and comfortable staffing the virtual reference desk. In a recent survey of Association of Research

Libraries (ARL) libraries, 69% of responding institutions felt that their staff needed additional training in order to make their chat reference services successful. According to the same survey, primary training needs to include not only technical training on the use of chat software, but also training in the transfer of more traditional reference skills to the virtual world (Ronan and Turner, 2002). Considering the value of training when implementing a virtual reference service, it is necessary to learn those methods that are most effective and those skills that are most needed by staff. To do that, the investigators surveyed staff after they had had the experience of working in the virtual environment. This paper reports the results of that survey as well as the training program that it measured and steps taken to create a virtual reference culture among librarians at Kent State University (KSU). Before examining virtual reference training at KSU, it is necessary to put it in its proper context through a review of the literature.

TRAINING FOR
VIRTUAL REFERENCE—BASIC ELEMENTS

A review of the literature on training for virtual reference reveals basic elements common to most training programs. These include core reference skills, real-time chat techniques, software-specific skills, and live virtual reference policies (Kawakami and Swartz, 2003; Meola and Stormont, 2002; Ronan, 2003; Ronan and Turner, 2002; Weissman, 2000; Williamson, 2003).

Core Reference Skills

Meola and Stormont (2002, 117) maintain, "live virtual reference is a new service rooted in traditional librarianship" and "answering live virtual questions is still answering reference questions: your reference librarians still need traditional core reference skills." Kawakami and Swartz (2003) concur, stating that individuals providing digital reference service at the University of California–Los Angeles (UCLA) must be experienced in traditional reference service and familiar with library policies. Meola and Stormont and Ronan (2003) suggest these essential proficiencies include reference interviewing and communication skills and knowledge of print and electronic resources. Meola and Stormont go on to add advanced search skills and the ability to evaluate sources for authority and bias.

Real-Time Chat Techniques

Virtual reference interactions may be more challenging because of the lack of visual and oral clues (Meola and Stormont, 2002; Williamson, 2002) and "the chance for miscommunication is greater" (Meola and Stormont, 119). Elias and Morrill (2003), Helfer (2003), Meola and Stormont, Ronan (2003), and Williamson (2003) recommend the following skills to provide effective communication in the chat environment: using short, concise, and frequent messages; learning how to type (but not worrying overly much about typos); adopting a friendly but professional tone; mixing scripted messages with live ones; and multitasking for efficiency.

Software Specific Skills

"Software specific skills include all procedures and features that must be mastered to answer a call using the specific software the library has chosen to use" (Meola and Stormont, 2002, 122). These skills include logging in, recognizing when a question comes in, answering a question, closing a session, logging out, simple technical fixes, and providing documented tips that are Web accessible (Jerant and Firestein, 2003; Kawakami, 2003; Kawakami and Swartz, 2003; Meola and Stormont).

Live Virtual Reference Policies

Written guidelines and policies that describe the elements of a virtual reference service help to provide consistency and quality of service in much the same manner that traditional reference policies do. They typically articulate the intended audience; level of service that may be expected; services provided (e.g., document delivery, information tools, and resources available); and user privacy policy. They ought to be documented and Web accessible (Martin, 2003; Meola and Stormont, 2002; Ronan and Turner, 2002).

TRAINING FOR
VIRTUAL REFERENCE—TRAINING METHODS

A number of different approaches, whether used singly or in combination, have been used to train virtual reference providers (Balleste and Russell, 2003; Kawakami and Swartz, 2003; Lankes and Kasowitz, 1998; Lipow, 2003; Martin, 2003; Meola and Stormont, 2002; Ronan and Turner, 2002; Tunender and Horn, 2002). These may include an on-the-job or learn-as-you-go introductory session, a train-the-trainer workshop held by the software vendor selected by the library, and in-house classes or workshops, which include training exercises followed up by mentoring and practice with more experienced colleagues.

Meola and Stormont (2002) also discuss training for a collaborative virtual reference service. Here, several libraries pool resources to purchase software and provide staffing. Training is coordinated across different sites, with a coordinator within each library. The service is available to patrons from every participating library, with the understanding that they may receive assistance from librarians outside of their institutions. Participating staff use a listserv to increase communication across the various sites and have access to Web documentation with tips and service policies. (KSU is part of a collaborative service through its membership in OhioLINK, but did not pay for the software used to participate in the statewide service; rather it is provided to all participating members of the consortium, and KSU pays for an individual seat to provide chat service exclusively to the KSU community.)

Transcript Analysis

Transcripts of virtual reference sessions may hold a great deal of information that is useful for training purposes. Ward (2003) describes their use as a tool for training graduate reference assistants, while Kawakami and Swartz (2003) suggest that they may be used for identifying additional training needs after an initial program has been in place. Smyth (2003) recommends using them for assessing the overall quality of service.

VIRTUAL REFERENCE AT KENT STATE UNIVERSITY

KSU is an eight-campus system, consisting of a main campus and seven regional campuses. Main campus enrollment is approximately 18,470 full-time students, while that of the regional campuses is 7,212 (Cartwright, Creamer, and Kandel, 2003). There are 13 librarians in the main campus library, eight of whom currently participate in the virtual reference service, and ten regional campus librarians, two of whom currently provide virtual reference. There are six graduate student assistants in the main library, all of whom provide virtual reference service.

KSU is a member of the OhioLINK consortium chat service, which consists of 84 Ohio colleges and universities, and the State Library of Ohio. The service is available to a potential 600,000 students, faculty, and staff users from OhioLINK member institutions only (OhioLINK User Services Committee, 2003). Three hundred librarians from 42 OhioLINK libraries participate 73 hours per week, with two librarians per shift (OhioLINK User Services Committee, 2003).

Library users may connect to the service via the OhioLINK home page, as well as from provided database-help screens and member library home pages. Initial training of service providers took the form of a "train-the-trainers" workshop conducted by OhioLINK librarians, with a follow-up, statewide training session titled "Reference Rendezvous." Online documentation is found in the OhioLINK Chat Service Manual (http:// library.utoledo.edu/userhomes/wlee/chatmanual.html) and at the OhioLINK WebRef Information site (http:// staff.lib.muohio.edu/~bbarr/webrefinfo/index.html).

Librarians at KSU provide virtual reference for OhioLINK in scheduled two-hour blocks for a total of eight hours per week. The main campus graduate reference students provide virtual reference for the KSU community 20 hours per week, typically during the weekday afternoons. Main campus librarians provide virtual reference for the KSU community in lieu of unfilled consultation office hours.

VIRTUAL REFERENCE TRAINING
AT KENT STATE UNIVERSITY

Several two-hour training sessions for librarians and library and information science graduate students were provided at KSU's main library in preparation for staffing the statewide OhioLINK chat seat and the local KSU chat seat. A modified session of a full-day train-the-trainer session provided by OhioLINK was employed at the KSU main campus. Local training was provided by KSU's chat coordinator and other librarians who attended the OhioLINK train-the-trainer session, focusing on technical skills, policies and guidelines, transferable reference communication skills in the chat environment, and non-transferable reference communication skills in the chat environment.

Training on technical skills covered three main components: software specific commands, multitasking abilities, and support venues. The chat software used by OhioLINK is Digi-Net Technologies' eLibrarian software (http://elibrarian.digi-net.com). Digi-Net is a privately held commercial corporation that develops software that allows companies to provide real-time customer support on their Web sites. The eLibrarian software was developed and marketed to other libraries as a result of Digi-Net's acquiring their first major library contract with OhioLINK. During training, KSU trainers provided staff with a hard copy of OhioLINK's online chat manual, a locally produced print chat cheat sheet, and hands-on time to develop skills using the eLibrarian software from both librarian and patron views. Multitasking skills were demonstrated during training by using the chat software while multiple Web browsers and other applications were running, which provided staff with a sense of what a typical chat session might entail. Multitasking between multiple chat sessions was discussed but not demonstrated until after staff became more proficient in providing chat service. Support avenues presented to staff providing chat service included vendor support and software upgrades, online and print documentation provided by OhioLINK and KSU's chat coordinator, a chat listserv run by OhioLINK, and tapping into the knowledge base of experienced chat staff.

Policies and guidelines developed both by OhioLINK and

by the Reference Services Team at KSU's main library were reviewed and discussed during training, focusing on staffing models, acceptable use, service guidelines, and standardized responses. Staffing model guidelines for staffing the consortia seat versus staffing the local institutional seat were presented. Acceptable use policies were reviewed during training, including intended audience, acceptable online behavior and enforcement, and privacy policies. Training covered various service guidelines, including types of questions that can be answered via chat, discerning when to provide the answer for the patron and when to direct a patron to the answer, and providing citations to sources used to answer questions. Standardized messages (automessages) and preselected Web addresses (push files) were set up and reviewed to establish a standard protocol for opening and closing a chat session and to speed up chat dialogue and Web sites sent to the patron. Staff were encouraged to send a mix of scripted and personalized chat messages when conducting a chat interview.

Reference communication skills that are transferable to the chat reference environment were discussed and demonstrated during training, including approachability, question negotiation, follow-up and closing, instructing versus answering questions, and referring. Staff could ensure approachability by making sure the chat software was connected and volume was turned on to hear incoming calls, sending a message acknowledgment when a call was picked up, and pacing oneself when dialoguing with the chat patron or when handling multiple calls. Training also focused on question-negotiation skills in the chat environment, including answering queries with a mix of open- and closed-ended questions, asking for clarification if needed, asking the patron if he or she is still online if a long pause is experienced between the patron's and the librarian's comments, and making sure that communication is ongoing throughout the chat session. Follow-up and closing remarks involved in the chat interview include asking if the librarian's response was what the patron was looking for, asking if the patron would like a transcript of the session, and closing with a scripted or friendly message.

The philosophy of instructing versus answering a chat reference query and the factors that may warrant one philosophy above the other were also addressed. The consortia's policy is to instruct users in how to locate the information on their own. This is the standard protocol followed except when certain factors may preclude that the query be answered without providing the patron with the intermediate steps of how the answer was obtained. Time-constraint factors, such as other calls in the queue, closing or shift changes, or other factors such as a frustrated patron, may necessitate that the answer be given rather than instructing the patron during the chat session. Training also addressed the various methods of referring chat queries. Referrals may be warranted for in-depth research queries that may not be appropriate in the chat medium; subject-expertise queries that may not be able to be answered by the particular chat staff; calls that are specific to another librarian's institution and cannot be answered easily or quickly by the chat librarian on duty, and out-of-scope questions, such as requests for assistance with using various software applications or needing password information for e-mail or other applications. Referral modes may vary to include a different chat librarian, an in-person referral, e-mail, or phone call.

Training also focused on nontransferable chat reference skills, particularly nonvisual cues, nonverbal cues, written communication skills, and chat-etiquette skills. The two main cues that are not present during the chat interview are visual and verbal cues. Visual cues such as eye contact and body language and verbal cues such as tone of voice that are not present in chat transactions all emphasize the written text as the main mode of communication. Written communication in the chat transaction is a vital link to the reference interview. Important aspects of the chat transaction include concise and organized text, use of ellipses to send messages in short chunks to reduce delay time. Long pauses equate with silence and, therefore, are not acceptable, and factors such as typos and grammar do not need to be letter perfect during the session. Staff also learned basic chat-etiquette skills, such as not typing in ALL CAPS, which is synonymous to shouting, and keeping it professional by not initiating chat acronyms or emoticons unless initiated by the patron.

NEEDS ASSESSMENT FOR VIRTUAL REFERENCE TRAINING AT KENT STATE UNIVERSITY

Several months after providing the local training sessions, we surveyed chat staffers at the Kent State University's Main Library to identify skill sets that are necessary for providing effective chat reference service. The survey population comprised reference librarians and library and information science graduate reference assistants and employed a survey method that consisted of four multiple choice questions, ten Likert-scale questions, and three open-ended questions (see survey appended at end of this chapter). The survey measured five skills sets, including technical skills, communication skills, instructional skills, database-searching skills, and Web-searching skills. The findings of the data are presented below.

DATA ANALYSIS OF VIRTUAL REFERENCE TRAINING AT KENT STATE UNIVERSITY

Staffing Levels and Staffing Frequency

Of the eight reference librarians and six library and information science graduate reference assistants staffing the chat service at the time of the survey, six from each category completed the questionnaire. The majority of the staff (11) provided chat service less than five hours per week and only one member of the staff provided more than six hours of chat service per week. These were mainly library and information science graduate students who staffed the service for the local KSU chat seat.

Time Provided for and Pace of Training Session

Of the 12 participants, 11 felt that the amount of time provided for chat reference training was just right while one person felt that not enough time was provided. The pace of training was just right for most staff, while one respondent felt that the pace was too fast to follow.

Skill Sets

The questionnaire asked chat staffers to indicate how important technical skills were to provide effective chat reference service on a four-point Likert scale. The majority of the respondents (11) believed that technical skills were *very important*, and 1 respondent believed that it was *important* to provide effective chat reference service. The questionnaire also asked chat staffers to rate the importance of communication skills in providing effective chat reference service. Nine believed that communication skills were *very important*, and the remaining three members of the staff believed that communication skills were *important* to be able to provide effective chat reference service.

Half (6) of the chat staff felt that instructional skills were *very important* in providing effective chat reference service. An additional three respondents felt that it was *important* to demonstrate instructional assistance when answering questions in the chat environment. These findings are in line with the consortia and KSU's reference philosophy of directing or instructing patrons on how to find the answer whenever appropriate.

All members of the staff felt that database-searching skills were either *very important* or *important* in providing effective chat reference service. The importance of database-searching skills is evidenced by the 200+ databases that the OhioLINK consortia provide KSU and over 80 other institutions, which are essential in providing reference service to our users. In the area of Web searching, nine of the chat staffers believed that being proficient in Web-searching skills was either *very important* or *important* in providing effective chat reference service. See Table 6-1 for the ratings of these skills.

Development of Virtual Reference Proficiencies

After training and staffing the chat service, half of the members of the staff (6) felt that their technical skills were developed through staffing the service employing a learn-as-you-go approach. Three chat staffers felt that their technical skills were developed through training only, while the remaining three felt that technical skills were strengthened through training.

Table 6–1
Respondent Ratings for Virtual Reference Skills

Skill Sets		Very Important	Important	Somewhat Important	Not Important
Technical	Count	11	1	0	0
	Percent	92%	8%	0%	0%
Communication	Count	9	3	0	0
	Percent	75%	25%	0%	0%
Instruction	Count	6	2	4	0
	Percent	50%	17%	33%	0%
Database searching	Count	9	3	0	0
	Percent	75%	25%	0%	0%
Web searching	Count	6	3	3	0
	Percent	50%	25%	25%	0%

A noteworthy finding regarding communication-skills proficiencies was that the majority of respondents (11) believed that their communication skills were already proficient before training or staffing the chat service. Only one felt that his or her communication skills were strengthened through training. One reason for these figures may be that respondents were taking into consideration the transferable reference communication skills that they were proficient in prior to chat-reference service.

All 12 respondents believed that they were already proficient in their instructional skills prior to chat training. This was most likely a result, in part, of a strong training program that is in place for traditional reference services.

Eleven staff felt that they were already proficient in their database- and Web-searching skills prior to chat training. Again, this was most likely a result of a strong training program in place for traditional reference services. See Table 6-2 for the development of these proficiencies.

Table 6–2
Development of Proficiencies

Proficiencies		Proficient before training	Strength-ened through training	Developed through training only	Developed by staffing service
Technical	Count	0	3	3	6
	Percent	0%	25%	25%	50%
Communication	Count	11	1	0	0
	Percent	92%	8%	0%	0%
Instruction	Count	12	0	0	0
	Percent	100%	0%	0%	0%
Database searching	Count	11	1	0	0
	Percent	92%	8%	0%	0%
Web searching	Count	11	1	0	0
	Percent	92%	8%	0%	0%

LESSONS LEARNED AT KENT STATE UNIVERSITY FOR FUTURE VIRTUAL REFERENCE TRAINING

Regarding technical skills, three important areas for additional chat reference training should include more time for trouble-shooting tips, advanced application and software-upgrade information, and basic typing skills for those who need it. Future chat training needs in the area of communication skills should continue to include role-playing scenarios and should also attempt to incorporate the use of chat transcripts and observation of experienced chat librarians. Below are some quotations from comments from several survey respondents:

> "Actual practice with 'patrons' (i.e., other librarians) was ESSENTIAL."
> ". . . some examples of good online reference transactions given."
> "A lot of learning to be a good reference librarian comes from watching other reference librarians. I wish I could watch someone do good reference chat."

Regarding instructional skills, chat reference training should emphasize what the current policy and practice is of answering questions versus directing chat patrons to answers. Also, reinforcing exceptions to this policy should be emphasized. Finally, regarding both database-searching and Web-searching skills, prior training or experience before chat training is essential to be successful in providing effective chat reference service.

CREATING A CULTURE IN WHICH VIRTUAL REFERENCE TRAINING IS VALUED

Successful training for any new initiative requires engaged participants. Staff engagement can be ensured by having staff on board for the new initiative, which can be a challenge when developing virtual reference service. Although implementers may not view a new virtual reference service as anything more than a new medium for traditional reference services, staff perspectives may differ drastically. What implementers view as a new channel for services, staff may view as a threat or a challenge to the professional and service philosophies that they value. These differing perspectives should not be viewed simply as growing pains for particular members of the staff. Although it may be easy to dismiss reluctance to train for virtual reference services as immutable antitechnology stances among some staff, the deeper roots of such reluctance must be considered in order to ensure successful professional development and service implementation. Staff engagement or reluctance regarding new initiatives in general and virtual reference services in particular can be examined by considering the professional culture within the department or organization when putting together a staffing model and training plan.

Organizational culture receives much attention within business research, especially within the professional literature for managers and corporate trainers. Although its heaviest uses are outside of the library environment, organizational theory and organizational culture are major concerns among library administrators and service implementers. Organizational culture began to appear in the professional literature as early as the late 1980s and is now so entrenched in library administrative considerations that it must not be ignored when developing new services. Lakos and Gray (2000) observe the importance of keeping organizational culture in mind when implementing new services. "Organizational culture is important because initiatives and changes undertaken without its consideration often have unforeseen consequences—and usually negative ones from the perspective of organizational effectiveness" (Lakos and Gray, 2000, 170). As library services in general and reference services in particular continue to change, new service initiatives are inevitable, thus professional development, training, and flexibility will be mandatory. Janes (2000) argues that a combination of interconnected information resources and delivery technologies, budgetary constraints, and user expectations make digital reference a viable service option and a potential trend in library services. As such, digital or virtual reference services will need to fit into a library's organizational culture. Before examining how virtual reference fits into a library's organizational culture, it is important to describe all that the concept encompasses.

Although definitions of organizational culture differ in some ways, most agree that it comprises the shared assumptions of staff regarding the values and norms of the organization. For Sannwald (2000), organizational culture defines "Who we are as an organization, or 'Us,'" "How we became 'Us,'" "What makes us 'Us' and not 'Them,'" "How we recruit new members and socialize them to become 'Us,'" and "How we perpetuate 'Us.'" A key aspect of organizational culture is that these assumptions work almost subconsciously. As a library tackles new problems or initiates new services, the ways in which these things are accomplished are woven into the fabric of organizational culture; therefore, future responses to similar problems or initiatives are not only informed by these experiences, they become almost automatic. As a result, organizational culture "represents the accumulated learning of a group" (Lakos and Gray, 2000), so it is often very well established and, therefore, difficult to change.

Although radical change is not necessary to implement virtual reference services such as e-mail reference or Web-based reference tutorials, synchronous services like the OhioLINK "Chat with a Librarian" service may require slightly more effort to fit into the library's culture, because of some of the demands of the service. Synchronous services like the "Chat" initiative require staff to fit the way that they provide services into the rubric of working with whatever software is selected. This requires a familiarity with the software and comfort level with communicating within it. Reluctance among staff at this level may easily be dismissed as technophobia; however, organizational culture can play a significant role. If a library has not emphasized professional development over the recent past and has not made efforts to keep staff at least familiar with the latest software, resources, and services in the library community, the implementation of a synchronous service and the software with which it operates may be a shock to some members of the staff. When training for the "Chat with a Librarian" service, the Information Services staff at KSU was well served by the department's emphasis on professional development. During the academic year, Information Services meets monthly for two-hour professional development sessions that focus on new resources, software packages, and services within the library, as well as across campus. Professional development and continuing education is, therefore, a strong component of the culture of the department.

The professional philosophy of Information Services also made it easy to fit the "Chat" service into the department's culture. Providing convenient service hours and taking advantage of new media to do so have been central to the mission of Libraries and Media Services (LMS) over the last five years. KSU has provided e-mail reference services via a Web-based form since 1998. In addition to this nonsynchronous e-mail service, Information Services librarians provided real-time virtual reference to the Honors College during the 2000–2001 academic year using a video software package called VCON, so the OhioLINK "Chat" service was not the library's first foray into synchronous virtual reference services. In addition to these larger initiatives, the department's culture evolved over the last few years to better accommodate working in a virtual reference environment. In anticipation of providing some sort of real-time service, staff began using prominent, free chat software to communicate internally. In addition to using the software to communicate with other members of the staff, librarians were encouraged to share their screen names as another piece of contact information with the students and faculty whom they assisted at the desk or within the academic departments with which they work through the Libraries' Liaison Librarian program. This interdepartmental correspondence helped to develop a comfort level with chat software in general as well as with communicating in the chat environment, which, with its lack of concern with strong grammar and its emphasis on succinctness can be challenging to beginners. Even this internal use of instant messaging software helped to move the culture within LMS toward that of many of its users in general and its virtual reference patrons in particular. As librarians and staff increasingly follow the same use patterns as students on campus, understanding student needs becomes easier.

CONCLUSION

Regardless of the training methods employed when implementing a virtual reference service, it is important to keep the needs and culture of the organization at the forefront. Reviewing the results of a needs assessment like the survey reported above should be the first step in identifying the needs of members of an individual institution. Before implementing a training program for a virtual reference service the staff acceptance of the new service and proficiency with the necessary skills should be reviewed. The instrument developed for this study can be modified to meet the needs of a particular institution and can serve as at least a starting point for assessing the needs of any virtual reference training program. The experience at KSU shows that although those needs and staff comfort levels can vary, understanding them can lead to a well-prepared staff and a staff that values virtual reference services not only as a new medium to reach students and a convenient way to do their work, but as a part of the culture of many emerging user groups as well as the professional culture of reference librarians in the new century.

REFERENCES

Balleste, Roy, and Gordon Russell. 2003. "Hollywood Technology in Real Life." *Computers in Libraries* 23, no. 4 (April): 14–16, 18.

Cartwright, Carol A., David K. Creamer, and Sally A. Kandel. 2003. *Factbook: Kent State University, 2002–2003—Characteristics and Composition, University Resources, Institutional Understanding*. Kent, OH: Research, Planning, and Institutional Effectiveness, Kent State University.

Elias, Tana, and Stef Morrill. 2003. "Our Virtual Reference Training Camp." *Computers in Libraries* 23, no. 4 (April): 10–12, 70–72.

Helfer, Doris Small. 2003. "Virtual Reference in Libraries: Status and Issues." *Searcher* 11, no. 2 (February): 63–65.

Janes, Joseph. 2000. "Why Reference Is About to Change Forever (but Not Completely)." In *Digital Reference Service in the New Millennium*, edited by R. David Lankes, J. W. Collins, and Abby S. Kasowitz (pp. 13–24). New York: Neal-Schuman.

Jerant, Lisa L., and Kenneth Firestein. 2003. "Not Virtual, but a Real, Live, Online, Interactive Reference Service." *Medical Reference Services Quarterly* 22, no. 2 (Summer): 57–68.

Katz, William. 1987. *Introduction to Reference Work: Basic Information Sources*, 1. New York: McGraw-Hill.

Kawakami, Alice K. 2003. "Testing the Road to Real-Time Digital Reference: Pilot Projects at the University of California, Los Angeles." In *Implementing Digital Reference Services: Setting Standards and Making it Real*, edited by R. David Lankes, Charles R. McClure, Melissa Gross, Jeffrey Pomerantz (pp. 75–81). New York: Neal-Schuman.

Kawakami, Alice, and Pauline Swartz. 2003. "Digital Reference: Training and Assessment for Service Improvement." *Reference Services Review* 31, no. 3: 227–236.

Lakos, Amos, and Chris Gray. 2000. "Personalized Library Portals as an Organizational Culture Change Agent." *Information Technology and Libraries* 19, no. 4 (December): 169–174.

Lankes, R. David, and Abby S. Kasowitz. 1998. *AskA Starter Kit: How to Build and Maintain Digital Reference Services*. Syracuse, NY: ERIC Clearinghouse on Information and Technology.

Lipow, Anne G. 2003. *The Virtual Reference Librarian's Handbook*. New York: Neal-Schuman.

Martin, Julie. 2003. "Ask a Librarian Virtual Reference Services at the Boeing Library." *Internet Reference Services Quarterly* 8, no. 1/2: 127–135.

Meola, Marc, and Sam Stormont. 2002. *Starting and Operating Live Virtual Reference Services: A How-To-Do-It Manual for Librarians*, no. 118. New York: Neal-Schuman.

OhioLINK Chat Service Manual. 2003. Available: http://library.utoledo.edu/userhomes/wlee/chatmanual.html.

OhioLINK User Services Committee. 2003. "OhioLINK's Chat with a Librarian History and Service Description." (Fall 2003) Available: http://library.utoledo.edu/userhomes/wlee/chathist.pdf.

OhioLINK Web Ref Information site. 2003. Available: http://staff.lib.muohio.edu/~bbarr/webrefinfo/index.html.

Ronan, Jana Smith. 2003. "Staffing a Real-Time Reference Service: The University of Florida Experience." *Internet Reference Services Quarterly* 8, no. 1/2: 33–47.

Ronan, Jana, and Carol Turner. 2002. *Chat Reference: SPEC Kit 273*. Washington, DC: Association for Research Libraries.

Sannwald, William. 2000. "Understanding Organizational Culture." *Library Administration & Management* 14, no. 1 (Winter): 8–14.

Smyth, Joanne. 2003. "Virtual Reference Transcript Analysis." *Searcher* 11, no. 3 (March): 26–30.

Tunender, Heather, and Judy Horn. 2002. "Bringing It All Together: Training for Integrating Electronic Reference." Presentation at the Virtual Reference Desk Conference 2002, "Charting the Course for Reference: Toward a Preferred Future," Chicago, November 2002. Available: www.vrd.org/conferences/VRD2002/proceedings/tunender-horn.shtml.

Ward, David. 2003. "Using Virtual Reference Transcripts for Staff Training." *Reference Services Review* 31, no. 1: 45–56.

Weissman, Sara. 2000. "Shoptalk: Answers to Real-World Problems." *Library Journal* 125, no. 1 (January): 28.

Williamson, Janet. 2002. "The Reality of Virtual Reference: A View from the Edge." *Feliciter* 48, no. 3: 110–111.

Chapter 7

Making the Digital Connection More Personal

Jessica G. Bell and April P. Levy

Without the physical presence of the library patron, it is easy to overlook interpersonal skills in digital reference services. However librarians cannot afford to lose sight of this basic component of the reference transaction. Based on learning theory and customer service literature, this paper outlines ways in which librarians can consistently include specific elements that attend to the human side of reference services in an electronic environment. It also addresses and comments on current, relevant professional standards.

INTRODUCTION

In 1876, Samuel Swett Green (1993) established the importance of the relationship between the librarian and library customer when he outlined the elements of reference service. Green recognized that the exchange of information in a library is intrinsically personal and the connection between librarian and patron indispensable. In the Internet age it is easy to lose sight of this essential human connection when library customers frequently do not stand before the librarian in person, but instead approach through digital means such as e-mail.

LESLEY UNIVERSITY

When the Lesley University (Cambridge, Mass.) libraries ventured into digital reference service, our librarians were mindful of maintaining the personal touch with online customers. However, we also recognized that ours were somewhat exceptional circumstances because of the university's culture. Lesley University has a population of over 9,400 students. Over 80% are women, and 60% of students study at off-campus sites in 18 states, in Israel, and online. Lesley offers degrees from bachelors through Ph.D. in subjects focusing primarily in the human services fields of education, counseling, and therapies, as well as programs in the arts. One point that surfaces repeatedly in Lesley University's descriptions of itself is its humanistic disposition. The mission statement declares "a distinctive and fundamental aspect of the education at Lesley is the conviction that people matter" (Lesley University, 1986). It logically follows that students who enroll at Lesley tend to share this humanistic perspective. With this in mind, we recognized the necessity of creating an electronic reference service that would adhere to the people-centered principles so pervasive in our university culture. First and foremost, we recognized that it would be unacceptable to use formal, businesslike, or curt messages to respond to users' needs. Instead we wanted users to feel supported, encouraged, and, most important, connected to the librarians themselves.

THEORETICAL FRAMEWORK

Though Lesley's population may be extreme in its insistence upon more human connection, we believe that our population is not unique. Creating a more personal environment in electronic reference transactions should be part of every service and, based on learning theory and customer service literature, may even be crucial to the overall success of digital reference services.

Learning Theory

Cognitive learning theory, at its most basic, involves an investigation of the internal influences on information processing and the ways in which people incorporate new experiences based on memories of past experiences. Based on this premise, it would seem logical to include emotional, or affective, influences as important components in this process. However, until fairly recently, most educational psychologists tended to relegate emotion to the background or considered it entirely separate from their inquiries into learning and cognition. Fortunately, that situation is beginning to change.

The introduction to a 2002 issue of *Educational Psychologist* states this change clearly: "In the 2000s, researchers interested in teaching, learning, and motivational transactions within the classroom context can no longer ignore emotional issues. Emotions are intimately involved in virtually every aspect of the teaching and learning process" (Schultz and Lanehart, 2002, 67). An idea that has been advocated by educators for years is finally becoming clear to educational psychologists. Paying attention to the emotional elements of learning interactions is not optional, but, rather, crucial to fully understanding the learning process.

Adult educators are among those particularly aware of the emotion-learning connection. The idea that teachers should strive for an emotionally supportive environment has long been a part of the andragogy literature. Knowles (1980), in what is still considered a standard of the discipline, advocates his optimal conditions of learning in which both the physical and psychological comfort of the student play a vital role. Daloz (1986) reinforces the need for emotional support in his examination of the relationship between student and instructor. He characterizes the relationship between adult learners and their teachers as a mentoring relationship. He goes on to describe the role of the teacher, giving two of the factors as engendering trust and providing encouragement, both of which require an emotional connection to the student to exist effectively. These theories are borne out in anecdotal evidence from adult learners themselves. Students who have positive learning experiences "typically describe experiences in which there was a strong, positive, emotional, or affective dimension" (Dirkx, 2001, 67).

These long held beliefs in the field of adult education are gaining a wider audience because of recent research conducted by neurologists supporting the existence of a strong link between emotion and learning in the brain. It seems that emotion and reason are not the polar opposites we have come to believe, nor can they even be easily separated. The neurologist Antonio Damasio (1994) uses the term enmeshed to describe the relationship between emotion and reason. He gives the example of decision making to further his point, conjecturing that emotions are a vital part of decision making, a process that heretofore had firmly been ensconced in the realm of reason. He defends this idea based on his study of brain chemistry, in which he finds that such basic emotions as fear and surprise, when not in the extreme, help focus the mind and therefore lead to better, faster decisions.

Sylwester (1995) references Damasio and goes on to consider decision making in a slightly different way. He talks about emotions as the first and most influential step in assigning a level of importance to things in our environments. From this premise he makes his main point that emotion "drives attention, which drives learning and memory" (72). Daniel Goleman (1997) also refers to Damasio, but talks more pointedly about the learning situation. He refers to the power of negative emotions, such as anxiety and anger, to disrupt learning in ways that are entirely separate from intelligence.

Perhaps as a result of this research into brain chemistry, education literature examining the relationship between cognition and emotion is on the rise. Laukenmann and colleagues (2003) studied whether a correlation could be drawn between emotional state and learning outcomes. The authors concluded that a sense of greater well-being led to greater interest and then to an increase in learning. However, they did not consider possible influences on that sense of well-being. Illeris (2003), who also emphasizes the intrinsic connection between learning and emotions, takes the theory further to include influences. He purports that learning and emotional functions are "crucially dependent on the interaction process" between learners and their environments (Illeris, 401).

Other researchers are coming to similar conclusions. Results show that the teacher's demeanor is key to determining both the students' own emotions and their motivation and cognition

(Meyer and Turner, 2002). More specifically, the teacher must plainly show concern for and support of students' emotional comfort as well as their progress in learning in order to bring about successful learning outcomes (Patrick et al., 2001). These psychologists and educators are no longer trying to keep the emotional and cognitive realms separate, but instead are recognizing the implications of their intersections as well as ways in which these realms may be manipulated by instructors.

The library literature also references the emotional component of information processing. Lipow (1999) and Straw (2000) both suggest the connection, but it is Morris (1994) who clearly states the significance of feelings or emotions in the research process and recommends that emotions be mediated by another human being. She says, "affect or emotion is intimately involved in the individual's cognitive response to information" (22). Morris quotes extensively from the works of notable researchers, particularly Brenda Dervin, Nick Belkin, Robert S. Taylor, and Carol C. Kuhlthau, to support user-centered reference service. Admittedly, librarians cannot expect to provide a consistent environment for individuals to the same extent a classroom teacher can, since reference interactions are often one-time encounters. However, if we consider the reference transaction a learning experience, we need to be cognizant of the emotional component and do what we can to support it.

In a digital environment, supporting customers' emotional and intellectual needs is a particular challenge. It can be difficult to see learners as whole people, as Knowles (1980) would have us do, and it is likely that our customers encounter the same problem in the way they view librarians. Regardless of the difficulty, clearly establishing a human connection and including positive emotional signals in digital reference interactions will result in more meaningful and productive outcomes for the customers.

Customer Service Theory

Those outcomes are reason enough for librarians to focus attention on this neglected side of reference service delivery. However, there are additional incentives: when customers perceive that their interactions with librarians are on a positive emotional level they overwhelmingly report satisfaction with these interactions. In fact, these positive perceptions seem to determine satisfaction to a large extent. In 1989, Joan Durrance conducted a study in which she used willingness to return as the measure of customer satisfaction and then defined possible librarian characteristics that influence that willingness: friendliness, interest, self-confidence, nonjudgment, and comfort. One of the most remarkable things to come out of these results was that friendliness was consistently the factor that determined whether a patron would return to the same librarian for additional help. The study found that patrons were far more forgiving in their ratings when librarians showed a lack of information-finding skills than when they performed poorly in interpersonal skills. Of the library users who rated friendliness of the library staff member as low, 88% indicated that they were "not likely to return" to that same staff member, regardless of how they had rated the accuracy of the response they received. In fact, 100% of the people who gave the lowest mark for friendliness said they would not return, again regardless of accuracy (Durrance). Further research on the evaluation of reference service was conducted by Dewdney and Ross (1994), who used Durrance's "willingness to return" measure as well as an assessment of the overall helpfulness of library staff members' responses to reference questions. The results of this research echoed Durrance's results, demonstrating a strong correlation between friendliness of library staff members and overall satisfaction of customers.

Management literature supports these results as well. Pugh (2001) found that the emotions displayed by the bank tellers he studied were "positively related to customer affect and customer evaluation of the quality of service received" (1024). Tsai and Huang (2002), in their study of sales clerks and customers at retail shoe stores in Taiwan, reported similar results, but also furthered the findings by confirming Durrance's "willingness to return" hypothesis. The authors offer a reason for why these relationships exist: emotional states are contagious. Interestingly, this principle may also explain why the poor interpersonal skills Durrance documented resulted in low willingness to return rates. The staff member's negative emotional message resulted in a corresponding negative emotional state in the customer, which produced feelings of dissatisfaction with the service encounter. It is clear that positive emotional displays, or friendliness, by librarians and staff will result in positive reports of satisfaction among customers.

THEORY INTO PRACTICE

Despite these findings linking friendliness and other positive emotions to better learning experiences and customer satisfaction, we still do not know if our digital reference customers recognize the value of more friendly, personalized interactions when they begin using our services. Many people argue that customers want anonymity online and regard any breach of that anonymity, including human contact, as an intrusion. It may be true that people value their privacy online, but Internet romances alone demonstrate that this privacy is not an absolute and that people are willing to relinquish some privacy when the situation is right. In fact, a market study by Jupiter Research (1999) found that 90% of online customers do indeed want human contact. Whether as a result of the Jupiter Research findings or perhaps from their own customers' suggestions, many Internet companies are making their customer service contact points much more prominent. In situations in which information exchange is sophisticated, like the travel industry, many companies offer chat services to help customers navigate the options and procedures.

In librarianship, David Tyckoson's (2003) recent article on the future of reference echoed these sentiments. He posits that "in an increasingly impersonal world, the librarian will continue to provide personalized service to patrons" (15). Personalization is nothing new for libraries or librarians; it is one of the qualities that defines librarianship and must be a trait we continue to emphasize. Tyckoson reinforces his point by saying "personal service is what will differentiate the library from other information providers" (15). Based on the trends in online retail, this may not be entirely true, but what is certain is that the level and quality of personal service libraries provide for free sets us apart. Librarians need to ensure they diligently maintain these distinguishing characteristics in the move to digital environments.

Despite knowing the reasons for preserving the human touch in online reference, it can be difficult to apply day in and day out. In the rush to serve customers in a timely manner, courtesy and human-focused service may fall by the wayside. For that reason, we offer some basic principles to follow and tips to practice.

Nonverbal Communication

First, a frequent complaint about digital encounters is their lack of nonverbal signals. In typical face-to-face reference transactions, librarians use kinesic cues and paralanguage to help send and receive an incredible amount of information. Based on communications literature, these methods of communication are typically broken into six categories (see Table 7-1 for examples of each): facial expression, gaze, body orientation and gestures, proxemics, clothes and appearance, and paralanguage (Sundaram and Webster, 2000; Knapp, 1980). Depending on whose results you read, linguists say that 70% to 90% of communication is based on these nonverbal signals (Smith, 2001; Sundaram and Webster, 2000). Although the impact of the loss of nonverbal signals has not been widely documented, we can deduce that their absence in the digital reference environment will significantly affect communication. Therefore, librarians will need to put greater emphasis upon the language they use in order to compensate.

Translating and adapting physical and auditory signals for e-mail is not seamless, but it is certainly achievable. Most positive, affective signals librarians use in a physical library convey welcomeness, enthusiasm, helpfulness, and friendliness. Incorporating these basic sentiments into reference e-mail messages goes a long way toward creating human connections with library customers (see Table 7-1 for suggested adaptations). Joseph Straw (2000) recognized the importance of making adaptations for e-mail in his article about the electronic reference interview. He advocates that "a well-written response not

Table 7–1
Positive Nonverbal Signals

Signals	Examples	E-mail adaptations
Facial expression	smile, quizzical, pensive, nodding	Include phrases like "Great question" or "This is a complicated issue" to provide emotional feedback
Gaze	eye contact (initial and maintained)	Using customer's name in greeting, include a photograph or cartoon of friendly librarians on form
Body orientation and gestures	standing, arms at side, shoulders straight, handshake	Friendly, welcoming Web form highlighting what the service *can* do, not restrictions
Proxemics	personal space, touching	Invite familiarity and comfort by offering hints for processes/information not asked, but remember to keep from sounding pedantic or too familiar
Clothes and appearance	professional dress, neatness	Well-designed Web form; keep e-mails informal, but not unprofessional
Paralanguage	tone of voice, laughing, pauses, utterances	Carefully write responses to be clear and completely answer questions and encourage further contact.

only answers a question eloquently, but it also tells the user about the importance that the library places on the question" (378). Although he may not have identified it as such, he was referring to the paralanguage components of the e-mail message.

Web Question Form

Another area that needs attention is a library's Web presence, particularly the page that describes reference services. The first step Ludcke Library at Lesley University took to create a friendly atmosphere was designing a friendly Web form for its Ask a Librarian e-mail reference service (Ludcke Library, 2003, Ask a Librarian Form). One of the choices we made was to include a photograph of the librarians who answer questions for the service. This establishes the initial human connection and suggests that people are waiting to receive customers' questions. Next to the photo is a list of what the service *can* do, rather than restrictions on use. For libraries where a photograph is not feasible, such as with a large number of librarians answering questions or librarians who do not feel comfortable appearing in a photo, another option is to use cartoons of friendly-looking people instead.

In the form itself, we have found that explicitly asking for details about our users and their questions has helped us. The Internet Public Library has had similar experience, finding that its detailed question form has generated positive results for their staff and customers (McClennen and Memmott, 2001). Lesley's form is a bit extreme in this area, because the Ask a Librarian service currently serves both reference and document-delivery functions. In future these functions will be separated but the reference question form will likely continue to ask for customers' state or country of residence as well as Lesley program and school. Knowing these specifics about customers helps us to understand customer needs and contexts.

Finally, listing the restrictions of a service is undoubtedly necessary, but they need not be the most prominent part of the page. At Lesley we chose to include, near the very bottom of the page, a fairly mild restriction that the service is available to the Lesley community and questions from others will be answered if feasible. The language of the restriction is more positive so as not to discourage questioners. As a private university we are flexible in answering questions from customers outside our community, so we can keep this restriction fairly vague. Even for institutions with more restrictive policies, rephrasing those policies in a less negative way will be more welcoming to all customers.

Tips for Friendly E-mail Responses

Ludcke Library has developed specific practices for making responses more human and friendly. While many of these commonsense suggestions are also practiced by other digital reference services, they are often not codified. We will try to do that here. The first practice is that librarians greet customers by name, which serves as the virtual equivalent of eye contact in a face-to-face interaction. If someone asks a question without including his or her name, a way to keep friendliness in the response is by starting the message with "I'm sorry I don't know your name." Greeting customers by name is practiced by many digital reference services, including Internet Public Library (Lagace and McClennen, 1998); Anytime Anywhere Answers of Washington State Library (2004); QuestionPoint (QuestionPoint User Group, 2003); and the Virtual Reference Desk Project (2003).

Next, librarians acknowledge questions with some level of emotion or a descriptive adjective in the first line. Some examples include "Good question," "Interesting topic," or "I'm sorry you are having trouble accessing our databases." Acknowledging the question makes an immediate emotional connection between librarian and customer. The importance of conveying overall interest and enthusiasm for customers' questions is emphasized in the Virtual Reference Desk Project's training documentation as well (Virtual Reference Desk, 2003, 20–21).

As the response continues, librarians offer more help and encouragement along the way. This is especially useful when describing a complicated or difficult process. Inserting statements addressing the difficulty of a process helps the customer not to feel as intimidated and is also a way to remind the librarian not to use too much technical jargon or long paragraphs with boring directions.

An issue that can be difficult is saying "No" to customers because it can make the tone of the interaction unpleasant. We try to do this in a graceful way, and perhaps turn the "No" into a positive experience. For example, if a customer who lives close to our campus requests that we mail some articles to her, we respond as follows, "Good news! The article you want is available in our library and you can come here to photocopy it." We then follow this statement with instructions on where to find articles, the library's hours, and where to ask for help in the library.

The librarians also try to respect customers' knowledge and avoid being patronizing. If a librarian is unsure whether a customer already knows something, she gives them the courtesy to suggest they might know, by prefacing explanations with, "You may already know this . . ." Finally, in closing a response, we include one last friendly remark, and encourage follow-up if necessary. We also sign our names to continue to reinforce the human connection. Providing a closing statement and signature is also a required part of the digital reference transaction as described in QuestionPoint's training documentation (QuestionPoint User Group, 2003, 20).

Lesley University's Ask a Librarian service occasionally receives questions from customers outside the Lesley community. In these cases, librarians follow the same friendly practices already discussed, answering questions to the extent we are able. We try to keep a positive style, provide some information that will help, and, if possible, connect these customers with a library they can use. This practice is good public relations for our service because it both reinforces our friendliness and allows us to symbolically "return the favor" to the many librarians who help Lesley's off-campus students near where they live. While not all services may be permitted to respond to questions from unaffiliated users, even a brief referral to another service useful to the customer is a valuable and positive addition to the practice of digital reference services.

As we have noted, Lesley University's practices for conveying friendliness and emotional connection are not unique; training documents from many other digital reference services require or recommend friendly personal greetings, responding in a tone that conveys interest and enthusiasm, and closing statements that reinforce the friendly connection and encourage further contact with the service. However, often these practices are mentioned in a general way, without specific recommendations, examples, or reinforcement in the training documentation.

This may be due to an assumption that librarians already know how to provide good customer service, or that friendliness is seen as less crucial than other aspects of answering digital reference questions. We believe that more direct recommendations for humanizing the digital reference interaction are beneficial additions to training documents as well as professional standards.

PROFESSIONAL STANDARDS

Making digital reference more personal and emotionally responsive is a goal toward which all libraries should strive, but it can be difficult without standards by which to measure success. The Virtual Reference Desk's *Facets of Quality* makes a promising start, but falls short of offering specific behavioral guidelines. In the section detailing standards for training, one recommendation states, "Ensure that trainees are practicing appropriate tone, 'approachability', and responsiveness in their replies," (Virtual Reference Desk, 2003, sec. 7) but then does not give specific standards for what that tone, etc., should be.

Fortunately the revised version of the Reference and User Services Association's (RUSA) "Guidelines for Behavioral Performance of Reference and Information Services Providers," to be released in June at the Annual American Library Association (ALA) Conference, provides some basic rules to follow. The current draft offers an adaptation of the original guidelines for face-to-face reference interactions and now includes the unique characteristics of remote, and specifically digital, reference. It is interesting to note that the revised guidelines still appear to favor in-person reference. There are a larger number and more specific standards offered for in-person reference. For example, the section that addresses approachability recommends that librarians providing in-person service "acknowledge[s] patrons through the use of a friendly greeting" (RUSA, 2004, sec. 1.5), but fails to recommend this friendly greeting for remote reference either in this section or any other part of the document. Clearly, the warm and friendly characteristics so readily recommended for in-person reference are still difficult to incorporate into remote reference.

The revised draft of the RUSA behavioral guidelines retains

the same general organization as the original, and, although not directly stated, presumably retains the justification as well. The introduction in the original document states that its focus is on "five areas in which behavioral attributes could be directly observed" (RUSA, 1996, introduction): approachability, interest, listening/inquiring, searching, and follow-up. Unfortunately, the affective components of the reference interaction are still largely overlooked (the example from a previous paragraph excepted) and entirely overlooked for the remote reference standards. Several of the areas hint at the need for librarians to appear emotionally responsive toward their patrons, but none sets a standard for what these components should look like in practice. Based on the literature and our experience, we offer a critique of the RUSA guidelines with recommendations for augmentation.

For the first area, approachability, the guidelines highlight the need to make the Web link to digital reference services easy to find. However, they do not talk about the library's Web page where the reference services are described. Whether it is a form for e-mail reference, a link to chat reference, or instructions on how to use the services, this page represents the demeanor and attitude of both the library and individual librarians a remote user can expect to encounter. Novotny (2001), in his article adapting the 1996 RUSA guidelines, remarked on the importance of such pages and observed that many libraries open their page with a list of rules that generally focus on the negative aspects of the service: who does not qualify as a user and types of questions that should not be asked. He calls this "equivalent to sitting at the reference desk with arms folded and a stern look" (114). Clearly, this is not the first impression to make if we want to be perceived as friendly. Addressing ways to help libraries make these pages more welcoming would be an appreciated addition.

To address the second area of the guidelines, interest, the draft RUSA (2004) document has included the importance of response time, something Novotny (2001) also highlights as the best way to show users that the questions they ask are important to the librarians answering them. RUSA did not rest there, however, as the new guidelines adapt the original recommendations about nonverbal cues to something called "word contact" (2.6), the written equivalent to initiating and maintaining eye contact, nodding, and other gestures used in communication. These efforts at "word contact" are crucial to establishing the personal connection with the user and are a terrific addition. The only recommendation we have here is for stronger wording to encourage friendly "word contact" by including statements to indicate interest in the users' questions.

The third area, listening and inquiring, refers to the reference interview, a major stumbling block in the asynchronous environment of e-mail. Thankfully the research conducted by Abels (1996) sheds some light on this issue. She found that the most successful e-mail reference interviews include a preliminary step that precedes the actual answer. She recommends that upon receiving an e-mail reference question, the librarian should first send the user a summary of the information need before attempting an answer. Novotny (2001) agrees with Abels that this confirmation is an essential part of the face-to-face interview, which needs its equivalent in e-mail interviews. The revised RUSA guidelines not only recommend such a confirmation for all reference transactions but also emphasize the need for an e-mail Web form that elicits answers to basic reference interview questions. Unfortunately, neither of these steps includes mention of a personal touch. It still rests with the librarian to offer answers in such a way as to impart respect for the user while recognizing frustration or any difficulties that may be present.

The final two guidelines, searching and follow-up, do not differ greatly from the face-to-face to the e-mail interaction. Regardless of environment, the librarian should always try to involve the person seeking assistance in the search process. If we consider the reference interaction as a learning interaction, then that involvement is essential whether transmitted orally or in writing. The same principle holds for follow-up. Additional assistance should always be offered and referrals made regardless of the medium. The RUSA guidelines cover these areas well.

OUR SURVEY

Because of the lack of literature dealing with the effects of friendliness or lack thereof in the e-mail reference environment, we based the decision to promote a friendly environment on our experience alone. To augment that experiential information, we surveyed the users of our service. Based on anecdotal data and a previous satisfaction survey, we were confident that survey respondents were happy with the service provided. However, from the literature, we knew to be wary of putting too much faith in the results of such surveys. They tend to be overly positive and lack a critical component (Bristow, 1992). We decided to use the "willingness to return" factor posited in Joan Durrance's (1989) study as a more reliable means of assessing user satisfaction with our e-mail reference service.

Method

On September 15, 2003, we posted a survey on the Web using Survey Monkey, the Web-survey hosting company. That same day we sent an e-mail message to 238 addresses, each of which represented a person who had used the Ask a Librarian service at least once since May 2003. The e-mail message asked the recipient to participate in a feedback survey and provided a link to the Web site where it resided. Eight of the e-mail addresses were no longer valid, so the survey was received by 230 previous customers. Responses were accepted for one month, closing October 15, 2003.

Survey Instrument

The questionnaire consisted of five multiple-choice questions and space for additional comments. The questions and response choices are listed in Table 7–2.

Survey respondents were required to answer the five questions; additional comments were optional. Questions 1 and 2 deal directly with the "willingness to return" issue, while the three other questions address customers' experience using the service. The analysis to follow will offer brief discussion of the

Table 7–2
Ludcke Library Ask a Librarian Survey

Response Choices	# of Respondents
How many times have you used the Ask a Librarian e-mail reference service?	
Never	2
1	27
2–4	37
5 or more	14
Would you use this service again?	
Yes	80
No	0
Describe your experience filling out the Ask a Librarian Web form.	
It was confusing.	2
It was easy to use.	70
The form asks for too much personal information.	8
What is the best part of the Ask a Librarian service for you?	
Being able to send my question anytime.	22
Connecting with a librarian who can answer my question.	16
Getting help I can't get elsewhere.	6
Getting an answer quickly.	19
Other	17
What was the worst part of the Ask a Librarian service for you?	
Having to wait for an answer.	19
Having to describe my problem.	13
The answer I received did not help.	5
Other	43

responses to the questions. Complete survey results including individuals' comments are available at Survey Monkey's Web site (Ludcke Library, 2003, Results of Ask a Librarian Feedback Survey).

Response Rate and Analysis

The survey received 80 responses, a 34% response rate. We considered this an acceptable rate for our analysis, but will aim for more responses in future surveys so that the data might represent more of our population.

In response to the question "How many times have you used the Ask a Librarian e-mail reference service," the most frequent response was 2–4 times, with 37 of the 80 respondents indicating that answer. The responses to this question indicated that 63% of the customers who completed the survey were already repeat users of our service.

In response to the second question, "Would you use the service again?" all 80 respondents indicated Yes. Even respondents who had used the service only once were willing to use it again.

The third question asked respondents to describe their experience completing the Ask a Librarian Web form. The majority of respondents (88%) chose "It was easy to use." Two respondents (3%) chose "It was confusing." Eight respondents (10%) chose "The form asks for too much personal information." A clear majority found the Ask a Librarian Web form easy to use, and asking for personal information was an insignificant concern for a fair number of respondents. It is possible that those who responded to the survey, which was administered via a Web form, might be more comfortable completing Web forms than those who did not respond.

In question 4, "What is the best part of the Ask a Librarian service for you?" there was not a large majority for any response. Twenty-two respondents (28%) indicated "Being able to send in my question anytime" was the best part of the service; 16 (20%) respondents chose "Connecting with a librarian who can answer my question" as the best part; 6 respondents (7.5%) selected "Getting help I can't get elsewhere," and 19 (24%) selected "Getting an answer quickly."

Seventeen respondents (21%) selected the "Other" response, which required respondents to add a comment. Of those 17, 11 indicated that they valued equally all four of the possible responses to the question. One comment indicated an appreciation for the emotional connection Lesley librarians make with customers: "I'd say all of the above and that the librarians really do care you are finding the resources you need."

In answering the fifth question, "What is the worst part of the Ask a Librarian service for you?" 19 (24%) respondents, indicated that "Having to wait for an answer" was their worst part. Thirteen (16%) respondents selected "Having to describe my problem." Five (6.3%) chose "The answer I received did not help me." The majority of respondents (54%) selected the "Other" response. Of these, 36 indicated that they did not think there was a worst part, with comments like "There is no worst part," "I have had no problems," "Nothing," and "There is not a bad part." Because a large number of respondents indicated there was no worst part of the service, we may conjecture that having to wait for an answer, describe their problem, or receiving an unhelpful answer are not significant hindering factors for the respondents.

Of the 80 survey respondents, 46 chose to make additional comments at the end of the survey. Seventeen (37%) of these comments acknowledged the helpfulness or friendliness of the librarians, suggesting the importance of that human connection. These are examples of such comments:

- "A REAL person answered my question, not a 'self-serve' technology device."
- "I really appreciated the quick turnaround for answers and how nice everyone is."
- "I recently used the 'Ask a Librarian' service and was more than satisfied with the prompt response and cordial attitude of the women who helped me."
- "I was very impressed with the quick response and de-tail [sic] explanation on how to use the e-Library and the friendly manner in which it was delivered. The librarians at Lud[c]ke have always been very helpful and this feature is just another way for them to show how great they are. Thank you for all your support. A very grateful student!!"

The large number of positive comments is heartening to Lesley's reference librarians, but we are mindful that our response rate does not reflect even half of those to whom we sent the survey. Therefore we cannot state with certainty that our service is well-received by most customers.

By applying Joan Durrance's (1989) findings as well as the

literature on the importance of emotion in learning and customer service to our situation at Lesley University, it appears
likely that a focus on personalized, friendly service contributes
to satisfied customers. While our survey results do not allow
us to make conclusions about our own service, we are pleased
that every person who answered the survey would use the service again, and most already have. We are happy that survey
respondents were satisfied with our service, and that several
commented upon it in ways that support the importance of the
friendly human connection we strive for, but we realize that our
relatively low response rate does not allow us to safely generalize about how our customers feel. In future surveys, we plan
to ask more directly what customers value about our Ask a Librarian service. We also plan to conduct an immediate feedback
survey that will allow customers to comment specifically upon
the service they received for a particular reference transaction.
We hope through these additional assessments we will find evidence that will support our experience and establish the great
importance of the human connection in digital reference
services.

CONCLUSION

Librarianship, as a profession, has never been particularly concerned with achieving customer satisfaction. We do not regularly emphasize to new professionals the importance of
interpersonal skills to successfully complete a reference transaction, but instead focus almost solely on information-seeking
skills. This is not to say that information seeking is less important, but as the results of the Durrance (1989) and Dewdney and
Ross (1994) studies show, no amount of accuracy can make up
for poor people skills. With libraries increasingly competing
with other information providers, we cannot afford to lose the
personal service for which we are known. If Tyckoson (2003) is
correct, it is this personalized approach that will keep us competitive and viable. To that end, the profession needs to augment existing standards more so than the revised draft RUSA
(n.d.) behavioral guidelines to clearly define how to create the
emotionally supportive, human-centered environment that will

contribute to satisfied customers. Library educators and practicing librarians need to put more emphasis on such human-centered skills, especially as digital reference continues to grow.

REFERENCES

Abels, Eileen G. 1996. "The E-mail Reference Interview." *RQ* 35, no. 3: 345–358.

Bristow, Ann. 1992. "Academic Reference Service over Electronic Mail." *College and Research Libraries News* 53, no. 10 (November): 631–632. Available: www.indiana.edu/~librcsd/reference/email/01.html.

Daloz, Laurent A. 1986. *Effective Teaching and Mentoring: Realizing the Transformational Power of Adult Learning*. San Francisco: Jossey-Bass.

Damasio, Antonio. 1994. *Emotion, Reason, and the Human Brain*. New York: Avon.

Dewdney, Patricia, and Catherine Sheldrick Ross. 1994. "Flying a Light Aircraft: Reference Service Evaluation from a User's Viewpoint." *RQ* 34, no. 2 (Winter): 217–230.

Dirkx, John M. 2001. "The Power of Feelings: Emotion, Imagination, and the Construction of Meaning in Adult Learning." In *The New Update on Adult Learning Theory*, edited by Sharan B. Merriam (pp. 63–72). San Francisco: Jossey-Bass.

Durrance, Joan C. 1989. "Reference Success: Does the 55 Percent Rule Tell the Whole Story?" *Library Journal* 114, no. 7 (April): 31–36.

Goleman, Daniel. 1997. *Emotional Intelligence*. New York: Bantam.

Green, Samuel S. 1993. "Personal Relations between Librarians and Readers." *Library Journal* 118, no. 11 (June): S4–S5 [reprinted, originally published October 1876].

Illeris, Knud. 2003. "Towards a Contemporary and Comprehensive Theory of Learning." *International Journal of Lifelong Education*, 22, no. 4: 396–406.

Jupiter Research. 1999. "Account Management: Reintermediating the Human Touch for Most Valuable Customers." Overview. Available: www.jup.com with registration for guest account.

Knapp, Mark L. 1980. *Essentials of Nonverbal Communication*. New York: Holt, Rinehart and Winston.

Knowles, Malcolm S. 1980. *The Modern Practice of Adult Education: From Pedagogy to Andragogy*. Englewood Cliffs, NJ: Cambridge Adult Education.

Lagace, Nettie, and Michael McClennen. 1998. "Questions and Quirks: Managing an Internet-Based Distributed Reference Service." *Computers in Libraries* 18, no. 2 (February): 24–27. Available: www.infotoday.com/cilmag/feb98/story1.htm.

Laukenmann, Matthius, Michael Bleicher, Stefan Fuss, Michaela Glaser-Zikuda, Philipp Mayring, and Christoph von Rhoneck. 2003. "An Investigation of the Influence of Emotional Factors on Learning in Physics Instruction." *International Journal of Science Education* 25, no. 4: 489–507.

Lesley University. 1986. "Mission Statement." Cambridge, MA: Author. (November 2003) Available: www.lesley.edu/about/mission.html.

Lipow, Anne Grodzins. 1999. "'In Your Face' Reference Service." *Library Journal* 124, no. 13 (August): 50–52.

Ludcke Library. 2003. Ask a Librarian Question Form. Cambridge, MA: Lesley University. Available: www.lesley.edu/library/guides/asklib.html.

Ludcke Library. 2003. Results of Ask a Librarian Feedback Survey. Cambridge, MA: Lesley University. Available: www.surveymonkey.com/DisplaySummary.asp?SID=269576&U=26957629029.

McClennen, Michael, and Patricia Memmott. 2001. "Roles in Digital Reference." *Information Technology and Libraries* 20, no. 3 (September): 143–148. Available: www.ala.org/ala/lita/litapublications/ital/2003mcclennen.htm.

Meyer, Debra K., and Julianne C. Turner. 2002. "Discovering Emotion in Classroom Motivation Research." *Educational Psychologist* 37, no. 2: 107–114.

Morris, Ruth C. T. 1994. "Toward a User-Centered Information Service." *Journal of the American Society for Information Science* 45, no. 1 (January): 20–30.

Novotny, Eric. 2001. "Evaluating Electronic Reference Services: Issues, Approaches and Criteria." *The Reference Librarian* 74: 103–120.

Patrick, Helen, Lynley H. Anderman, Allison M. Ryan, Kimberley C. Edelin, and Carol Midgley. 2001. "Teachers' Communication of Goal Orientations in Four Fifth-Grade Classrooms." *The Elementary School Journal*, 102, no. 1: 35–58.

Pugh, S. Douglas. 2001. "Service with a Smile: Emotional Contagion in the Service Encounter." *Academy of Management Journal* 44, no. 5 (October): 1018–1027.

QuestionPoint User Group. 2003. "Library of Congress QuestionPoint User Guidelines." Washington, DC: Library of Congress. (March 2004) Available: www.loc.gov/rr/digiref/QP_best_practices.pdf.

Reference and User Services Association. 1996. "Guidelines for Behavioral Performance of Reference and Information Services Professionals." Chicago: Author. (August 2003). Available: www.ala.org/ala/rusa/rusaprotocols/referenceguide/guidelinesbehavioral.htm.

Reference and User Services Association. 2004. "Final Draft: Guidelines for Behavioral Performance of Reference and Information Service Providers." Chicago: Author. (March 8, 2004). Available: www.library.uiuc.edu/ugl/_rusa/FinalDraftBehavioralGuidelines2.doc.

Schultz, Paul A., and Sonja L. Lanehart. 2002. "Introduction: Emotions in Education." *Educational Psychologist* 37, no. 2: 67–68.

Smith, Carol. 2001. "Customer Service: Part VI Face to Face with Customers." *Professional Builder* 66, no. 6 (June): 95–98.

Straw, Joseph E. 2000. "A Virtual Understanding: The Reference Interview and Question Negotiation in the Digital Age." *Reference & User Services Quarterly* 39, no. 4 (Summer): 376–379.

Sundaram, D. S. and Cynthia Webster. 2000. "The Role of Nonverbal Communication in Service Encounters." *Journal of Services Marketing* 12, no. 4/5: 378–389.

Sylwester, Robert. 1995. *A Celebration of Neurons*: *An Educator's Guide to the Human Brain*. Alexandria, VA: Association for Supervision and Curriculum Development.

Tsai, Wei-Chu, and Yin-Mei Huang. 2002. "Mechanisms Linking Employee Affective Delivery and Customer Behavioral Intentions." *Journal of Applied Psychology* 87, no. 5: 1001–1008.

Tyckoson, David. 2003. "On the Desirableness of Personal Relations between Librarians and Readers: The Past and Future of Reference Service." *Reference Services Review* 31, no. 1: 12–16.

Virtual Reference Desk. 2003. "VRD Volunteer Training—Incubator Version." Syracuse, NY: Information Institute of Syracuse. (March 2004). Available: www.vrd.org/incubator_training/printable_incubator_training.pdf.

Washington State Library. Statewide Virtual Reference Project. 2004. "Anytime Anywhere Answers: Building Skills for Virtual Reference. First Week: Practice for Training. Chatting at the Virtual Reference Desk." Olympia, WA: Author. (March 2004). Available: http://66212.65.207/textdocs/getchatty.pdf.

PART III

Virtual Reference Services and Policies

OVERVIEW

As virtual reference moves from a cutting-edge phenomenon to a more common and accepted practice, it is especially important that the practices and processes that have proven effective be appropriately documented. The following three chapters focus on virtual reference services, examining the policies, best practices, future initiatives, and a re-examination of the specifics of what these services should include.

M. Kathleen Kern and Esther Gillie empirically study the virtual reference policies of academic libraries, public libraries, and consortia and how accessible they are to potential users. Alison C. Morin uses her experience working on the Library of Congress QuestionPoint User Guidelines to discuss the importance of best practices and guidelines in driving digital reference forward. Henry Bankhead's chapter critically examines the services offered through digital reference and challenges us to think beyond question answering and incorporate other reference services, such as instruction, readers' advisory, and roaming reference.

As we push the envelope of what services virtual reference can provide to its users, these chapters reinforce the importance of documenting practices. We are encouraged to do this internally—to share guidelines and strengthen the digital reference community—and externally so that users are aware of our offerings and our limitations.

Chapter 8

Virtual Reference Policies: An Examination of Current Practice

M. Kathleen Kern and Esther Gillie[1]

Most libraries have a variety of internal and publicly available policies that guide their interactions with users. As virtual reference services are developed it is important that their policies are communicated to the users. This study conducted a survey on the policies of 135 virtual reference services, including those run through consortia and academic and public libraries. Only 118 of the 135 services had virtual reference policies accessible online. Using these 118 services that had one or more policies online, the policies related to user restrictions, question restrictions, privacy, and user behavior are analyzed.

This research examines policies to answer the following questions: Do libraries communicate with their users about the parameters of virtual reference services? What service parameters are common? Are there differences in policies by type of organization? Finally, is there a divergence between the theory as represented by the published literature of virtual reference and practices as delineated in institutional policies? Recommendations for policy development are made based on common content of service.

INTRODUCTION

Policies are an important tool in communicating intentions and restrictions of our services. Policies are also valuable in managing services and maintaining consistency when the virtual reference service is staffed by multiple staff members or multiple libraries. The literature of virtual reference services lacks an examination of publicly available service policies for online reference. It is important to understand other libraries' best practices to guide the future development of services.

Current writing on the theory of virtual reference services suggests parameters on question types and other limitations to services. The Reference and User Services Association (RUSA) of the American Library Association (ALA) has, in draft form, "Guidelines for Implementing and Maintaining Virtual Reference Services" (2003) (hereafter "Virtual Reference Guidelines"). These guidelines, based on Bernie Sloan's recommendations concerning electronic reference service, include basic policy considerations, such as who will be targeted to use the service, the level of service offered (i.e., what type of questions will be addressed, what the time parameters will be, whether document delivery will be provided, and who will staff the service), and privacy considerations.

Meola and Stormont's How-To-Do-It Manual (2002) includes a section on drafting policy that discusses three aspects: audience, level of service, and privacy. There is a growing body of anecdotal literature that discusses how particular libraries instituted online chat service, and many of these articles provide recommendations about policy similar to the Virtual Reference Guidelines.[2] Additional considerations mentioned include compliance with the Americans with Disabilities Act (ADA) and ensuring that the policy for the chat service agrees with stated policy for regular reference service (and that parameters for the virtual service are used to update traditional reference service policy). This theory about what virtual reference service policy should be is fairly well defined.

There is not much current information about what policies are actually being implemented by libraries or whether there is any standardization or differentiation by type of institution. In

Bao's (2003) study only 36% of the academic libraries that offer interactive reference service had a policy statement of eligible users and eligible questions. In other words, 64% had no policy statement. This finding is in direct opposition to the Virtual Reference Guidelines section 3, which states that libraries should make their reference service policies available to the public.

METHODOLOGY

Policies can be internal or publicly available. Internal policies, while important, are meant for staff use, and not easily communicated to the user and, thus, were not considered as part of this study. To address the question of whether libraries are communicating their policies with their users, policies that were publicly available online were examined. Data came exclusively from the public policies and an examination of the library Web site.

The general categories of policy statements were drawn from the Virtual Reference Guidelines and the Meola and Stormont (2002) book. Placement of policies online and statements about who staffs the service were also analyzed as indicators of the level of policy communication with users. We decided that placement of policy was an important element in communication after examining a few virtual reference services. In addition to the statements about eligible users and eligible questions, which were examined previously by Bao (2003), we also examined the presence of privacy policies—an increasingly important component of user policies. The data-collection form went through several iterations as policies were examined and common elements identified (see Figure 8-1).

The intent of this research was to cast a broad look at virtual reference policies in a variety of libraries and information organizations in North America. Our goal was to identify at least 100 institutions that represented various sizes, geographic locations, and types of institutions, including public and private. Because the universe of virtual reference services is quickly expanding, no comprehensive list of virtual reference services exists. This made defining a sample of libraries with virtual reference services challenging. This study builds on the exist-

Figure 8–1
Data Collection Form

Type of Service: Public Academic Ask-A Service Consortium
Size of Library/Carnegie Classification (if applicable):
Are policies online? Yes / No
User restrictions Yes / No / Targeted
   Description of limits:
Question type restrictions Yes / No
   Description of limits:
User behavior policy:
Privacy statement present: Yes / No
Prominence of policy (placement)
   Text is part of chat Web page
   Linked directly from chat Web page
   Linked more than one click from chat Web page
   Click-through to get into service
   Other:

ing initial attempts to identify virtual reference providers. Most of the libraries and consortia examined in this study are from the lists maintained by Bernie Sloan (2003) and McKiernan (2003). We used all of the consortia, academic, and public libraries from these lists, provided they met our criteria. We selected only English-speaking services within North American institutions, though we did not restrict ourselves to institutions within the United States. We did not include corporate libraries as those are generally less accessible to the general public. Within these lists, we selected only those institutions for which we could locate their virtual reference page. If a library had more than one service offered, such as specialized collections may offer, only the main service was selected. The AskA Services are from the list provided by the Virtual Reference Desk. Compared to academic libraries and consortia, there were few public library services on the Sloan (2003) and McKiernan (2003) lists. To expand the nine public libraries from these lists, public libraries that were part of the represented consortia were added to the sample. Only one public library from each consortium was included to maximize geographic and organizational distribution. Some of the services on these lists are no longer active; only services active at the time of the data collection (September 2003–November 2003) were included.

This survey examines 61 academic libraries and 20 public libraries of various sizes. Virtual reference consortia are a growing factor in virtual reference, and policies from 33 consortia are included. AskA Services are another part of the virtual reference landscape. The Virtual Reference Desk (2002, see sec. 2) defines AskA services as, "Internet-based question-and-answer services that connect users with experts and subject expertise." While librarians are experts in finding information, AskA services, or Ask an Expert services seek to connect users with subject experts such as nuclear physicists and marine biologists. Additionally they most often target the K–12 environment (i.e., students, teachers, and parents). Twenty-one AskA services are included to provide an indication of policies from these more highly focused virtual reference services. Since many types of virtual reference services are part of this research, the more general terms "service" or "institution" will be used instead of the more narrow term "library."

Live virtual reference policies were examined when live virtual reference services were offered. However, all of the AskA Services were e-mail only. The listings for consortia, academic, and public libraries reported all of the libraries examined as having live reference services. As these offerings change, at the time of our data collection 6 of the 61 academic libraries offered only e-mail service. These e-mail services were included, nonetheless, since the e-mail-only AskA services were in our study. The remainder of the listed services had both chat and e-mail or chat only. For institutions with chat services, the chat policies were examined. For those services offering e-mail only, the e-mail policy was examined.

We collected basic demographic information to help ensure a reasonably even distribution of public libraries and sizes and types of academic institutions. Public libraries were categorized using the National Center for Education Statistics (NCES) population classification (1998), U.S. academic libraries using the Carnegie Classification (2003), and Canadian academic institutions using Maclean's (2003) three-peer groupings.[3] For the most part, these classifications did not figure into the data analysis, as results were not significant. Where results by library size classification were unique enough to be interesting, they are reported.

COMMUNICATION OF POLICY TO USERS

During data collection, it was noted that policy information often resides in an FAQ or elsewhere on a service's Web site but is not always labeled as a "policy." Any policy-type information that was present on a services Web site was examined, regardless of the heading under which it was found. Consequently, our study may employ a more liberal definition of "policy" than other studies that have encompassed virtual reference policies. We were concerned with external policies—what is communicated with the user—and not with internal policies, which are known only to the people who staff the reference service. Policy, as we applied it, is the communication to the users of information regarding who may use the service, what they can ask of the service, and what the expectations of privacy for the virtual reference transcript are.

Presence of Policy

Out of 135 libraries examined, 118 (87%) had some sort of virtual reference policy statement online. Size and type of library seemed to have little relevance to the availability of policies. The least likely group to have policies available was academic libraries, with 80% of this group having a policy statement online. For the remaining groups, policies were online for 90% of the public libraries, 94% of the consortia, and 95% of the AskA Services.

Of the academic libraries without policies online, seven were doctoral-granting, two were masters-granting, two were baccalaureate, and one was a community college. Size of institution was not a factor in availability of policy for either academic or public libraries. The two public libraries without a policy statement were midsized, falling in the 50,000 to 99,000 population range. There was no significant difference in policy availability between public and private academic institutions.

The presence of policy was surprisingly high, in comparison with what was reported in studies by Bao (2003) and Janes (2001). The currency of our data may be a factor in the dramatic increase in policies seen during our study as compared to earlier studies. This would indicate a major change in institutions' approach to public policies as their services mature. However, our broader definition of policy, differences in the institutions surveyed, and the low threshold for the amount of policy present (only *one* type of policy needed to be online) make it difficult to compare our results with those of Bao and Janes.

The 118 institutions with publicly available virtual reference policies serve as the study group for all of the other analyses of virtual reference policies. No further data from the 17 institutions without policies were used.

Policy Placement

While libraries, consortia, and AskA services are fairly uniform in providing user policies, there is not uniformity about the prominence of policies on the services' Web sites. The majority of the policies were prominently placed where the user could easily find them. About half (53%) of the virtual reference Web pages placed their policy on the entry page, where there was also a link into the service. Another 21% of the virtual reference services placed their policy information on the same page as the actual reference query form or as the chat window. Combined, this means that almost three-quarters (73%) of the policies were placed where the user must at least pass by the page, if not read it, in order to enter the virtual reference service. These two categories are combined for the rest of the policy placement analysis and referred to as "top level."

The remaining 27% of services placed their policies somewhere off of the main service page, with 11% providing a link from the service page to policy information. Another 16% removed their policies even further, placing them more than one link away from the main service page. In the cases where the policies were buried this deep, they were most commonly part of an FAQ or "about this service" page that was categorized and required the user to click through several layers to reach the service policies. Interestingly, there was one library that had an implicit policy where a user restriction existed (by requiring the user to enter a library ID), but no policy statement could be found explaining the restriction. Since this library had no publicly available written policy statement of any type, this library was not part of the 118 libraries with policies that we examined.

There was some relation between type of institution and policy placement. AskA services placed their policies most prominently, with 90% at the top level. Academic (76%) were slightly more likely than public libraries (72%) and consortia (58%) to place policies at the top level of their service. Consortia and pubic libraries were the most likely to have links to their policies placed deep within their Web sites, with 22% and 20%, respectively, placing their policies more than one click away from this main entry point to the service. This variation in placement may be due to consortia Web pages often not being the primary point of entry into a virtual reference service, and participating libraries may have their own interfaces and even their own policies, causing consortia policies to seem less relevant or less easily defined.

When evaluating placement of policies, we analyzed only the most readily found policies. That is, if there were separate policies for privacy and user restrictions, the placement of the most prominent policy was counted. It is useful to note that it was not uncommon for privacy policies to be placed a click or even more away from the main virtual reference page even when other policies were placed on the entrance to the service. Since public libraries are the most likely to have only a privacy policy, this may account for the 20% of the public libraries with their policies more than one click away from their main service Web page. While libraries can have little control over user attention to policies, they can control how readily the policies are communicated. Some libraries opted for succinctly stating their policies on a top-level page with a more detailed policy statement available one click deeper into the service's Web site.

Table 8–1
Comparison of User Restriction Policy by Type of Service

	Yes	Targeted	No policy
Academic (N=49)	43%	45%	12%
Public (N=18)	39%	22%	39%
AskA (N=20)	10%	55%	35%
Consortia (N=31)	36%	39%	26%

DEFINING PARAMETERS OF SERVICE

Audience (User Restrictions)

User restrictions were the most common policy element. User restrictions were part of the policy for 90 (76%) of the services. Twenty-eight services had either no restriction on what users are served or did not include this information as part of their policies. (One service did have a restriction since library ID was required to use the service, but provided no type of policy statement, so this library was not included in the policy analysis.) Three of the libraries with user restrictions restricted use by patron log-in, but did not have a written user policy; however, they did have other policies such as privacy and question type.

In our data collection we coded user restriction as "yes," "targeted," or "no" (see Table 8-1). "Yes" indicated that the service was limited only to certain groups, and specific groups were barred from using the service. "Targeted" applied to wording that was more flexible, such as "service is intended primarily for" or "priority given to." Wording that targeted user groups was most prevalent with 42% of all services using preferential, rather than restrictive, wording.

Without interviewing libraries about their actual practice, it is difficult to know the extent to which user restrictions and targeted users affect who can ask questions of the service. In several cases, user restrictions are enforced by requiring the user to provide a library ID number in order to access the service. More commonly, institutional affiliation or a library card is required by policy, but not by software implementation. Wording that targets or gives preference to user groups provides the library with flexibility, but also an enforceable policy for users who may be clearly "out of scope." It also allows users to determine if they fall within the parameters of the service. Many public institutions have a mission to serve the public with their collections, if not their services, and may accordingly want their service to remain open to accommodating questions about library policies and collections.

Public libraries had the least restriction on users served: 39% did not have a policy limiting eligible users. AskA services were also not very restrictive in their user policies and were the most likely to word their policy in terms of a target rather than a restriction. They often serve anyone, with the restriction placed on the type of question asked. Some of the AskA services do target or limit by user affiliation such as K–12 students or teachers as a target audience. Academic libraries were the most likely to provide a policy on user audience, with all of the private academic institutions posting a policy about served groups. They were also the most likely to be restrictive with their wording. Several of the academic libraries required authentication of affiliate status before entering the service, and where this existed, it was mostly, but not always, reflected in a policy statement. Consortia had a spread that reflects the varied constituency of consortia and also, perhaps, a reliance on local member policies.

Level of Service (Question Restrictions)

Policies about level of service encompass what types of questions a virtual reference service will answer and the limits on the amount of time that will be spent on a query. This policy communicates to the user what can be expected of the service. More frequently, the wording of this policy was in the form of question restrictions. Question restrictions were much less common than user restrictions. Forty-eight percent of the services had level of service as part of their policies and 73% had no stated parameters for questions that could be asked of the ser-

Table 8–2
Comparison of Question Restriction Policy by Type of Service

	Yes	No
Academic (N=49)	33%	67%
Public (N=18)	44%	56%
AskA (N=20)	80%	20%
Consortia (N=31)	26%	74%

vice. AskA Services were the most likely to communicate question restrictions, with 80% limiting the type of questions that they would answer (see Table 8-2). This is in keeping with the mission of most AskA Services to provide answers to questions within a specific subject area. Only 33% of the academic libraries had any question restrictions, whereas 44% of the public libraries had question-type restrictions as part of their policies. Limits on question types were least frequent among the consortia at 26%. Again, as consortia often allow member libraries to have separately stated policies, this might account for the low percentage in the consortia group. Multitype consortia might also broaden the types of questions answered, as when public and academic libraries share a service or even specialized libraries (such as legal or medical) are in a reference consortium with public or academic libraries.

The types of limitations placed on user questions varied, but the most common restrictions were not answering legal or medical questions. This follows the policies of some in-person reference services and reflects the legal and ethical unease of many librarians with respect to these types of questions. Other common restrictions were no circulation, fines, or interlibrary loan questions. No homework help was an occasional restriction for public libraries. Occasionally academic libraries restricted questions to only brief or factual questions and no extensive research. AskA services were very specific about the types of question areas that they were willing to answer, such as Scientific

American's Ask An Expert service's policy, which states that they only accept questions related to science.

Janes' earlier work found a higher prevalence of libraries limiting the types of questions that they would field via their virtual reference services. With many libraries reporting low use of their virtual reference services (Janes, 2001), the question-type restriction may be seen as an unnecessary filter. It is possible that libraries are removing question restrictions as a barrier to service and bringing virtual reference more in line with their other reference services by providing the same type of assistance across all services.

Privacy

User privacy is a growing area of concern for libraries in the post-USA Patriot Act era. Circulation records and computer-use logs are perhaps most commonly thought of as vulnerable, but virtual reference transactions may also be at risk. Van Fleet and Wallace (2003) detail the many ways that virtual reference has potential for user and librarian vulnerability. Beyond the legal implications, virtual reference transactions may also be open to viewing by the librarian or expert staff, management, and software vendor. How long records are kept and what personal information is tied to a transaction varies by software, vendor, and institution, but these issues exist for all virtual reference services and users. Neuhaus (2003) provides a detailed analysis of privacy issues in virtual reference along with recommendations for policy. Privacy policies let the users know that records of their reference interactions exist, to what purposes they will be used, and to what extent their confidentiality is protected.

For this study, we examined whether a privacy statement was present. We did not analyze the content or scope of the policies. Policies might cover such things as retention of records; what kind of information is retained; use by library staff for training, research, and evaluation; or user ability to request that transcripts be deleted. Policies were varied in their detail and content, and this might be an area for further study.

We found that the policy statements of virtual reference ser-

Figure 8–2
Percent of Services by Type with Privacy Policies

Co-occurrence of types of polices (N=118)

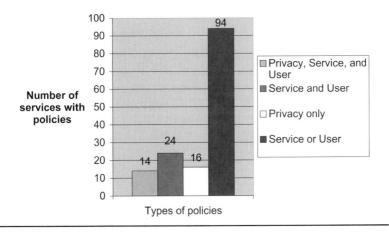

vices often address privacy of records, but attention to this area of concern could be greater. In their article on technostress and virtual reference, Van Fleet and Wallace (2003) assert that "examination of virtual reference service sites indicates a laudable concern for confidentiality and privacy" (189). As far as this concern being reflected in service policy, we found that some libraries are displaying a laudable concern, but this concern is not uniform across library types (see Figure 8-2). Sixty-two percent of the services had privacy policies. Public libraries were the leader in this area with 90% (all but 2) communicating privacy policies to their virtual users. This was also an area in which consortia were strong; 77% provided privacy policies. Of the AskA services, 65% had statements about privacy and use of records. Academic libraries were the weakest in this area, with only 49% providing any statement about use, retention, or privacy of user records, and with little difference between private and public academic libraries. While it is possible that privacy of virtual reference transcripts is covered by a broader library policy on user confidentiality, it seems vital to provide this information to users in an up-front and easy-to-find manner, close to the point where service is provided.

User Behavior

Policies about acceptable (or unacceptable) user behavior are common in libraries of all types. We examined virtual reference policies for indications about proscribed or suggested user behavior. Very few, only eight, of the institutions had any statement about user behavior in the virtual reference interaction. This is less than 7% of the services with any type of policy. One of the public libraries had a behavior policy, one of the consortia, and six of the academic libraries. We did not know what to expect from the behavior policies as we did not find this type of policy for virtual users addressed in any of the literature on virtual reference.

Behavior policies fell into two broad categories: guidelines for good communication and policies designed to prevent or terminate misuse of the service. Some policies that sought to guide users into good style for online communications are illustrated below:

- "Please be patient while waiting for a librarian to respond to you" (University of Florida).
- "Communicate in short sentences" (Pennsylvania State University).
- "Refrain from typing in all capital letters. It is hard to read, and can be interpreted as yelling and/or rude" (Louisiana State University).

Virtual reference can be an open door for anonymous questions, and the potential for abuse of this service exists. Libraries often have user conduct policies that allow for the removal of disruptive or threatening in-person users. A few virtual reference services had policies available to users regarding inappropriate behavior. Some examples:

- "You agree not to send any question that otherwise violates any applicable local, state, national, or international law" (Baltimore County Public Library).
- "Harassment of other people will not be tolerated. Emoted violence and obscenities are considered inappropriate" (University of Florida).

Table 8–3
Policies Containing Audience or
Service-Level Restrictions
by Type of Service

	Number	Percent
Academic (N=61)	44	72%
Public (N=20)	9	45%
AskA (N=21)	20	95%
Consortia (N=33)	21	64%

It is likely that many more libraries have internal policies for staff concerning how to deal with inappropriate virtual reference interactions, but they are not posted for the user to view. It remains a question whether it is helpful to communicate the limits of acceptable behavior to the user or if this is potentially inviting trouble. Having a publicly stated behavior policy may be helpful to institutions in enforcing refusal of service or disconnection of inappropriate chats.

COMMON CONTENT

While almost 80% of the virtual reference services had some type of policy online, only 14 (10%) had policies that encompassed all three areas of audience, level of service, and privacy (see Figure 8-3). None of the consortia or public libraries examined had policies in all three categories. This is not surprising given the low occurrence of policies about target audience and level of service within these two groups. Twenty-four services had a co-occurrence of policies that define parameters of service (user and question). This is only 20% of the 118 services with policies online, and 18% of the 135 services examined. None of the public libraries had both user and question policies, reflecting the openness of public library virtual reference services in regard to user restrictions. For the academic librar-

Figure 8–3
Co-occurrence of Types of Policies
{II=118}

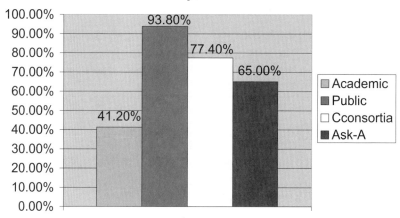

Percent of services by type with privacy policies

Type of Service

ies, 25% of all of the academic libraries had both user and question policies.

Looking at service policy more broadly, 70% of the services had a policy defining parameters of service—either user *or* service level (see Table 8-3). The 72% figure for academic libraries contrasts with Bao's 2003 (data from 2001) study, which found only 36% posting a service policy. Public libraries had the lowest occurrence of any type of service policy, keeping their parameters of service open to all inquirers and inquiries.

There is marked variance in comprehensiveness of publicly available policies. Few services have covered all three areas noted in Meola and Stormont (2002) and Sloan (1998). Examination of overlap reveals that many services have only one or two policy elements. It is more constructive to look at the presence of any kind of service policy, as it is likely that in practice very few services offer an absolutely unrestricted service. Presence of either an audience or service level indicates that thought has been given to the policy and that the institution is concerned with communication of policies to users.

The policy needs of services may vary by institution type or service mission. Lack of a particular statement within the service policy is not a deficiency if the absence of policy is intentional and reflective of actual practice. (Privacy, however, is an issue that all virtual reference services should address in their communication with their users.) Institutions may be cautious about creating limitations to their service and not want to publicize service policies, particularly if volume is low or the service is new and both librarian and user expectations are uncertain. Institutions choosing not to have service policies should take care that they do not have hidden, internal policies that affect the user but are not communicated. Hence, if a library does not have a statement regarding intended audience, it should match this by providing service to all users regardless of affiliation.

CONCLUSIONS AND RECOMMENDATIONS

The majority of institutions post information concerning audience, service level, and privacy on their virtual reference Web sites. Our empirical findings indicate that the practice of virtual reference services with regard to communicating policies is converging with recommendations found in professional guidelines and the library science literature. While the numbers are encouraging, there are some areas of improvement across the board and within service type. A few trends in policy stand out as noteworthy:

- Policies are more prevalent than was previously found.
- The most common type of policy is audience restriction or statement of target clientele.
- Academic libraries are the most restrictive of user affiliation, and public libraries are the least restrictive.
- Academic libraries are the least likely to communicate any type of virtual reference policy to their users.
- AskA Services have the most defined question policies.
- Privacy policies do not occur as often as they should; more than one-third of the services do not have privacy statements.

All institutions should remember that policies should not exist internally without external communication. If a librarywide policy exists that encompasses virtual reference, the user should be able to easily find it from the virtual reference Web site. Overall, when policies were found to be available, they were at the top level of the services' Web sites and readily visible. Communicating policy to users need not be weighty, and a brief statement of service parameters may increase readability. When a longer explanation is needed, a short, clear statement with a clearly worded link to a more comprehensive policy is an option. Privacy policies should enter the consciousness of all virtual reference services. It is common for these to be further removed from the main page for the service, but they should also be easy to locate.

The most important challenge for virtual reference policy is to match the practice of service to the policy and match the policy to the mission. Institutions without policies need to reflect on whether a policy is needed to define their actual practices: does the absence of an audience policy actually mean that anyone in the world can "ask a librarian"? Institutions with policies need to consider whether the policy reflects the service that is provided; does a policy that states that questions are limited to ready reference match what is provided by the librarians staffing the service? Matching policy and mission may require looking beyond borders of virtual reference to examine the missions and policies of an institution's entire reference service. Where virtual policies differ from in-person policies, the reasons should be clear to the staff and the users. The virtual reference policy should make sense within the institution and relate to broader reference policies.

As virtual reference services mature, institutions will continue to develop their policies. Specific content for these policies will be as diverse as current reference policies. Further study might examine the connection between the stated policy and the actual service provided by staff and explore where policy and practice disconnect.

NOTES

1. The authors wish to acknowledge the Research and Publication Committee of the University of Illinois at Urbana-Champaign Library, which provided support for the completion of this research.
2. For a general outline of decisions to be made, see Kibbee, Jo, David Ward, and Wei Ma, 2002, "Virtual Service, Real Data: Results of a Pilot Study," *Reference Services Review* 30 no. 1: 25–36. For a discussion of policy issues to be considered when planning a chat service, see, for example, Francoeur, Stephen, 2001, "An Analytical Survey of Chat Reference Services," *Reference Services Review* 29 no. 3: 189–204.
3. For further explanation of academic library size classification see: Maclean's Magazine peer groupings at www.macleans.ca/universities/article.jsp?content=20031106_133202_2948 <accessed November 30, 2003>; Carnegie Classifications at www.carnegiefoundation.org/Classification/ <accessed November 30, 2003>; and NCES peer groups at http://nces.ed.gov/pubs98/98310.pdf <accessed November 30, 2003>.

REFERENCES

Bao, Xue-Ming. 2003. "A Study of Web-Based Interactive Reference Services via Academic Library Home Pages." *Reference & User Services Quarterly* 42, no. 3 (Spring): 250–256.

Janes, Joseph. 2001. "Digital Reference Services in Public and Academic Libraries." In *Evaluating Networked Information Services: Techniques, Policy, and Issues*, edited by Charles R. McClure and John Bertot (pp. 175–195). Medford, NJ: Information Today.

Louisiana State University Libraries Middleton Virtual Reference Services. 2002. "Virtual Reference Etiquette Policy." Louisiana State University. (August 7, 2002). Available: www.lib.lsu.edu/virtual /policies.html.

MARS Ad Hoc Committee for Digital Reference Guidelines. 2003. "Draft Guidelines for Implementing and Maintaining Virtual Reference Services." American Library Association. (May 2003). Available: www.ala.org/rusa/mars/dig_ref_guidelines.htm.

Maryland AskUsNow! 2003. "Disclaimer" Maryland: Author. (August 26, 2003). Available: www.askusnow.info/about/.

McKiernan, Gerry. 2003. LiveRef. Ames, IA: Iowa State University. (March 9, 2003). Available: www.public.iastate.edu/~CYBERSTACKS/LiveRef.htm. Viewed August–November 2003.

Meola, Marc, and Sam Stormont. 2002. *Starting and Operating Live Virtual Reference Services*. New York: Neal-Schuman.

Neuhaus, Paul. 2003. "Privacy and Confidentiality in Digital Reference." *Reference & User Services Quarterly* 43, no. 1 (Spring): 26–36.

Penn State University Libraries, Penn State Virtual Reference Service. 2003.

"Rules." Author. (August 18, 2003). Available: www.de2.psu.edu/faculty/ saw4/vrs/about.html.
Reference and User Services Association. 2004. "Final Draft: Guidelines for Behavioral Performance of Reference and Information Service Providers." Chicago: Author. (March 8, 2004). Available: www.library.uiuc.edu/ugl/ _rusa/FinalDraft/BehavioralGuidelines2.doc.
Sloan, Bernie. 1998. "Electronic Reference Services: Some Suggested Guidelines." *Reference & User Services Quarterly* 38, no. 1 (Summer): 77–81.
Sloan, Bernie. 2003. "Collaborative Live Reference Services." Urbana-Champaign: University of Illinois. (November 11, 2003). Available: http:// alexia.lis.uiuc.edu/~b-sloan/collab.htm. Viewed August–November 2003.
University of Florida, George A. Smathers Libraries RefeXpress. 2001. "Rules of Conduct." University of Florida. (February 19, 2001). Available: http:/ /smathersnt11.uflic.ufl.edu/rxrules.html.
Van Fleet, Connie, and Danny P. Wallace. 2003. "Virtual Libraries—Real Threats: Technostress and Virtual Reference." *Reference & User Services Quarterly* 42, no. 3 (Spring): 188–191.
Virtual Reference Desk. 2002. "About VRD.org" (May 13, 2002). Available: www.vrd.org/about.shtml.

Chapter 9

Approaching Best Practices and Guidelines for Digital Reference

Alison C. Morin

While reference services all over the globe have encountered major changes, the corresponding best practices and guidelines have been left comparatively underdeveloped. Although the transition from implementation to a sustainable digital reference service can take years, best practices and guidelines can help ensure consistent service by reflecting practical customs, procedures, and habits during the implementation period. Leading library organizations are setting a precedent for creating best practices for reference services. More than a handful of libraries and library consortia are developing best practices for contemporary reference services. In this article, a member of the authoring body of the Library of Congress QuestionPoint User Guidelines writes about the experience of developing these guidelines and offers some sensible suggestions for getting started.

INTRODUCTION

Best practices and *guidelines* are sometimes confused with terms such as *standards* and *policy*. Language like this is often borrowed from the corporate world and adapted for the library environment with little definition and a lot of room for assumption. In a literature search, best practices prove to be a concept that does not easily lend itself to definition. Best practices came out of benchmarking programs during the 1990s. At first, best practices were affiliated with product manufacturing, but they have since been adapted for measuring quality and productivity. Best practices and guidelines are different from standards. Standards, as we refer to them today, are thought to be universal, definite and concrete, coming from leading organizations like the National Information Standards Organization (NISO) and Virtual Reference Desk (VRD). Best practices and guidelines are also different from policy, which results from decisions by organizational management.

Best practices and guidelines outline a process, practice, or method that can improve effectiveness and efficiency in several situations. One reason to create best practices and guidelines is to help collaboration. Consortia use best practices to optimize and balance services. On the local level, best practices and guidelines can be useful for divisions that share an e-mail account to standardize the handling and retention of reference transactions. Putting best practices and guidelines in writing provides the opportunity to define quality services and introduce new assessment measures. Best practices and guidelines can help to delineate tasks, save staff time by outlining scenarios and options, set expectation levels clearly, smooth staffing transitions, and identify gaps in understanding.

The business literature offers many illustrations of how best practices are created and utilized in the corporate environment. For example, Ford Motor Company started capturing best practices for the final automobile assembly phase from its best performing manufacturing plants in 1995 (Harney, 2002). Best practices were compiled and distributed to other plants. Soon other employee groups were contributing best practices, and, in 1996, this data was shared on Ford's intranet for the benefit of all Ford Motor Company employees.

Ford's example demonstrates three things about best practices: specificity, employee support, and customization. In the same way that Ford began to capture best practices for just one phase of automobile assembly, best practices for libraries should be task specific. Best practices and guidelines should be specific and situational, attempting to outline a variety of scenarios and options. As a guide to performing daily operations, they should move beyond implementation and into practical customs, habits, and procedures that ensure consistent behavior and delineate tasks.

At Ford, employees collated their own best practices, and once the best practices from one branch were shared with the rest of the corporation, more employees began to contribute (Harney, 2002). The purpose of composing best practices is to support the employee's work and provide a general framework within which work should be performed. In libraries, best practices and guidelines should be developed definitely for reference librarians, possibly for library management, but certainly not for patrons. Best practices should not be confused with policies that state service expectations to the patrons up front. In his article "Best Practices in Process Improvement," Tom Dolan (2003) wrote, "The Internet makes it easy for people to contact others with similar challenges and identify common solutions" (23). While the digital frontier is taking shape, solutions are more readily being shared and collaboration among all levels of service is increasing.

BEST PRACTICES FOR DIGITAL REFERENCE WORK

There is a longstanding tradition that defines what the profession deems "good" reference work; however, the manner in which reference staff accomplishes the task of generating a "good" response for a patron varies from institution to institution. In digital reference services, reference staff use different systems and software, and in many instances, may use multiple systems. Most librarians have a personal e-mail account, a group or division e-mail account, chat software, Web-browsing software, as well as a variety of online databases and Web resources—all necessary tools to perform their jobs. Best practices and guidelines can help librarians to be more effective and self-assured when utilizing a combination of digital reference tools. The way in which these tools are used together is going to dictate how best practices differ from one another. In addition, tools in use will be a result of a lot of institutional decisions or policies.

At present, the suppliers of digital reference technology are offering a range of products with promising new features and functions. The addition of these emergent tools has prompted evolution in the reference librarian workflow. Digital tools have allowed us to move from individual reference to the opportunity for teamwork, even internally. With evolving communication tools and an evolving reference culture, the whole librarian and patron interaction is sometimes left to fall somewhere in-between. Inevitably, this leads to new reference practices.

Joe Janes and Chrystie Hill (2002) wrote an article reporting the results of an informal exploratory study of digital reference librarians. When Janes and Hill asked about guidelines, they found that most digital reference librarians were still engaged in the debate about the merits of various aspects of digital reference: how to staff it, when to offer it, and what software to use. Janes and Hill found that most guidelines are internal, and informal documents developed around patron expectations and the types of incoming questions. More than half of the librarians surveyed reported having no guidelines, or broad or basic guidelines. Existing "guidelines" consisted of stock answers or frequently asked questions. The primary reason explaining this practice was that librarians believed the basic reference principles still apply. In a later article (2003a), Janes explained, "[We see] attempts to make what has been done in the past fit the apparent present and very near future by tweaking or adding to what is familiar and traditional" (23).

Furthermore, Janes maintains that in-person, telephone, e-mail, and chat services are all "just reference" (Janes, 2003b). Librarians may not be able to continue to make a distinction between reference and digital reference. Advances in technology have allowed the ability to quantify, monitor, identify, track, and manage reference inquiries with greater precision and ease than before. Of course, for the most part, basic principles still apply; yet our abilities to provide reference services have greatly expanded and evolved. New tools and new challenges need to be recognized in conjunction with these basic principles in order to improve services. In many cases, services have grown to encompass more patrons and a more diverse assemblage of them. The aim is to include traditional principles in the best practices and apply these practices in a modern context.

Leading library organizations are setting a precedent for creating best practices for reference services. Before digital reference was in full swing, the American Library Association's (ALA's) Reference and User Services Association (RUSA) outlined "Information Services for Information Consumers: Guidelines for Providers," which addressed information services from many different perspectives (1990). Virtual Reference Desk (VRD) took the lead years ago to build new guidelines based on the fact that digital reference has significantly impacted libraries, librarians, and patrons. VRD put out "VRD Guidelines for Information Specialists of K–12 Digital Reference Services" (Kasowitz, 1998).

ALA's RUSA Machine-Assisted Reference Section (MARS) drafted virtual reference guidelines in July 2003. These guidelines focus on the implementation and maintenance of digital reference services, further suggesting that the digital reference community is not prepared to generate guidelines for enduring services at this time. The focus on implementation is probably based on a perceived demand for steps toward an authoritative representation of services and a glimpse of which direction technology may be headed.

During the International Federation of Library Associations and Institutions (IFLA) Annual Conference in 2001, IFLA's Reference Work Section submitted a project proposal to identify the best practices of digital reference. In their proposal, the Reference Work Section stated, "It is felt that digital reference services are still in their infancy and changing due to changes in technology, so that best practices instead of standards are more appropriate. . . . This subgroup will come up with IFLA guidelines that will be useful for libraries and groups of libraries that are beginning or evaluating a digital reference service" (IFLA Reference Work Section, 2002b).

In the December 2002 report on the project, the Reference Work Section explained, "While interest in creating digital reference standards and guidelines exists, official guidelines and policies have not been developed to date. This is most likely due to the fact that libraries offering digital reference services are at different stages" (IFLA Reference Work Section, 2002a). The report further stated that, "the unique nature of digital reference introduces a new realm of issues and challenges. The need for

guidelines and standards becomes even more important as con-
sortium-wide digital reference services continue to evolve"
(IFLA Reference Work Section, 2002a). IFLA later released their
digital reference guidelines in November 2003 (IFLA Reference
Work Section, 2003).

More than a handful of libraries and library consortia are
developing best practices for contemporary reference services.
Consortia such as Illinois, Maryland, New Jersey, the Washington Research Libraries, and the Internet Public Library (IPL)
have guidelines for digital reference librarians and services on
the Web (MyWebLibrarian.com, 2002; Maryland AskUsNow!,
2002; QandANJ, n.d.; Washington Research Libraries Consortium, n.d.; Internet Public Library, 2002). The University of
Florida has guidelines that explore the integration of digital reference tools and a separate document for chatiquette (Turner,
Hirsh, and Ochoa, 2003). The University of California at Los
Angeles (UCLA) has composed both best practices and guidelines (UCLA Library, 2003). Washington State Library has devoted an entire Web site to best practices (Washington State
Library, n.d.).

There are different types of best practices, each with a different emphasis. For example, Maryland's AskUsNow digital
reference service offers comprehensive guidelines (2002) that are
similar to the Library of Congress' QuestionPoint User Guidelines (QuestionPoint User Group, 2003) in that they are fairly
inclusive. These guidelines define local priorities, set definitions
for cooperative relationships, and set guidelines for staffing and
training. A separate section for "Software Selection" allows the
consortium to set guidelines independently of any single digital reference software package.

New Jersey's QandANJ digital reference service has more
instructional guidelines that may be used as an educational tool
for new staff or collaborative partners (QandANJ, n.d.). These
guidelines outline how to handle specific situations, such as
"When to use the 'Call Back' Resolution Code." Instructional
guidelines may also include specific instructions, such as using
employee personal names in chat, formatting answers, spell
checking, and signatures.

QuestionPoint offers Member Guidelines for participants in

the Global Reference Network (QuestionPoint, n.d.). These are primarily performance-based behavioral guidelines that may be used for service review and assessment. These guidelines are similar to ALA RUSA and VRD standards in scope. Behavioral guidelines have to do with quality, appropriate responses, and the recognition of a professional code of ethics.

The Washington Research Library Consortium (WRLC) has created technical guidelines that detail the operation of both soft and hard tools used in digital reference services (WRLC, n.d.). These guidelines outline system requirements and a step-by-step approach to signing on to chat. Technical guidelines may include one or a compilation of tools, but are generally tool specific.

Because every institution represents a unique situation, there are a number of ways to assess what types of guidelines are appropriate to use. When composing best practices and guidelines it is best to first review digital reference guidelines for comparable reference services. After looking at what other groups have done, consider what works and what does not. By having a template for comparison, ultimately higher goals may be set. Then identify the organization's mission and goals and compare it to patrons' needs. Look at how reference and other services are being used.

Next, try to determine what is emphasized by existing reference policies and guidelines. Take inventory of the effect of any new software and recent organizational changes and investigate how it can be utilized to improve processes. You want to ensure that you are using all your knowledge and your technology to succeed. Then determine what current reference practices are by looking at librarians' tacit knowledge in the tasks reference librarians are performing and why. If the guidelines are to move beyond implementation, look at the customs and habits of practitioners.

THE EXPERIENCE AT THE LIBRARY OF CONGRESS

The Library of Congress' recent experience with the best practices and guidelines development process is a primary example. The Library of Congress has been engaged in digital reference since 1994, when an e-mail address for public inquiries about the catalog was first mounted on the OPAC. The Library of Congress' digital reference service has come a long way since the days of using Pine® (Program for Internet News and E-mail). In 2003, Library of Congress staff answered 55,964 online reference requests and hosted over 1,400 chat sessions using QuestionPoint™ software.[1] With the combination of an increasing volume of electronic reference requests and the addition of new software to an already existing service, reference practices and librarian workflow have been greatly affected. Many of the Library of Congress' reference and correspondence policies, originating in the 1970s, no longer provide adequate guidance. The implementation of new services and new technologies since then has presented the opportunity to document some reference practices for the first time, as well as re-examine and revise existing guidelines and best practices.

The Library of Congress Web site presents an overwhelming amount of options and resources to patrons and staff. The Library of Congress currently has 20 distinct research centers, as well as other special programs, centers, and divisions. Each of these has a variety of collection formats, subjects, and staffing. Adequately representing each reference service and corresponding resources in an accessible manner is a challenge. As a result, the Library of Congress' Public Service Collections Directorate created the Advisory Group for Digital Reference (AGDR) Committee.[2] AGDR is comprised of 13 primarily senior, nonmanagerial reference staff who are charged to help determine the future direction of reference as it relates to the electronic reference environment at the Library of Congress. One of their first assignments was to create a more practical guide for reference librarians that would align different policies and help make reference services consistent among all of the Library of Congress' research centers.

Because the AGDR represents various research centers with differing policies, practices, and management, the drafting and approval process took over six months. For the nonmanagerial staff involved, one major hurdle was the perceived lack of authority to compose such a document on behalf of the institution. Even after the guidelines had been drafted, feedback continued to be lacking for the same reason. Though the committee had been tasked with the project, they felt uncomfortable making recommendations for practice, as much of it has to do with issues of policy. The AGDR felt that all guidelines relating to issues of reference policy had to be extracted and placed in a separate section. As a result, the Library of Congress QuestionPoint User Guidelines (QuestionPoint User Group, 2003) is largely focused on implementation and software education instead of actual reference practice.

At the Library of Congress, the link to our Ask a Librarian service was elevated to the library's home page at the same time that many reference librarians first experienced digital reference using QuestionPoint. Librarians were immediately inundated with a large volume of questions and a completely new tool to deal with them. As the use of both Ask a Librarian and QuestionPoint started at the same time, many reference librarians initially had difficulty separating the experience of the service from the software.

The AGDR Committee worked together to educate each other about the tools, policies, and how each can intersect. Many reference librarians are seeking digital reference tools to aid in performing reference services in the same way that they are accustomed to, rather than using technology to explore and enhance services. Part of the process of developing guidelines included confronting the desire for perfect solutions. There will always be certain limitations.

Each Library of Congress research center has implemented and used QuestionPoint a little bit differently. Some are using chat, some are not; some are using the QuestionPoint Knowledge Base, some are not; some have organized triage, and others do not. In the first year, QuestionPoint released monthly enhancements to the system that sometimes dramatically changed the librarian workflow and system interface. It was difficult to pin down software-related best practices until the system became more established and stable.

All of these issues presented the AGDR Committee with several decisions to make. How—or should—reference practices and reference policies be separated? Should the guidelines focus on the implementation of the digital reference service, the provisions of the service, the performance of the service, or all three? And at what stage is the service between implementation and sustainability? Shall the guidelines reflect what reference librarians are realistically doing or what they should be doing? Should guidelines be added for librarians who provide reference services as supervisors or administrators? Will these guidelines be used as a training guide to explain services to new employees? If so, will that be of value to current staff? Are the guidelines software specific? How detailed do guidelines need to be in order to be useful? How broad do guidelines need to be in order to accommodate our differences? After discussion, few of these questions were fully answered. Some issues had to be abandoned, such as guidelines for licensed database usage. Some issues were never introduced because they are inapplicable to the Library of Congress, such as the marketing of reference services.

The Library of Congress QuestionPoint User Guidelines attempt to encompass the effect the Library of Congress Web pages, digital reference software, and chat has had on staffing, reference skills, established service groups, transaction retention, use of reference sources, citation style, and service assessment. Hoping to prove useful to over 400 reference librarians, the resulting guidelines became increasingly comprehensive. Below is an outline of the Library of Congress QuestionPoint User Guidelines main headings:

Section I. Digital Reference Policy Issues

Section II. QuestionPoint Implementation

A. QuestionPoint Administration

    1. Staffing Digital Reference Services
    2. Integrating Digital Reference Services into Regular Reference Procedures
    3. Duties of the QuestionPoint Institution Administrator
    4. Handling Inappropriate Patrons
    5. Quality Assessment
    6. Database Licensing Agreements

7. QuestionPoint News
8. Promoting Digital Reference Services

B. Accessing LC Reference Services on the Web

1. Ask a Librarian Pages

Section III. QuestionPoint Functionality and Best Practices

A. QuestionPoint System Orientation

1. General Guidelines
2. Technical Advisories
3. Viewing QuestionPoint Questions

B. Establishing Quality Reference Services

1. General Standards
2. Quality Answers
3. Citing Resources
4. Answer Structure

C. Acting upon QuestionPoint Questions

1. Local LC Questions
2. Global Reference Network Questions (via Global Routing)
3. Standard Chat Questions

CONCLUSION

The Library of Congress encounters many of the same challenging issues as other libraries. One AGDR committee member stated, "You can not write [guidelines] until you have had experience with the system for a while and discover what works and how things should be done" (personal communication, 2003). However, it may be that the guidelines are most effective precisely when the system and services are in the developing stages. Best practices and guidelines can help retain the knowledge of past and existing services even while they are in transition. In addition, the transition from implementation to a more sustainable digital reference service can take years.

Once best practices and guidelines are created, it is not the end of the process. One of the biggest problems with best practices and guidelines is that once they are analyzed and gathered, best practices have to be embraced and implemented by staff. For example, "In a 2003 [American Productivity & Quality Center] survey of 123 firms practicing [knowledge management], only 31 (25%) were actively supporting the adoption (not just collection or sharing) of best practices," (American Productivity & Quality Center, 2003, 4). Accordingly, implementation and dispersal takes a long time. Dr. Gabriel Szulanski, now an associate professor of strategy and management at INSEAD, studied the phases and barriers of best practices in 1994. He found that a practice could linger for years unrecognized and unshared (O'Dell and Grayson, 1998). For this reason, support from the top and middle management is especially important for the distribution and enforcement of guidelines. In 2003, Szulanski went on to explain:

> Difficulties to the transfer of best practices within firms are traditionally ascribed to interdivisional jealousy, lack of incentives, . . . insufficient priority, lack of buy-in, a heavy inclination to re-invent the wheel, . . . refusal of recipients to do exactly what they are told, resistance to change, turf protection and many other manifestations of the Not-Invented-Here or NIH syndrome" (American Productivity & Quality Center, 2003, 4).

Outside of digital reference, libraries are using best practices and guidelines in other areas, such as digital acquisitions, young adult services, digitization, digital archiving, library instruction, and information literacy. Best practices and guidelines may be another area that reflects the increased collaboration between libraries. Outside of libraries, best practices are increasing in popularity. Best practices and guidelines can be most effective when custom-fitted to an institution and its services. The process of analyzing and composing best practices can be meticulous and evasive, yet proves to be an edifying and educational task that provides many opportunities for improving reference services to meet user needs. For libraries, taking stock of all digital reference plans, practices, and policies can help identify where your service has been and where your service is headed.

NOTES

1. QuestionPoint grew out of the Library of Congress's Collaborative Digital Reference Service and has been jointly developed by OCLC (Online Computer Library Center) and Library of Congress.
2. AGDR was formerly known as the Library of Congress QuestionPoint User Group (QPUG).

REFERENCES

American Productivity & Quality Center. 2003. "Transfer of Best Practices: How to Accelerate the Adoption of Proven Practices." Houston: Author. Available: www.apqc.org/site/images/Transfer%20of%20Best%20 Practices%20Proposal–11–3–03.pdf.

Dolan, Tom. 2003. "Best Practices in Process Improvement." *Quality Progress* 36, no. 8 (August): 23–28.

Harney, John. 2002. "Making Knowledge Mobile." *E-Doc* 16, no. 5 (September/October): 46–49.

IFLA Reference Work Section. 2003. "IFLA Digital Reference Guidelines" The Hague: IFLA. (November, 2003). Available: www.ifla.org/VII/s36/pubs/drg03.htm

IFLA Reference Work Section. 2002a. "IFLA Digital Reference Standards Project." The Hague: IFLA. (December 2002). Available: www.ifla.org/VII/s36/pubs/drsp.htm.

IFLA Reference Work Section. 2002b. "Minutes: Interim Standing Committee Meeting 1 August 2002, Glasgow, Scotland." The Hague: IFLA. (August 2002). Available: www.ifla.org/VII/s36/annual/min02.htm.

Internet Public Library (IPL). 2002. "Policy: Answering IPL Reference Questions." Ann Arbor, MI: Author. (January, 2002). Available: www.ipl.org:2000/backroom/refvols/q-ans.pol.html.

Janes, Joseph. 2003a. "What Is Reference For?" *Reference Services Review* 31, no. 1: 22–26.

Janes, Joseph. 2003b. *Why Does Digital Reference Matter?* Produced by the Library of Congress. 89 min. February 10, 2003. Real Player media file. Available: www.loc.gov/rr/program/lectures/video/janes-pres.ram.

Janes, Joseph, and Chrystie Hill. 2002. "Finger on the Pulse." *Reference & User Services Quarterly* 42, no. 1 (Fall): 54–66.

Kasowitz, Abby S. 1998. "VRD Guidelines for Information Specialists of K–12 Digital Reference Services." Syracuse: Virtual Reference Desk. (April, 1998). Available: www.vrd.org/training/guide.shtml.

MyWebLibrarian.com. 2002. "Guidelines and Standards." Illinois: author. (January, 2002). Available: www.myweblibrarian.com/For_Librarians/ Standards.html

Maryland AskUsNow!. 2002. "Maryland AskUsNow! Plan." Author. (October, 2002). Available: http://askusnow.info/Maryland_AskUsNow_Plan.doc.

O'Dell, Carla, and C. Jackson Grayson, Jr. 1998. *If Only We Knew What We Know.* New York: The Free Press.

Q and A NJ. n.d. "Quick Service Tips." New Jersey: Author. Available: www.qandanj.org/manual/svc_quick.htm.

QuestionPoint. n.d. "Member Guidelines." Dublin, OH: Online Computer Library Center. Available: http://questionpoint.org/ordering/ memberguidelines.html.

QuestionPoint User Group. 2003. "Library of Congress QuestionPoint User Guidelines." Washington, DC: Library of Congress. (June 4, 2003). Available: www.loc.gov/rr/digiref/QP_best_practices.pdf.

Reference and User Services Association (RUSA), Machine-Assisted Reference Services (MARS). 2003. "Draft Guidelines for Implementing and Maintaining Virtual Reference Services." Chicago: American Library Association. (July, 2003) Available: www.ala.org/ala/rusa/rusaourassoc/ rusasections/mars/marssection/marscomm/draftvirtual.htm.

Reference and User Services Association (RUSA). 1990. "Information Services for Information Consumers: Guidelines for Providers." *Reference & User Services Quarterly* 30, no. 2 (Winter): 262–265.

Turner, Carol, Erika Hirsh, and Marilyn Ochoa. 2003. "QuestionPoint Documentation." Gainesville, FL: University of Florida George A. Smathers Libraries. Available: www.uflib.ufl.edu/hss/qp/qpdocument/ qp321.html.

University of California at Los Angeles (UCLA) Library. 2003. "Best Practices for Digital Reference Librarians at UCLA." Los Angles: Author. (June, 2003). Available: www.library.ucla.edu/digref/practices.htm.

Washington Research Libraries Consortium (WRLC). n.d. "Guidelines for WRLC Virtual Reference Librarians." Upper Marlboro, MD: Author. Available: www.wrlc.org/virtualref/vrguidelines.html.

Washington State Library. n.d. "Digital Best Practices" Olympia, WA: Author. Available: http://digitalwa.statelib.wa.gov/newsite/best.htm.

Chapter 10

Not Just Q and A: An Inclusive Examination of Digital Reference Services

Henry Bankhead

Digital reference has traditionally focused primarily on ready reference. The function and importance of bibliographic instruction, readers' advisory, and roaming reference in the digital reference environment will be explored.

INTRODUCTION

Since the advent of the Internet and the personal computer, and the development of a host of new technologies, many libraries and librarians are becoming involved in providing digital and virtual reference. Digital reference has become increasingly more common in public, academic, and special libraries. Since digital reference services are still relatively new technologies, this general analysis will combine examples from different types of libraries in order to construct an overview of digital reference services without regard to any particular setting. Touching on the definition and history of digital reference, this paper will show how virtual reference services are expanding beyond the basic function of question answering and entering into the other traditional functions of reference. It will give an inclusive description of the functioning of the different forms of digital reference in the four basic areas of traditional reference services. This will be followed by a discussion of the implications of digital reference in relation to the functioning of reference services in general, and to librarianship as a profession. The conclusion will be an examination of how digital reference may evolve in the near future and beyond.

TRADITIONAL ROLES IN REFERENCE

Sloan (2001) defines digital reference as providing reference services using a medium that is computer based. A better, more straightforward definition would be that digital reference is any reference service provided in a digital medium. The online, direct question-and-answer service that occurs in real time is known as virtual reference, or live digital reference. Digital reference, however, is more than just question and answer. The consideration of digital reference must therefore take into account the full range of the reference librarian's duties that are undertaken in a digital environment. Tyckoson (2003) gives a modern interpretation of the four traditional functions of the reference librarian outlined by Green (1876): answering direct questions, instruction in the use of the library or bibliographic instruction, readers' advisory, and roving reference. The scholarly discussion of digital reference has seemed to focus almost exclusively on the first function of question answering, the ready reference function, while largely ignoring the others. With the advent of new software, however, digital bibliographic instruction is becoming more widespread. Patterson (2001) details how a sophisticated virtual reference program is effective in teaching information literacy. Readers' advisory service is almost invisible in the literature regarding digital reference service. This is because readers' advisory questions are co-mingled with reference questions in the same way that readers' advisory service is combined with ready reference at the physical reference desk. Digital roving reference occurs when reference librarians use digital technologies to market their services in order to attract users. As Broughton, Hunker, and Singer (2001) observe, "real time reference service allows what is, in effect, virtual roving" (9). Online librarians are able to become more fully available to users, which is the epitome of roving reference.

A BRIEF HISTORY OF DIGITAL REFERENCE

Digital reference predates the World Wide Web. The history of digital reference has its origins in reference questions posed and answered by e-mail. One of the first was the EARS (Electronic Access to Reference Services) system which started in 1984, according to Weise and Borgendale (1986). This system allowed the Health Sciences Library of the University of Maryland to answer reference questions using electronic mail. Gray (2000) remarks that because scientists were some of the earliest users of e-mail services, academic science libraries were among the first to use e-mail for reference. Janes (2002) points out the progression of e-mail reference from basic e-mail in the early nineties to later Web forms that were designed to help the user frame useful reference questions. With the advent of widespread Internet usage in the late nineties, digital reference services started taking advantage of the popularity of the phenomenon of instant messaging and chat to experiment with service in real time. Coffman (2001) points out the growth of live, virtual reference services from only five libraries in 1999 to more than 200 a year and a half later. Now, the most recent advance is to provide reference service at all hours. Dougherty (2002) states that the Metropolitan Cooperative Library System of Southern California began providing 24-hour reference service in 2000. Recently this cooperative service has formed a partnership with the Q and A Café virtual reference service in Northern California to provide real-time reference services to a mix of public and academic libraries across the state (Train, 2002).

THE COMPLETE SCOPE OF DIGITAL REFERENCE

Digital reference, as defined earlier, however, must also include the other traditional aspects of reference services, according to Tyckoson (2003) and Bunge (1999), but translated into the digital environment. An examination of digital reference services, therefore, should include an examination of these other aspects of providing reference services. We will provide a brief overview of how digital technologies are used to provide mainstream ready reference services. This will be followed by a discussion of how instruction in library resources (bibliographic instruction), the suggestion of appropriate materials (readers' advisory), and the marketing of library resources (roving reference) are provided using some of the same digital technologies.

Digital Ready Reference

Ready reference is the reference function most closely associated with reference services provided in the digital environment. E-mail, live-chat, and Voice over IP (VoIP) are used to provide ready reference services. E-mail is currently the most pervasive form of digital reference (Sloan, 2001). The most salient feature of e-mail reference as opposed to live reference is the significant delay between question and answer. This delay, however, can be seen as a benefit. Straw (2000) points out how the e-mail reference interview "can allow for a more thoughtful process of question negotiation" (377). Live chat reference services take advantage of already existing communication technologies, such as AOL Instant Messenger or specially customized call center software, according to Francoeur (2001); this allows patrons and librarians to communicate through typed messages in real time. Though communication is totally text based, as with e-mail, the advantage is the increased speed with which the user and the librarian can interact and exchange information as compared with e-mail. VoIP is an emerging technology in virtual reference that allows the librarian and user to communicate more easily by voice over the Internet (Francoeur). This gets rid of the need for typing messages and the attendant typo-ridden text, "which makes the best of us look like fools" (Coffman, 2001, 150). A potential drawback, however, is that text transcripts of the interaction are not automatically produced, though Coffman has provided us with an innovative work-around with the idea of using voice recognition software to convert sound files from each virtual session into text.

Digital Bibliographic Instruction

Bibliographic instruction works well in the digital environment. The latest digital reference question answering software is also useful for providing live, in-person instruction about library resources, either formally or informally. In addition, self-help instruction services provided on library Web sites are available to help learners at all hours.

Live Service

Though Katz (2001, 269) mocks the worth of bibliographic instruction, advocating providing answers rather than "diddling with instruction," teaching people how to use library resources, especially digital resources, remains an important aspect of reference services. In academic settings where students need to be taught to use the complex resources available, digital bibliographic instruction becomes an important component of digital reference services. Jaworowski (2001) and Viggiano and Ault (2001) describe the success of a live chat bibliographic instruction program that began in 2000 and is used by a distance-learning network of Florida colleges and universities. Viggiano and Ault recommend the use of course software such as Blackboard and WebCT to allow librarians to teach distance learners in an environment with which they are familiar. Ruppel and Fagan (2002) also note the usefulness of live chat services as a medium for bibliographic instruction. Informal bibliographic instruction, however, may occur at any point during a regular virtual reference transaction in any type of library setting. Broughton and colleagues (2001) explain how virtual reference librarians can easily "take full advantage of the teachable moment" (6) in order to instruct users about the available resources. According to Gray (2000) virtual reference gives the opportunity to provide informal library instruction "in the learning moment" (370). Alfino and Pierce (2001) argue that, although the online reference has a "bias toward discrete information requests" (483), it is a setting where librarians can offer "guidance in shaping and pursuing an inquiry" (484). The live digital environment is an effective arena for providing instruction in the use of the range of library resources.

Self-Help Service

Digital bibliographic instruction can also be effectively delivered via Web-based tutorials that are not live. Germain and Bobish (2002) describe the benefits of two interactive Web-based bibliographic instruction tutorials, one at the University of Albany and one called TILT (Texas Information Literary Tutorial) at the University of Texas at Austin. Since tutorials such as these are self-paced, they allow both local and remote students a flexible way to learn to use the library's catalog and databases as well as to learn to evaluate the accuracy of materials they may find. The Clark Library at San Jose State University (Calif.) has an extensive online tutorial that instructs students in the use of the library. It is called *InfoPower* (2002) and was adapted from the TILT tutorial mentioned above. Gray (2000, 374) explains the potential for such "highly interactive tutorials" in teaching information literacy. These types of tutorials provide a general grounding for students with regards to available resources upon which librarians can build with individualized instruction. Gorman (2001) points out the need for digital bibliographic instruction across a range of library environments, remarking that the "young are not all 'computer literate' . . . and today's students are not all young" (182).

Digital Readers' Advisory

Readers' advisory, though a tradition in the public library setting, is often overlooked in the digital reference environment. Katz (2001) states that "while many reference librarians view readers' advisory services as outdated as yesterday's celebrities, citizens still require help in selecting books" (278). Digital readers' advisory takes the form of personal and self-help services.

Personal Service

Patrons who seek the personal help of a librarian in selecting fiction, but who are unable or unwilling to go to a physical library, may employ one of the digital ready-reference services described above to seek advice about selecting books. It can be assumed that readers' advisory questions posed during live chat sessions and by e-mail become co-mingled with factual reference inquiries. As Bunge (1999) reminds us, historically the separate readers' advisory function became a part of the general service provided by reference librarians. Therefore, it can be inferred that the same is true in the digital reference environment. Feldman and Strobel (2002) and Holt (2001) observe the formalized use of live chat to provide readers' advisory services. Personalized, but not live, readers' advisory is also offered by public libraries through e-mail based on forms that patrons can fill out on library Web sites (Personalized Reading Picks, 2001; Readers' Advisory Online, n.d.). Since a large portion of the material circulated in public libraries is fiction (Shearer, 1996), one could conclude that live chat and e-mail services specifically tailored for readers' advisory will become more visible as digital reference services mature. One such service was recently implemented by the Cleveland Public Library. It is a 24/7 live chat service called "Read This Now" that is specifically for the purpose of providing readers' advisory (Hoffert, 2003). Cleveland's program makes use of "genre geniuses"(Fox, personal communication, October 9, 2002) to try to route users to appropriate librarians in the same way that the more mainstream virtual reference services employ subject specialists. Live chat specifically devoted to readers' advisory is rather new, and the Cleveland Public Library is the major innovator in this type of endeavor. They provide this service to all the members of the CLEVNET library consortium and other participating Ohio libraries.

Self-Help Service

Self-help digital readers' advisory services are widely available on the Internet. On most public library Web sites one will find booklists, recommended readings, and reviews. Nordmeyer (2001) provides extensive discussion of readers' advisory Web sites. An example of a more interactive digital readers' advisory service is the Readers' Robot (Kierans, 2002) provided by the

Thompson–Nicola Regional District Library System of Kamloops, B.C., Canada. This innovative digital creation helps suggest books to users in a variety of genres based on a set of choices they make about books they like the most from a multiple-choice list. Self-help readers' advisory Web sites offer a wide range of resources to patrons but lack the personalized service that real live and live virtual librarians can offer.

Digital Roving Reference

Broughton, Hunker, and Singer (2001) explain how the metaphor of roving reference, bringing reference services to users, functions well in the live digital environment; this is because librarians can be "available anywhere the user can access a computer" (9). Kawakami (2002) points out that librarians also market their online reference services according to how accessible they make the icons that link to the service on Web pages; she states that "burying the link is a sure way to sink the serviced" (29). Lipow (1999) states that "rather than thinking of our users as remote, we should instead recognize that it is we who are remote from our users" (¶ 22). This motto epitomizes the proactive application of roving reference to the digital environment. As virtual reference advocates such as Anne Lipow publicize digital reference services with phrases such as "in your face digital reference" (¶ 27), the roving reference aspect of digital reference will become more commonplace. Francoeur (2001) describes an innovative service whereby reference librarians, alerted when users are visiting the library Web site, can "send an icon floating across the user's browser" (196) offering to provide live help if needed. This is an interesting example of roving reference transposed into the digital environment. Another approach is to take digital reference technology out of the library and into the greater user community. One idea is for librarians to take laptops with wireless local area network and Internet connections into student union buildings and other areas where students congregate, in order to offer reference help. An example of this is the "Ask Us Here" service of the Simon Fraser University Library in Burnaby, British Columbia, Canada (Graebner, 2003).

IMPLICATIONS OF DIGITAL REFERENCE

Librarians have strong feelings about digital reference. Some may believe that it is the best thing happening in libraries today, while others may see it as the end of the profession as we know it. Digital reference services have implications in relation to accessibility, convenience, control, privacy, and efficiency. The negative implications of digital reference are impersonality through the loss of human contact and the potential loss of professionalism through the reduction of the quality of the reference transaction because of the limits of digital interaction.

Accessibility

Increased accessibility is one of the major implications of digital reference services. Janes (2002) comments that the new live chat services could better serve younger people who are very comfortable with instant messaging. Digital and virtual reference services create new points of access for people who, for whatever reason, do not wish to go to the library in person (Francoeur, 2001). Patterson (2001) makes the important observation that people who are physically unable to go to a library can receive reference help through online services. Digital reference may also provide better access for non-native speakers. Gray (2000) asserts that non-native speakers frequently may be more adept in communicating in the written language, making text-based services an easier way for them to access reference services. Because so many people use the Internet on a daily basis, providing digital reference services, especially virtual services, is vital to ensuring access. This is because, as Lipow (1999) points out, the traditional role of reference is "to assist information seekers at the point of their information need" (¶ 2).

Convenience

Because of increased access, increased convenience for users is another result of providing reference services online. Francoeur (2001) relates how students in the library will often avail themselves of virtual reference services from librarians working in the same library because leaving their computer station would mean they would have to give up their access to the computer terminals, which are in short supply. Lipow (1999) writes that convenience often dictates what source users will opt to use in seeking information. Stemper and Butler (2001) concur, remarking that students will often "place convenience before quality" (173). Seeking convenience does not necessarily imply laziness or ineptitude on the part of the users, however. Lipow emphasizes the importance of this convenience to information seekers in order not to interrupt the process of the work in which they are engaged. Digital reference services, especially services that are available at all hours, offer librarians the opportunity to make reference services as convenient as possible for users who may require information that is remote from their location or is physically inaccessible at particular hours.

Control

Another implication of digital reference services is control, specifically the migration of control from the librarian to the user. Wilson (2000) asserts that certain types of personalities who were averse to accessing the reference librarian in the traditional hierarchical paradigm in which the librarian was a gatekeeper may be much more inclined to use online reference services, which place the librarian and the user in a more egalitarian relationship. Koyama (1998) describes Internet users who "feel free of the captive nature inherent sometimes in the personal interview controlled by the librarian" (51). These types of users will also feel free to terminate an unsatisfactory reference chat session with the click of a button. This is sometimes disconcerting to digital librarians, as evidenced in the remarks of Janes (2002) who describes the phenomenon of the "disappearing questioner" (13) and the consequent pressure to keep users online. The reality is that online, the anonymous user has ultimate control. Thus, virtual librarians must let go of traditional preconceptions of reference service in order to embrace this new paradigm and provide quality reference service that will keep users online.

Privacy

Increased opportunity for certain types of privacy is another result of digital reference services. Though providing an e-mail address is a requirement, e-mail reference allows a degree of confidentiality for users who desire to remain personally anonymous. Rockman (2002) points out that some virtual reference arrangements may require certain items of personal information, but that the latest programs allow users to remain completely anonymous. A potential breach of privacy that could be the result of virtual reference is the retention of transcripts that record each session; though the nonpersonal information in such transcripts can be useful additions to FAQs and knowledge bases, Francoeur (2001) reminds us that "librarians need to consider whether chat transcripts or e-mail responses can be reviewed by supervisors and under what circumstances" (201). Policies about what types of identifying data can be saved need to be well established to protect users' privacy. Koyama (1998) asks the important question about whether confidentiality can exist if librarians can recognize repeat users and identify their searches. These capabilities may be functions retained in software originally designed for commercial use. Custom engineered reference software should be designed to protect users' privacy.

Efficiency

Certainly one of the important potentials of digital reference is increased efficiency. Networking of virtual reference providers can allow librarians to serve a larger pool of users. Ferguson (2000) explains the organizational efficiencies in providing services, training, and collaboration in an "integrated information service" (306). Intelligent structuring of the workflow involved in collaborative digital reference can be used to produce such efficiencies as outlined by Penka (2003). McClennen and Memmott (2001) conclude that well-structured digital service "allows for increased efficiency by letting staff members focus on one aspect of the job at a time" (148) This type of well-designed structure, coupled with networked collaboration of librarians across a range of institutions, and even time zones, can lead to an overall increase in the reference services that libraries are able to offer. Francoeur (2001) describes the potential increased efficiency in this type of collaborative environment. Whether this translates into actual cost savings depends on how well libraries implement digital and virtual services. Coffman (2002) contends, however, that the costs of collaboration may be more than the benefits that it produces, especially for smaller institutions.

Impersonality

Fritch and Mandernack (2001) point out that "technology is not always the preferred or best method for human users" (296). Gorman (2001) states, "it borders on the fatuous" (173) to think that virtual services can replace personal services, noting that, "technology can enhance but will never supplant human-to-human reference service" (172). Certainly digital reference is no ultimate replacement for human contact, but it can provide some alternatives for users. There are inherent problems with digital reference services that make communication difficult, most namely, as Straw (2000) points out, the lack of body language and physical cues that are a large part of human interaction. Janes (2002) contends, however, that live reference has the potential of "stimulating the conversational aspects of the familiar reference encounter" (13). This might work to overcome some of the inherent limits on communication in the technology. The success of digital and reference services may depend on how creative and expressive librarians can be in a text-based medium. Fritch and Mandernack maintain that reference librarians must focus on providing "high quality, personalized, proactive reference services" (299) by whatever means are available. This may mean using the emoticons and smiley faces that add more functionality and meaning to instant messaging. Since most digital reference transactions are text based, it behooves librarians to pay close attention to how they communicate in this arena. Straw reminds us of the value of well-worded messages in communicating to the user not only information but "the importance the library places on the question" (376). As the physical library and the digital library become less separated, in-person service and digital service may effectively complement each other. Digital reference services will exist in a broad continuum of library services that include in-person services.

De-professionalization

Dilevko (2001) rails against the dehumanizing nature of digital reference services criticizing the paradigm that places librarians, stripped of their professionalism, into overworked call-center environments, where efficiency is more valued than quality. Alfino and Pierce (2001) take a somewhat larger view stating that librarians' traditional neutrality to information content "could deprofessionalize librarianship by making librarians deskilled technicians serving increasingly automated expert information systems" (475). As referred to above in the section on bibliographic instruction, Alfino and Pierce acknowledge that this traditional neutrality can carry over into the online reference environment, but they urge librarians to do more than just answer questions. They advocate for librarians to assume the role of "public intellectuals" (478) in order to become engaged in "qualitatively rich interactions with patrons" (485) that are not neutral and that involve subjective judgments. This is, in a sense, the be–all and end–all of reference librarianship, providing the human dimension of reflection and inquiry that machines cannot. Whether online or in person, reference librarians must engage with patrons to provide their own subjective viewpoint on information they provide. As Gorman (2001) points out "a good reference librarian will not only answer a question accurately but will also suggest other readings in that or related areas" (178). In the face of increasing technical complexity, reference librarians, especially those operating in the digital environment, must transcend the role of mere information providers and embrace the role of well-rounded, knowledge-filled intellectuals. Reference is more than question and answer; libraries are more than information repositories. In order to maintain the profession of librarianship and the existence of libraries, librarians must become proactively involved with patrons in the spirit of inquiry.

WHAT THE FUTURE HOLDS

The future of digital libraries contains many possibilities, three of which seem particularly interesting. The first will work to make the reference interaction more real; this is the addition of video capabilities on the Internet on a wider scale in the near future to assist in conducting person-to-person reference interactions from remote locations. The second is the possibility of making the reference interaction totally virtual; with advances in three-dimensional (3D) graphics, reference services can be offered in totally virtual, 3D worlds, where virtual librarians can take advantage of virtual worlds in order to provide users with visual, textual, and auditory interactive content. The third idea has been around for a while but still has great potential; this is the use of some type of autonomous software agent or artificial intelligence to provide reference services or to assist humans with some of the repetitive tasks involved in providing digital reference services.

Video

Videoconferencing technologies and software do exist, but they are not in general use for reference services. Smith (2001) points out how the use of videoconferencing allows law librarians to conduct remote reference interviews. Chowdhury (2002) views videoconferencing as a current technology that "may be deployed depending on the nature, number, location, available IT resources etc. of the end users" (278). Fritch and Mandernack (2001) mention the videoconferencing software *CUSeeMe* as a useful tool for providing remote reference services. Francoeur (2001) states that the library of Macquarie University in Australia is currently providing reference services using Microsoft's Web-conferencing software, which allows both users to see each other provided they have inexpensive Web cams. For the average person, however, who lacks a high-speed Internet connection and video equipment, video technologies may not be feasible, observes Rockman (2002). Since video technology has the potential of adding a more complete human element to live reference services, it seems likely that it will be adopted if and when broadband services become more cheaply available.

Virtual Worlds

Reference librarians could provide reference services in three-dimensional, virtual worlds. In this type of environment, users are able to navigate about the virtual space using a three-dimensional representation of a body, called an avatar, which has a first-person view of the surroundings. Users are able to see and communicate with other users' avatars. This communication is accomplished with text messaging in the same manner as it is employed in virtual reference services. Schroeder (2002) explores the wider ramifications of human communication using avatars. For those who are comfortable in such artificial environments, providing virtual reference services in this type of space could have certain advantages. Information services made available in a virtual visual space could allow librarians to manipulate and present a large mass of information with relative ease. Puterbaugh (n.d.) outlines just such an endeavor called the Virtual Bibliographic Instruction Project, which will offer library tours as well as live reference services and bibliographic instruction for Eastern College (St. Davids, Pa.) students using a three-dimensional representation of the actual library at Eastern College created in the Active Worlds Educational Universe. This is a long-term project that is currently underway, but it serves to illustrate the potential of the idea. Though the main focus of the current virtual library seems to be unmediated access to information, reference assistance in virtual space might be crucial in particular information domains or for non-expert users. Peters (2000) posits an environment in which "real world library services and digital library services may meld into a seamless whole" (348). Reference services in virtual worlds could contribute another dimension to "hyper-personalized" reference services that mediate between live interaction, technology, and convenience for geographically remote users.

Artificial Intelligence?

In the mid-nineties, Koller and colleagues (1996) detailed the technological potentials for artificial intelligence in digital librarianship and described the emergent technologies of the time. While fully autonomous artificial intelligence has not yet become a reality, Janes and Silverstein (2003) remark that there are some useful software programs that can aid human operators in better negotiating question answering in the digital environment. The idea is to automate the more repetitive functions, such as filtering, tracking, routing, and archiving questions. Zick (2001) also describes cooperative relationships between reference librarians and software, explaining that intelligent software agents can help librarians provide better service. These agents can be trained to perform lower-level tasks, freeing the librarian to meet more demanding information needs. As Arms (2000) states, librarians have "expertise in the idiosyncrasies of the information available" (¶ 30). This type of expertise is not at all within the scope of the autonomous devices currently available. Thus, collaboration between the librarians and software agents could be mutually beneficial. As Janes and Silverstein (2003) remark, "successful automation will allow more time for human intermediators to do the job that computers currently cannot" (Summary section, ¶ 4). Automated processes can help librarians deliver reference services in a digital environment, but will not replace them.

CONCLUSION

We have seen that digital reference services are complex and varied and entail much more than question-and-answer services. Question answering, however, is the most pervasive part of digital reference, though the other reference functions of bibliographic instruction, readers' advisory, and roving reference should not be overlooked in the digital environment. The provision of online digital resources is also a significant part of digital reference. The increase in popularity of live, all-hours, reference and the continuing widespread use of e-mail reference services is evidence of the need for these value-added digital services in increasing access and providing additional convenience for users. Increased efficiency and the potential for increased privacy are additional reasons why libraries of all types should consider adding digital reference if they are not already doing so. Libraries, however, should take pains to ensure that they will maintain the privacy of users of digital reference services. As voice and video become available online, the impersonal nature of text-based communication may be overcome. In addition, three-dimensional worlds and autonomous software agents may provide increased options to provide a kind of "hyper-personalized" live reference assistance for remote users. The future of digital reference will be determined by how well librarians take control of new technologies and innovations to better serve users rather than letting these technologies control them. In order to maintain the worth and nature of the profession of librarianship, reference librarians, in the digital domain and elsewhere, must transcend the role of mere information providers and engage with patrons in a mutual process of investigation.

REFERENCES

Alfino, Mark, and Linda Pierce. 2001. "The Social Nature of Information." *Library Trends* 49, no. 3: 471–485.

Arms, William Y. 2000. "Automated Digital Libraries: How Effectively Can Computers Be Used for the Skilled Tasks of Professional Librarianship?" *D-Lib Magazine* 6, no. 7/8 (July/August): Article 1. Available: www.dlib.org/dlib/july00/arms/07arms.html.

Broughton, Kelly, Stephanie D. Hunker, and Carol A. Singer. 2001. "Why Use Web Contact Center Software for Digital Reference?" *Internet Reference Services Quarterly* 6, no. 2: 1–12.

Bunge, Charles A. 1999. "Reference Services." *The Reference Librarian* 66: 185–199.

Chowdhury, Gobinda G. 2002. "Digital Libraries and Reference Services: Present and Future." *Journal of Documentation* 58, no. 3: 258–283.

Coffman, Steve. 2001. "We'll Take It from Here: Further Developments We'd Like to See in Virtual Reference Software." *Information Technology and Libraries* 20, no. 3: 149–152.

Coffman, Steve. 2002. "What's Wrong with Collaborative Virtual Reference?" *American Libraries* 33, no. 11: 56–58.

Dilevko, Juris. 2001. "An Ideological Analysis of Reference Service Models." *Library Trends* 50, no. 2: 218–236.

Dougherty, Richard M. 2002. "Reference around the Clock: Is It in Your Future?" *American Libraries* 33, no. 5: 44–46.

Feldman, Sari, and Tracy Strobel. 2002. "Advancing Your Library's Web-Based Services." ERIC Digest. (ERIC Document Reproduction Service No. ED465379). Available: www.ericfacility.net/ericdigests/ed465379.html.

Ferguson, Chris. 2000. "'Shaking the Conceptual Foundations,' Too: Integrating Research and Technology Support for the Next Generation of Information Service." *College & Research Libraries* 61, no. 4: 300–311.

Francoeur, Stephen. 2001. "An Analytical Survey of Chat Reference Services." *Reference Services Review* 29, no. 3: 189–203.

Fritch, John W., and Scott B. Mandernack. 2001. "The Emerging Reference Paradigm: A Vision of Reference Services in a Complex Environment." *Library Trends* 50, no. 2: 286–305.

Germain, Carol A., and Gregory Bobish. 2002. "Virtual Teaching: Library Instruction via the Web." *The Reference Librarian* 77: 71–88.

Gorman, Michael. 2001. "Values for Human-to-Human Reference." *Library Trends* 50, no. 2: 168–182.

Graebner, Carla. 2003. *Ask Us Here*. Simon Fraser University Library. Available: www.lib.sfu.ca/about/projects/ask_us_here/index.htm.

Gray, Suzanne M. 2000. "Virtual Reference Services Directions and Agendas." *Reference & User Services Quarterly* 39, no. 4: 365–375.

Green, Samuel S. 1876. "Personal Relations between Librarians and Readers." *Library Journal*, 1 (October): 74–81.

Hoffert, Barbara. 2003. "Taking Back Readers' Advisory: Online Book Talk, from Simple Lists to 24/7 Live Chat, Gives Librarians a New Way to Promote Reading." *Library Journal* 128, no. 14: 44–47.

Holt, G. 2001. "Conceptualizing a Center for the Reader." *The Readers' Advisor's Companion*, edited by K. Shearer and R. Burgin (pp. 269–285). Englewood, CO: Libraries Unlimited.

InfoPower 2002. Instruction Tutorial. San Jose, CA: Clark Library, San Jose State University. Available: http://130.65.100.214/.

Janes, Joseph. 2002. "Live Reference: Too Much, Too Fast? Joe Janes takes a hard look at this new service." *School Library Journal* 48, no. 11: 12–14.

Janes, Joseph, and Joanne Silverstein. 2003. "Question Negotiation and the Technological Environment." *D-Lib Magazine* 9, no. 2 (February): Article 3. Available: www.dlib.org/dlib/february03/janes/02janes.html.

Jaworowski, Carlene. 2001. "There's More to Chat than Chit-Chat: Using Chat Software for Library Instruction." Paper presented at Information Strategies, Fort Myers, Florida, November 16, 2001. Available: http://library.fgcu.edu/Conferences/infostrategies01/presentations/2001/jaworowski.htm.

Katz, Bill. 2001. "Long Live Old Reference Services and New Technologies." *Library Trends* 50, no .2: 263–285.

Kawakami, Alice K. 2002. "Delivering Digital Reference: Alice K. Kawakami Gives a Real-World Take on How to Manage Virtual Reference." *Library Journal* 127, no. 7: 28–29.

Kierans, Kevin. 2002. Readers' Robot [interactive readers' advisory Web site]. Thompson–Nicola Regional District Library System. Available: http://www.tnrdlib.bc.ca/rr.html.

Koller, Daphne, Yoav Shoham, Michael P. Wellman, Edmund H. Durfee, William P. Birmingham, and Jaime Carbonell. 1996. "The role of AI in Digital Libraries." *IEEE Expert* 11, no. 3: 8–13.

Koyama, Janice T. 1998. "http://digiref.scenarios.issues." *Reference & User Services Quarterly* 38, no. 1: 51–52.

Lipow, Anne G. 1999. "Serving the remote user: reference service in the digital environment" [keynote address]. Paper presented at Ninth Australasian Information Online & On Disc Conference and Exhibition Sydney Convention and Exhibition Centre, Sydney, Australia, January 20, 1999. Available: www.csu.edu.au/special/online99/proceedings99/200.htm.

McClennen, Michael, and Patricia Memmott. 2001. "Roles in Digital Reference." *Information Technology and Libraries* 20, no. 3: 143–148.

Nordmeyer, Ricki. 2001. "Readers' Advisory Web Sites." *Reference & User Services Quarterly* 41, no. 2: 139–143.

Patterson, Rory. 2001. "Live Virtual Reference: More Work and More Opportunity." *Reference Services Review* 29, no. 3: 204–209.

Penka, Jeffrey T. 2003. "The Technological Challenges of Digital Reference." *D-Lib Magazine* 9, no. 2 (February): Article 2. Available: www.dlib.org/dlib/february03/penka/02penka.html.

Personalized Reading Picks. 2001. Santa Clara, CA: Santa Clara County Library. Available: http://santaclaracountylib.org/services/personalized.html.

Peters, Thomas A. 2000. "Current Opportunities for the Effective Meta-Assessment of Online Reference Services." *Library Trends* 49, no. 2: 334–349.

Puterbaugh, M. D. n.d. "VBI Chatworld: The Virtual Bibliographic Instruction Project." Eastern University, Warner Memorial Library. Available: www.eastern.edu/library/www/Services/Chat/vbi_awedu.htm.

Readers' Advisory Online. n.d. Massillon Public Library. Available: www.keynetWeb.com/MPL/forms/form9.htm.

Rockman, Ilene F. 2002. "Internet Speed, Library Know-How Intersect in Digital Reference." In *The Bowker Annual of Library and Book Trade Information* (pp. 234–248). New York: R. R. Bowker.

Ruppel, Margie, and Jody C. Fagan. 2002. "Instant Messaging Reference: Users' Evaluation of Library Chat." *Reference Services Review* 30, no. 3: 183–197.

Schroeder, Ralph, ed. 2002. *The Social Life of Avatars: Presence and Interaction in Shared Virtual Environments.* London: Springer.

Shearer, Kenneth D. 1996. "Reflections on the Findings and Implications for Practice." In *Guiding the Reader to the Next Book,* edited by K. D. Shearer (pp. 170–183). New York: Neal-Schuman.

Sloan, Bernie. 2001. "Evaluating Digital Reference: The Script; Bernie Sloan Live from DC [transcript of Internet slide show]." (January 13, 2001). Available: http://alexia.lis.uiuc.edu/~b-sloan/evaldigref.htm.

Smith, Beth. 2001. "Enhancing Reference Services through Technology." *Legal Reference Services Quarterly* 19, no. 1/2: 133–146.

Stemper, James A., and John T. Butler. 2001. "Developing a Model to Provide Digital Reference Services." *Reference Services Review* 29, no. 3: 172–188.

Straw, Joseph E. 2000. "A Virtual Understanding." *Reference & User Services Quarterly* 39, no. 4: 376–379.

Train, Mary Beth. 2002. "Move Over, Google Searchers: Q and A Cafe Is Here." *FaultLine: A Publication of the San Andreas Chapter, Special Libraries Association* 23, no. 1 (September/October). Available: www.san-andreas-sla.org/faultline/qanda.htm.

Tyckoson, David. 2003. "On the Desirableness of Personal Relations Between Librarians and Readers: The Past and Future of Reference Service." *Reference Services Review* 31, no. 1: 12–16.

Viggiano, Rachel, and Meredith Ault. 2001. "Online Library Instruction for Online Students." *Information Technology and Libraries* 20, no. 3: 135–138.

Weise, Frieda O. and Marilyn Borgendale. 1986. "EARS: Electronic Access to Reference Service." *Bulletin of the Medical Library Association* 74, no. 4: 300–304.

Wilson, Myoung C. 2000. "Evolution or Entropy?" *Reference & User Services Quarterly* 39, no. 4: 387–390.

Zick, Laura. 2001. "The Work of Information Mediators: A Comparison of Librarians and Intelligent Software Agents." *First Monday* 5, no. 5 (May 1): Article 8. Available: http://firstmonday.org/issues/issue5_5/zick/index.html.

PART IV

Broader Context of Virtual Reference

OVERVIEW

Though virtual reference services can be viewed and evaluated independently, they undoubtedly are impacted by the organizational and societal contexts in which they are implemented. The following chapters address the broader aspects of virtual reference: education, privacy, and the various perspectives we can take in the study of virtual reference.

Robert S. Martin looks at the mission of the Institute of Museum and Library Services and how it serves the goals of national public policy. He challenges us to look beyond the current horizon to one where libraries, museums, and public broadcasting entities are all collaborating to transform the nature of learning. Glen Bencivengo brings us from the past to the present by analyzing the USA Patriot Act, the development of federal surveillance, and its implications with regard to virtual reference transactions. In his work on the Digital Reference Research Agenda, R. David Lankes defines virtual reference and locates its research within a number of lenses: policy, systems, evaluation, and behavior.

Each of these chapters helps us to see virtual reference in a broader context, hopefully providing insights that will enable more enlightened strategic decisions in an ever-changing world.

Chapter 11

Virtual Services for Real People: Building and Sustaining a Knowledge Society[1]

Robert S. Martin

I am very pleased to have the opportunity to be with you to-day for this Fifth Virtual Reference Desk Conference. For reasons that I hope will become clear, the Institute of Museum and Library Services takes an active interest in the development of virtual services and in the work that each of you participating in this conference do.

I want to begin today with a disclaimer. When I was asked to serve as the keynote speaker, I was a little taken aback. I am not an expert in this field; in fact, I have almost no experience in the virtual reference field. Although I am by no means a technophobe—my wife mistakenly thinks that I am an early adapter—I have no knowledge about planning or implanting digital services. I was assured by those arranging the program that I was not expected to bring expertise to the event. Indeed, you who are the participants in the conference are the experts. What I was asked to do was to bring the broad, national overview. So I will take the opportunity to give you my perspective on what the development of virtual reference services means, and how I think that it relates to other major trends.

INSTITUTE OF MUSEUM AND LIBRARY SERVICES

Before I begin, however, I want to digress for a moment to talk about the agency that I represent, the Institute of Museum and Library Services (IMLS). Since I became director of the Institute of Museum and Library Services over two years ago, I have spent a lot of time meeting with and speaking to librarians all around the country. I am always surprised to learn how many librarians do not know much about IMLS. I have found it useful, therefore, whenever I speak to devote some time to talking about IMLS, explaining a little about who we are and what we do. While I know this is a sophisticated audience, and I am confident that most of you already know a good bit about IMLS, I still would like to spend a few minutes talking about some recent developments.

You probably know that IMLS is an independent federal agency and that it is the primary source of federal grants for the nation's libraries and museums. Our grants to museums and libraries build institutional capacity, support core library and museum services, and encourage excellence.

IMLS was created in 1996 by the Museum and Library Services Act, which merged the federal programs for supporting the nation's museums and libraries, transferring the library programs out of the Department of Education and grafting them on to what had been the Institute of Museum Services.

This action by Congress in 1996 has just been reaffirmed by the enactment of the Museum and Library Services Act (MLSA) of 2003, which reauthorizes the IMLS. This legislation enjoyed strong support from the Bush administration and broad bipartisan support in Congress. The bill passed the House of Representatives by a margin of 416 to 2 and cleared the Senate by unanimous consent, and was signed into law by President Bush in an Oval Office ceremony on September 25, 2003. Enactment of the MLSA is a major affirmation of the important role that museums and libraries play in our society and the significant part that IMLS plays in strengthening museums and libraries.

Funding for our programs has continued to grow. The FY 2003 appropriations provided a significant increase in funding, from $194.5 million for our core programs in FY 2002 to $210.7 million in FY2003, an increase of about $15 million, or 7.7%.

Actually, the total appropriation for IMLS in FY02 was $245 million, which can be divided into three categories: $181.7 million for library programs funded under the Library Services and Technology Act, $29 million for museum programs funded under the Museum Services Act, and about $35 million in directed appropriations. If you ignore the final category—over which IMLS has no control and to which applicants have no access—the total funding for our core programs is $210.7 million.

You are probably aware that the majority of our funding for libraries is distributed in formula grants to the state library administrative agency in each state. In most states, LSTA funds are used in a variety of important ways: supporting resource sharing, providing training and staff development opportunities, statewide licensing of digital information services. So while you may not be aware of IMLS's role, the funding we provide to your state library may be very important to the services that your library provides your community.

I know that you are aware of the competitive grants that we provide through the National Leadership Grants program. These grants to institutions foster innovation and creativity and develop best practices.

Another element of the IMLS programs that is very important to some states is the Native American Library Services grants, which provide funds for core library operations, technical assistance, and innovative project grants for libraries serving Native Americans and Alaskan Native villages. These Native American Library grants may be small in size, but they have a significant impact on the library services available in these communities.

Part of the increase in our FY 2003 appropriation was an additional $10 million for IMLS to support recruitment and education for the next generation of librarians. On October 28, 2003, we announced the first grants in this program, grants to 27 institutions, totaling almost $10 million. The president has requested that the funding for this program be doubled to $20 million in 2004, and we remain hopeful that Congress will do so.

EDUCATION

So why did Congress create the IMLS in its present form? What was the rationale for combining the federal programs of support for museums and libraries into a single independent agency? I think that the record is clear that this evolution was the result of a simple recognition on the part of several members of Congress that libraries and museums share a common mission: education. Museums and libraries are both social institutions that provide resources and services that support public education.

The educational purpose of libraries in the United States is beyond question. What we know today as the American public library first came into existence in Boston about 150 years ago. There was no doubt in the minds of the founders of the Boston Public Library that its mission was to be primarily educational. In their report to the Boston City Council, the trustees of the library proposed that the public library in Boston would be "the crowning glory of our system of City schools" and "the utmost importance as the means of completing our system of public education." Communities that followed the Boston model and founded libraries in the 1850s and 1860s were explicit in citing the library's purpose to support and extend the agencies of formal education in the community.

The education theme has remained a constant in the discourse of the American library profession. In 1955, for example, testimony in support of the first federal legislation to support library development, the Library Services Act, consistently argued the educational importance of the public library, asserting that libraries were second only to schools in the capacity to educate citizens. Librarian of Congress L. Q. Mumford testified that "for most people the public library is the chief—and sometimes the only—means of carrying on their education after they leave school."

In recent years, however, the importance of education has almost disappeared from the rhetoric of librarians, replaced by a focus on information. Libraries and librarians are indeed good at organizing and providing access to information. But providing information and supporting education are not the same things. There is a difference between information and knowledge. There are many other agencies that also provide access to information, and a number of other professions that claim that expertise. The most important role of the library is supporting, enhancing, and facilitating the transfer of knowledge—in other words, education.

We often hear it said that today we are living in an information age. But in a world drowning in information, we are hungry for knowledge. That is why today, in the 21st century, we must be more than an information society. We must become a *learning* society. And that is why at IMLS we are dedicated to the purpose of creating and sustaining a nation of learners.

A learning society requires that we do more than develop the hardware, software, telecommunications networks, and other services and systems that supply and catalog content. It requires additional structure and context to enable learners around the globe to put knowledge to good use. And I think that virtual reference services are an important part of that process.

COLLABORATION

Virtual reference service is only possible today because the Internet provides a backbone and channel for robust communications. The Internet model is inherently one of collaboration and cooperation. Building a virtual reference service as a single site or within a single service would be difficult, if not impossible. It would also be counterproductive, and would overlook the valuable work already being done by existing Internet services. In short, for virtual reference service to work effectively, it must be built upon a foundation of collaboration.

At IMLS we believe that collaboration is emerging as the strategy of the 21st century. It is aligned with how we are thinking about our communities as "holistic" environments, as social ecosystems in which we are part of an integrated whole. The kind of collaboration we wish to encourage is not a joined-at-the-hip symbiosis, and it certainly is not a parasitic relationship. Instead it is a mature and reflective recognition of intersecting nodes of interest, activity, and mission. It is the potential for creating synergy out of cooperation, building a structure in which the whole is greater than the sum of the parts.

Librarians have a consistent history of collaboration. Sharing resources is fundamental to the practice of the profession. Indeed, the concept of sharing underlies the very foundation of the modern library as a social agency. Libraries were established in order to pool scarce resources for the common good. The society libraries of the American colonial period arose from the simple fact that books were too scarce, and too expensive, for any one individual to be able to acquire access to all they needed, so readers brought their individual collections together to share them in common. This ethic of sharing has remained strong in the practice of American librarianship ever since.

But collaboration is not easy. It requires that we—as individuals and as institutions—behave in ways that may feel unnatural. One definition of collaboration that I recently heard offered is that collaboration is "an unnatural act, practiced by non-consenting adults." The dictionary, in fact, offers the following as one definition: "cooperating treasonably, as with an enemy occupying one's country." This notion may be at the heart of some of the difficulties that we encounter in attempting to collaborate. A better definition for our purposes is "working together in a joint effort."

Differences among institutions, however, can be profound. The assets and personnel, academic preparation of professionals, even the very vocabulary we use to describe operations, can be dramatically different. The characteristics and proximity to the communities served can vary widely. Values and assumptions of mission and service can be different.

In short, the cultures of organizations can differ dramatically. These differences are challenging and they do not go away. It is imperative that these differences be recognized forthrightly. Over time, they can evolve into sources of synergy rather than contention. One goal of successful collaboration is assurance that the integrity of each institution is sustained by the partnership.

IMLS has provided a strong incentive to overcome these barriers and develop the potential of collaborative efforts. As Nancy Allen and Liz Bishoff (2002) observed in a recent publication:

> Through IMLS funding, a growing number of academic libraries are partnering with museums, historical societies, and other scientific and cultural heritage organizations. The IMLS presented these communities with financial incentives to develop joint projects and to work together to create new approaches to meet the common goals and purposes of creating better and more accessible collections that meet the needs of a knowledge society (57).

There are numerous examples of such projects, funded directly by IMLS and indirectly by state library administrative agencies using LSTA funds. They vary enormously in scope and range, in terms of the size and diversity of the institutions involved, the types of materials included in the projects, and the value-added matrix in which they are embedded. Many of these projects have been funded under our National Leadership Grant program in the Museum-Library Collaboration category, which requires collaboration between at least one museum and one library. It is interesting to note, however, that many of the collaborative projects funded by IMLS are in other grant categories in which collaboration is not required. It is clear that the library and museum communities have embraced collaboration as one of the most important tools they have for achieving their goals, for creating value for their communities.

Naturally at IMLS we are interested in fostering collaboration between and among museums and libraries. It is inherent in our structure, and mandated by our statute. But we also think it is imperative to reach out beyond the museum and library and to find those intersecting nodes of interest, activity, and mission among other players in the community.

To give you an idea of how essential we think this kind of approach is to success, last year I created a new position on our staff, director for strategic partnerships. The charge to that officer is to identify opportunities for useful collaborations, with other federal agencies, with nongovernmental organizations, with other funders like foundations and corporations, and with the relevant service organizations. We agreed to define the long-term success of this approach when these agencies start to come to us for help in involving museums and libraries in their programs because they recognize what museums and libraries can do to help them achieve their goals. That has already begun to happen.

One of the potential partners in which we have the most interest at present is public broadcasting. Robert Coonrod, the president of the Corporation for Public Broadcasting (CPB) gave the keynote address at our 2003 Web Wise conference in Washington. He provided a broad overview of the changes that broadcasters are going though, in large part as a result of the impact of digital technology (Coonrod, 2003). Those changes lead to the inescapable recognition of a pending convergence. Public broadcasters are becoming more and more like libraries and museums—just as libraries and museums are becoming more and more like broadcasters. Coonrod encouraged us to begin to explore what he called "community-based public service media collaboratives." We already have ready examples of such collaborative projects in the landscape, many of them funded by IMLS. We are now actively exploring collaborative projects between IMLS and CPB.

PENDING CONVERGENCE

In November 2003, IMLS and CPB jointly sponsored a conference in Washington, focusing on supporting community-based collaborations that foster learning and civic engagement for the 21st century. This "Partnership for a Nation of Learners," as we called it, is designed to support and promote collaborations that link active learners to an expanded network of community-based resources, with a special interest in collaborations that respond to specific community needs, produce public benefit, and promote civic engagement through the learning that occurs.

The meeting brought together representatives not only of the broadcaster, museum, and library professional communities, but also a range of funding organizations and nongovernmental organizations with an interest in the topic. We are still assessing the outcomes of that meeting, but some very interesting issues surfaced in the discussions. And I would like to discuss two of the major elements that I think, combined, lead to an inescapable conclusion of a major transition.

The first of these is the recognition of a pending convergence of libraries, museums, and broadcasters. For some time now I have been writing and speaking about the blurring boundaries between and among cultural institutions, focusing primarily on the boundaries between museums, libraries, and archives.

IMLS sponsors an annual conference called WebWise that focuses on digital library and museum projects, many of them funded by IMLS. A couple of years ago, we heard consistent reports indicating that in the digital environment, libraries are beginning to behave more like museums and museums are behaving more like archives. In the traditional nondigital environment, libraries organize their collections and present them for use in response to a user's specific need or inquiry. A user comes into the library and asks, "What do you have on topic X?" For example, "Show me everything you have on impressionist painting, on Native American ritual objects, on Paleolithic protozoa."

Conversely, museums traditionally organize selections from their collections in topical or thematic interpretive and didactic exercises we call exhibitions. A user comes into the museum and looks at what the museum staff has selected, presented, and interpreted. A museum-goer would not normally come into the museum and say, "Show me all of your impressionist paintings, show me all your Native American ritual objects, show me all your Paleolithic protozoa."

In the digital environment, these behaviors are almost precisely reversed. Museums for the first time can present their entire collections, cataloged and surrounded with metadata, retrievable in response to a user's specific interest or inquiry. And libraries have begun to organize selected items from their collections in thematic presentations that tell a particular story, and even call these presentations exhibitions.

It is important to note that the users of these digital collections do not care, and may well not even be aware, that the originals of the digital surrogates that they use are in a museum, a library, an archives, or some other kind of institution. The boundaries indeed are blurring.

Recently, I have learned that, in the digital arena, there has been a transformation that results in public broadcasters behaving more like museums and libraries. Formerly we have been accustomed to thinking about broadcasters as providing access to rich educational resources, but in a strictly synchronous manner. If we wanted to enjoy the educational content that they provide, we were expected to tune in on Thursday evening at 8:00 P.M. to see the latest program on the rings of Saturn, on the explorations of Lewis and Clark, or on the plays of Shakespeare. But increasingly now, this "broadcast" content is no longer "broadcast" in the conventional sense. It is accessed through cable or satellite connection. And, increasingly, we can also access and download the entire program from a Web site.

What's more, new digital devices like TIVO are transforming the way that audiences interact with television programming, enabling the "viewer" to capture the broadcast, retain it for use at a later time, to be retrieved and used at the convenience of the receiver.

Traditional synchronous access to broadcast programming is declining and asynchronous use is becoming the norm. "Broadcasting" no longer adequately describes what broadcasters do; it instead describes the technology that they formerly used to do what they do. The essence of their business is not "broadcasting"; it is creating and providing access to educational content and opportunities.

There is one other important transformation for broadcasters. In the traditional context, the programming that is made available at 8:00 P.M. on Thursday evening is typically 50 minutes of content. This represents really only an executive summary of hours of material that have been captured or created and edited down to fit the available programming slot. But it is now common to make at least some of that additional material available to the user, via the broadcaster's Web site. We have all heard the instruction at the end of a show or segment that we can find additional information at a specified URL.

In short, broadcasters are now trying to find ways to organize and present for use the vast quantities of raw material, surround it with metadata, and make it retrievable in response to a specific user inquiry. In short, in the digital environment, broadcasters are behaving more like museums and libraries.

The second element of the major transformation that we are

witnessing is a rapid transformation in our approach to structuring education, what some have called the "de-institutionalization of learning."

We have all heard discussion recently about a crisis in our education system. But really, what we are experiencing is perhaps a crisis in our system of schooling. We must remember that "schooling" is not the same thing as "education," and that "education" is not the same thing as "learning." What we at IMLS are interested in is the broadest of these terms and categories, learning.

As our system of schooling continues to struggle, alternative approaches to learning are expanding. In recent years there has been a tremendous growth in homeschooling. (The term "homeschooling" is in fact a misnomer, since the last thing that the practitioners of this form of learning is interested in doing is recreating a school in the home.)

In fact, in our society we learn in three different sectors. We learn in the school. We learn in the workplace. And we learn in the home and community. The last of these three sectors is now frequently referred to as the free-choice learning sector, underscoring that learners in this environment are motivated by individual needs and interests.

In the past century, we have devoted most of our resources to strengthening our schools. There is reason to believe that in the near future there may be a rapid and dramatic transformation in the way society structures learning—opportunities and support for learning. There will be an equalization across the three sectors, with less emphasis on schooling and increasing emphasis on the other two sectors. And this presents a major challenge—and a great opportunity—for libraries, museums, and public broadcasters.

We have long heard about virtual libraries and museums without walls. Now we have the opportunity to truly begin to develop new approaches to services that stretch the previous conceptions of how we structure and deliver services. We can, in short, develop customized learning experiences that are tailored to the unique needs and interests of the individual learner. And we can capture, store, re-use and re-purpose those unique experiences. And we can focus not only on the needs of communities-of-place, but also address the requirements of communities-of-interest.

THE FUTURE OF LIBRARY SERVICES

So what does this mean for libraries in general, and for reference services in particular? I think that we need to review, rethink, perhaps revise, almost certainly re-articulate our missions. This morning I heard Joe Janes comment that the substance of virtual reference work is not just about reference—it is about revisioning broadly the range and scope of all library services. I think he is right; we are on the cusp of a true revolution in library services. We have the potential to use digital technology to revolutionize public services in libraries in ways clearly analogous to the way technical services were revolutionized in the 1970s and 1980s.

When automation was first applied to technical services it was simply a way to computerize the existing card catalogs, making 3×5 cards appear on a computer screen. Indeed, I can recall an early computerized catalog in which the familiar 3×5 card was replicated on the computer screen, complete with the hole in the bottom. That was what library patrons (and librarians) were used to, so that is what we gave them.

But the development of MARC enabled the sharing of work as well as information. The idea of cataloging each book only once and then sharing that work of cataloging—an idea that originated at least a century ago with Herbert Putnam's Library of Congress card catalog service—finally made practical sense.

Shared cataloging resulted in the development of bibliographic databases that in turn empowered resource sharing. I think it is hard for many of us to remember how much more difficult research—especially humanistic research—was in the days before the development of such bibliographic tools. The archaic "bibliographic apparatus" of printed catalogs made it extremely difficult for scholars and students to determine the existence and location of a specific bibliographic entity. Work that we can now accomplish in a few minutes of searching in an online database formerly required months, even years, of diligent effort. In short, MARC transformed not only catalog-ing, but almost the whole of library services.

I believe that virtual reference systems have a similar trans-formative potential. If we can develop systems that can capture and organize the intellectual work of responding to a specific reference inquiry—intellectual work that responds to the spe-cific need of a unique user—then we can collate and re-purpose that work to address the needs of other users. We can better un-derstand the needs of all users, and we can develop approaches to truly collaborate to provide services. We can do it right, do it once, and re-use the work many times.

CONCLUSION

Virtual reference is but a small part of a much broader evolu-tion in libraries, museums, and archives, as we continue to ap-ply networked digital information technology to develop new approaches to providing resources and services that enable and empower learners of all ages. Virtual reference services are more than boxes and wires connected via the Internet. The important thing about these services is that they use digital technology to connect *people* with needs to *people* who can answer questions and support the development of skills. And as we develop these virtual services, we must remember that we must design them to serve the *real* needs of *real* people.

NOTE

1.   Robert S. Martin, director of the Institute of Museum and Library Ser-vices, gave the keynote address at the Fourth Virtual Reference Desk (VRD) conference. This paper is a slightly modified version of that ad-dress.

REFERENCES

Allen, Nancy, and Liz Bishoff. 2002. "Collaborative Digitization: Libraries and Museums Working Together." *Advances in Librarianship* 26: 43–81.
Coonrod, Robert. 2003. "Creating the Digital Future" [keynote address]. Paper presented at Web-Wise Conference, Washington, DC. February 26–28, 2003. Available: www.imls.gov/pubs/WebWise2003/wbws03cp2.htm.

Chapter 12

A Lawyer's View of Privacy, Surveillance, and the USA Patriot Act

Glen Bencivengo

What is one's expectation of privacy in the electronic realm, especially in light of the USA Patriot Act Amendments to important federal statutes? How do the USA Patriot Act and federal surveillance techniques impact on the confidentiality of virtual reference transactions? What are the implications of proposed federal legislation to libraries and other professionals engaged in providing information to the public? How do changes in technology affect our notions of privacy, and what is the legal response to these technological advances? These and other questions will be discussed.

Since the passage of the USA Patriot Act in October 2001, librarians and civil libertarians have become increasingly concerned about patron privacy rights. This is especially true for those engaged in virtual reference programs. Much has been written about maintaining the confidentiality of virtual reference transactions. Because of the Patriot Act, librarians have been forced to review their privacy policies and question the validity of any assurances they make to patrons concerning the privacy of these transactions. By passing the Patriot Act, specifically section 215, Congress opened a Pandora's box of prob-

lems for librarians, problems that must be addressed if information professionals are to remain true to their ethical codes.
Technological advancements, especially the Internet, have made
possible not only innovative reference service, but also increased
potential for governmental abuse. Fourth Amendment jurisprudence has been influenced by the telecommunications revolution, which, in turn, has influenced our notions of privacy.
Federal statutory law has become increasingly complex, especially in view of the many amendments to these laws made by
the Patriot Act. What Court and Congress now decide cannot
be ignored by librarians because these decisions have a direct
bearing on the daily activities and endeavors of all those engaged in providing reference service to patrons in need of information.

PRIVACY AND SURVEILLANCE

One will not find an explicit privacy right in the Constitution.
Rather the United States Supreme Court has held that the various guarantees found in the Bill of Rights create "zones of privacy." Privacy is a "penumbra" right, inferred from the specific
language of several of the first Ten Amendments (Griswold v.
Connecticut 381 U.S. 479, 1965). The founding fathers wrote the
Fourth Amendment, for example, to address concerns over the
privacy of an individual's home and a fear of unfettered governmental power and discretion (Ku, 2002). Americans can avail
themselves of the amendment's protections only when they
have "reasonable expectations of privacy." Without such an expectation, there is no privacy right to protect. Technological advancements have affected rights of privacy. Nowhere is this
more apparent than in Fourth Amendment search and seizure
law and in the constitutionality of electronic surveillance. What
the United States Supreme Court has defined as an unlawful
search and seizure has been influenced by the nature of surveillance technologies implemented.

The Supreme Court was first asked to consider the constitutionality of electronic surveillance as early as 1928, almost fifty
years after the invention of the telephone (Horn, 2002). In
Olmstead v. United States (277 US 438, 1928), the Court decided

that the warrantless wiretapping of telephones did not violate the Fourth Amendment. The court based its argument on the notion that the amendment protected only tangible property. The tapping of telephone wires did not constitute a search and seizure because the surveillance did not constitute an actual search or seizure of physical property (Horn).

However as case law continued to develop, the Supreme Court started to take a different path and began to extend constitutional protection beyond the seizure of tangible items. The Court came to realize that developing technologies demanded a new way of thinking. Two landmark cases played important roles in shaping federal wiretap law.

The first was Berger v. New York (388 U.S. 41, 1967). In this significant case, the Supreme Court struck down a New York statute authorizing electronic eavesdropping by law enforcement officials investigating certain types of crimes (Horn, 2002). The Court held that conversations fall within the meaning of the Fourth Amendment. Thus, the seizure of conversations constituted a Fourth Amendment violation. The court went on to enumerate the constitutional criteria that electronic surveillance legislation should contain. For example, there is the requirement of "particularity." This means that law enforcement could not use a general warrant to conduct searches, but must specify in the warrant details regarding the person, place, or thing to be seized, as well as the nature of the crime in question and the type of conversation sought (Horn). The court held that there had to be "precise and discriminate" procedures in place to minimize the unauthorized interception of conversations.

The Court reaffirmed the standards that electronic surveillance should contain in the other landmark decision, Katz v. United States (389 U.S. 347, 1967). In this case, FBI agents had placed taps on the outside of a telephone booth. The Court held that in electronically listening to and recording the individual's words, the FBI had violated the privacy upon which the individual justifiably relied and this constituted a search and seizure within the meaning of the Fourth Amendment. Justice Harlan in a now famous concurring opinion created a two-prong test to determine when the Fourth Amendment confers protection. First, a person (for the amendment protects people, not places) must have exhibited an actual, that is, a subjective, expectation of privacy. Second, that expectation must be one that society is prepared to recognize as reasonable. This concurring opinion, which was later accepted by a majority of the Court, illustrates the evolving nature of Fourth Amendment jurisprudence. Privacy as protected by the Fourth Amendment came to be viewed as a right to be free from unwarranted governmental surveillance. It is this privacy right that many critics contend is threatened by the broad powers granted to federal law enforcement under the Patriot Act.

OMNIBUS CRIME CONTROL AND SAFE STREETS ACT

Recognizing the need to set uniform standards and to adapt to changes in technology, Congress passed Title III of the Omnibus Crime Control and Safe Streets Act of 1968 less than one year after the Berger and Katz cases. Following the constitutional standards set out in those two decisions, Congress prohibited all wiretapping and electronic surveillance except by persons authorized under law. Title III was enacted in response to the Supreme Court's recognition that electronic surveillance did not constitute a violation of the Fourth Amendment as long as such surveillance was conducted in a legal manner.

While recognizing that electronic surveillance was an essential law enforcement tool, Congress was also concerned about protecting individual privacy rights. It therefore not only incorporated the criteria set forth in Berger and Katz, but also created a standard for surveillance that went beyond the requirements of the Fourth Amendment (Horn, 2002).

Title III was enacted as a means to implement a uniform procedure for conducting constitutionally acceptable electronic surveillance. Title III applies to criminal investigations and authorizes surveillance upon a judge's finding of probable cause that a serious crime has been or is about to be committed. The requirements for obtaining a court order under Title III are stringent. Law enforcement officials must obtain authorization from a senior official at the Justice Department before they can apply to the court for an order. The application must specify the identity of the person under surveillance and the nature and the exact location of the intercepted communications and must describe the type of communications law enforcement is seeking to intercept. They must prove they have probable cause to believe the person in question is involved in criminal activity relating to one of the enumerated offenses under Title III and that communications concerning that specific activity will be obtained through the interception. Surveillance must be conducted in a timely manner so that the interceptions of communications not otherwise subject to surveillance are minimized.

In the years after 1968 Congress began to recognize improvements in communications technology. Concerned that the privacy of such communications could not be guaranteed absent legislation, but also aware that these very improvements posed a challenge to law enforcement, Congress passed legislation that broadened the power of the federal government.

ELECTRONIC COMMUNICATIONS PRIVACY ACT

In 1986 Congress passed the Electronic Communications Privacy Act (ECPA), which amended Title III, extending protections against unauthorized interceptions of "electronic communications." These communications included those via computer. In a nutshell, ECPA should be considered the wiretapping act for the Internet (Mitrano, 2002).

Under Chapter 121 of this act, Congress created requirements for the authorized access of *stored* wire and electronic communications. Significantly, governmental access to stored communications requires adherence to a far less demanding standard than under Title III. In fact, authorization could take a number of forms: subpoena, warrant, administrative or court orders, or even an authorized Executive Order letter (Mitrano, 2002). While the greater degree of content sought will require a higher form of authorization, under section 2703(d) of the act, the government need only show that there are reasonable grounds to believe that the contents of a wire or electronic communication are relevant and material to an ongoing criminal investigation. This standard falls short of the probable-cause requirement of the Fourth Amendment and the more stringent standards of Title III.

Indeed, critics argue that ECPA gives law enforcement the upper hand because it enables the avoidance of Title III requirements. By simply waiting until an electronic communication becomes *stored* in the computer network, rather than intercepting the communication in route, law enforcement can avail itself of the lower standards made legal by ECPA.

ECPA also adopted a procedure governing the use of pen registers and trap-and-trace devices. These devices can capture e-mail and Web addresses, but not content. ECPA does require law enforcement to obtain court orders to use these devices. However the standard to obtain these orders is lower than Title III or the Fourth Amendment. To obtain a court order for a pen register or a trap-and-trace, the government must certify only that the information likely to be obtained is relevant to an ongoing criminal investigation being conducted by that agency. In addition, any attorney for the government may make such an application to the court without prior approval from senior officials at the Department of Justice.

FOREIGN INTELLIGENCE SURVEILLANCE ACT

The other important statutory response to the increased complexity of telecommunications is the Foreign Intelligence Surveillance Act (FISA). Passed by Congress in 1978, FISA permits law enforcement officers to seek orders for surveillance from a special court if the electronic surveillance targets a foreign power or an agent of a foreign power. Each application for surveillance authorization must be made by a federal officer with approval of the Attorney General. The FISA Court, which consists of appointed federal district court judges, will authorize a surveillance if it finds that there is probable cause to believe that the target of the surveillance is a foreign power or agent. The court subjects the application only to minimal scrutiny and, most importantly, none of the criteria necessary for the application's approval rise to the level of the Fourth Amendment probable-cause requirement, that is, that a criminal or unlawful act has been or is about to be committed. Furthermore, the officer seeking the application is theoretically not seeking evidence of criminal activities on which to base a prosecution, but rather is seeking information regarding foreign intelligence activities that may compromise national security. Federal courts have upheld the foreign intelligence exception to the Fourth Amendment requirement as long as the interests of the executive are paramount, the object of the surveillance is a foreign power, its agents, or collaborators, and when the surveillance is conducted primarily for foreign intelligence reasons.

THE USA PATRIOT ACT

Well over one hundred pages long, the USA Patriot Act amends at least 15 federal statues. It was passed in the wake of the September 11 tragedies with little debate. Many Congress members later reported that they had not studied the bill carefully. There is a paucity of legislative history about the statute.

The USA Patriot Act creates a new crime of domestic terrorism, which is defined as activities that involve acts dangerous to human life that are violations of the criminal laws of the United States or of any state; appear to be intended to intimidate or coerce a civilian population; influence the policy of a government by intimidation or coercion or affect the conduct of a government by mass destruction, assassination, or kidnapping; and occur primarily within the territorial jurisdiction of the United States (Mitrano, 2002). Since it is unclear what "intimidation" and "influence" mean, it should be noted that this language potentially could apply to lawful political dissent.

The USA Patriot Act (the "Act") amended ECPA in significant ways. Prior to the Act, law enforcement officials required traditional subpoenas in order to acquire routing information (Mitrano, 2002). But since the Act, "rubber stamp" subpoenas have replaced the traditional standard. Some critics have objected to the lower standard that law enforcement may now employ to obtain authorization for pen registers and trap-and-trace devices that capture this routing information (Mitrano). The constitutionality of this language is in question because there is not a one-to-one equivalency between telephonic and electronic communications. There is a possibility that content-subject lines of e-mails or URLs may be trapped or traced. Lower courts will eventually decide on the constitutionality of this language. Whether or not the Supreme Court will grant certiorari (i.e., decide the matter) for these possible cases is open to question (Mitrano).

This amendment to ECPA permitting a lower standard for an application of a subpoena may very well mean an increase in requests for information by law enforcement. Colleges and universities will not be liable for disclosing information, but this does not mean that institutions of higher learning should not have policies and procedures in place for the handling of the possible increase of legal papers served on them by law enforcement (Mitrano, 2002).

Another USA Patriot Act amendment to ECPA is the "emergency disclosure" language of section 212. This language amends section 2702 of ECPA to allow operators or owners of a network system to disclose information to anyone without fear of liability if they reasonably believe they have accessed information that would endanger people (Mitrano, 2002). This amendment raises confidentiality concerns with regard to virtual reference. Suppose in the course of business, network administrators or the company providing the platform for a library's virtual reference project access information they deem to be dangerous or that would result in some bodily harm. Under this new statutory language they could disclose that information to virtually anyone without fear of subsequent liability under ECPA.

The USA Patriot Act amendments to FISA are of important consequence. The Act changed the language of section 1804(a)(7)(B) of FISA. Currently a federal law enforcement officer no longer has to demonstrate that "the purpose" of the surveillance is to obtain foreign intelligence information, but may obtain surveillance authorization from the FISA Court under the less stringent showing that "a significant purpose" of the surveillance is to obtain the information. This seemingly slight change to section 1804 may mean an increase in FISA Court–ordered investigations carried out in the name of foreign intelligence. Note that as the FISA Court rarely rejects surveillance applications, it is very likely that the court will authorize all forthcoming applications under this more lenient standard.

One major concern raised by civil libertarians to this amendment is the possibility that the broad scope of section 1804 will permit intelligence and law enforcement agents to bring applications for surveillance before the FISA Court when the major purpose of the surveillance is the investigation of purely domestic criminal activities. In effect, this would mean that the amended FISA could be used as a means to undertake surveillance without demonstrating the heightened standard of probable cause required under Title III for criminal wiretaps. FISA could be employed to approve investigations of criminal activities, including purely domestic criminal acts in explicit violation of Title III and the Fourth Amendment. This danger has not gone unnoticed by some members of Congress. Senator Leahy, for example, recognized that by amending the language of FISA, the USA Patriot Act would make it easier for the FBI to use a FISA wiretap to obtain information when the government's prime motivation for the wiretap is for use in a criminal investigation. The senator acknowledged that "this is a disturbing and dangerous change in law" (Rackow, 2002).

CRIMINAL INVESTIGATIONS

There is increasing evidence that the Justice Department intends to use the Act as a tool for purely domestic criminal investigations. Furthermore this intent has received Court approval. In an extremely detailed and interesting Per Curiam opinion by the United States Foreign Intelligence Court of Review (FICR) decided in November 2002 (U.S. FICR, 2002), it was held that because of the crucial change of language to section 1804 of FISA, it is now permissible for the FBI to obtain FISA search or surveillance warrants against individuals who are targets of domestic criminal prosecutions and a source of valuable intelligence. Put another way, this FISA Appellate Court determined that FISA, as amended, does not oblige the government to demonstrate to the FISA Court that its primary purpose in conducting electronic surveillance is not criminal prosecution (U.S. FICR, 2002).

As reported in the media, the Justice Department has already begun using the USA Patriot Act in criminal investigations that have little or no connection to terrorism. With the Act breaking down the wall between intelligence and criminal investigations, the Justice Department is actively prosecuting individuals with little or no terrorist connections. The FBI, for example, has used its expanded authority to track the private Internet communications of a major drug distributor. While Attorney General Ashcroft publicly has portrayed his expanded power as a means of fighting terrorists, internally Justice Department officials have emphasized "a much broader mandate" (Lichtblau, 2003), one that would include pursuing domestic criminals. Senator Leahy, for one, is concerned about these developments and is quoted as saying that government cannot take "shortcuts" around criminal laws, which have higher standards of evidence, by invoking intelligence powers to demand access to records. He stated that "we did not intend for the government to shed traditional tools of criminal investigations, such as grand jury subpoenas, [which are] governed by well established precedent [and] monitored by federal judges" (Lichtblau, 2003). Despite these admonitions, Justice Department Officials remain undeterred and plan to continue to use the amended language of FISA with its lower standards of evidence and weaker requirements to pursue "garden variety criminals" (Lichtblau, 2003).

These planned actions by the Justice Department are troubling when one remembers that FISA was enacted in 1978 in part to erect a wall between foreign and domestic intelligence gathering. This was done after it was revealed that the FBI had conducted extensive surveillance of United States citizens during the 1960s and 70s. By requiring that the primary purpose of a wiretap or search was to obtain foreign intelligence, which requires a higher probable-cause standard, FISA forbade the use of the surveillance authority in criminal cases. However, the expanded authority granted the FBI by the USA Patriot Act amendments may resurrect the practice of investigating Americans with unpopular political views, ironically the same practice that prompted the original limiting language in FISA in the first place. At the very least it appears clear that the Justice Department plans to take an aggressive posture in its use of FISA as a law enforcement tool.

SURVEILLANCE/PEN/TRAP ORDERS

The USA Patriot Act expands FISA court orders to allow roving surveillance. This would enable government investigators to intercept all of a suspect's wire or electronic communications relating to the conduct under investigation regardless of the suspect's location. The use of multipoint wiretaps under a FISA warrant presents even greater concerns than those used in criminal investigations because the standard of proof required to obtain such a far reaching warrant is so much lower. The danger is that a multipoint surveillance increases the incidental surveillance of individuals who are not the target of FISA investigations. This incidental surveillance, combined with the sharing of information mandated by the USA Patriot Act, may very well have a negative impact on the protection of civil liberties (Bradley, 2002).

The USA Patriot Act also amends portions of FISA pertaining to pen/trap orders. The Act expands the government's ability to obtain a FISA Court order for pen register or trap-and-trace surveillance. The amendment replaces a strict standard with the requirement that the government merely certify that the information sought is relevant to an ongoing criminal investigation. If the government makes such a showing, a judge must grant the order. These changes, as well as those made to the provisions concerning the collection of documents, are a significant alteration to the mechanics of FISA because the language of the Act seems to eliminate judicial discretion. The judge must grant the order, language which seems to mandate judicial issuance of a FISA warrant (Bradley, 2002). Also, the changes made to the provisions for pen registers would permit a much broader collection of information than previously permitted under FISA. The FBI could collect not only the e-mail addresses of a communication, but also the subject header and information about URLs accessed. They could also obtain information about search queries and Web sites viewed by the suspect. All of this has obvious implications for virtual reference interactions.

SECTIONS 215, 216

As all librarians should know by this juncture, section 215 of the USA Patriot Act expands FISA, allowing federal law enforcement to compel the production of any tangible things (including books, records, papers, documents, and other items) sought in an investigation to protect against international terrorism or clandestine intelligence activities. The extension of physical searches is not limited to foreign powers and their agents and may include United States persons as long as the investigation is "not conducted of a United States person solely upon the basis of activities protected by the First Amendment." This seemingly simple language has some inherent confusion. What constitutes a "United States person": A person living in the United States? A citizen of the United States? What are activities protected by the First Amendment? This particular language belies the fact that First Amendment jurisprudence is complex and often shifting (Mitrano, 2002). It is not always crystal clear what activities are protected. Another important issue is that section 215 prohibits the record keeper served with the FISA warrant from disclosing the order to anyone other than those persons necessary to produce the tangible things requested.

It is worth repeating that a federal agent need only believe that the investigation relates to terrorism or clandestine activities in order to succeed in obtaining the necessary FISA Court order. This expanded power would permit the government to legally seize floppy disks, data tapes, computers with hard drives, and library records stored in any medium. Since section 216 of the Act makes it also relatively easy for law enforcement to obtain pen registers and trap-and-trace orders (there need be no showing of probable cause), librarians should be prepared to deal with these types of governmental requests, especially since the Act allows for nationwide execution of these orders. A pen/trap order can now follow a suspect to any jurisdiction. The order could be used to place a pen/trap device on a computer and intercept noncontent information and a library may not be aware of it. Many times the actual interception of electronic information takes place at the ISP, and now these providers are ordered to keep silent by nondisclosure provisions of section 216.

It should be noted again that the Act has extended the availability of wiretaps that may intercept electronic communication content. FISA wiretap orders may make their way into library networks because the threshold to obtain such orders, while higher than trap/trace orders, is still lower than traditional probable-cause standards.

PRIVACY AND THE INTERNET

Librarians are all aware that they have an ethical obligation to maintain the privacy and confidentiality of patron transactions. The ALA takes the position that "in a library (physical or virtual) the right of privacy is the right to open inquiry without having the subject of one's interest examined or scrutinized by others" (American Library Association, 2002). However in light of the USA Patriot Act, can librarians ensure the confidentiality of virtual reference transactions? The answer to this question is no. For despite any assurances to the contrary, librarians engaged in virtual reference, live chat, and e-mail with patrons cannot guarantee the confidentiality of these transactions. The federal government now has the power to obtain FISA warrants that would permit it to seize written records and computers. Written transcripts of virtual reference sessions could be seized legally by law enforcement officials. Furthermore, the Act supersedes any ethical codes librarians may have. Indeed, the Act preempts existing state library privacy statutes (*Safeguarding Our Patrons' Privacy*, 2002).

The issue of Internet privacy rights is complex and the legal literature is replete with articles on the topic (see Cooper, 2001, Haglund, 2003, Hector, 2003, Safier, 2000). Technology influences our notions of privacy, as case law indicates. For example, in Smith v. Maryland (442 U.S. 735, 1979), the United States Supreme Court ruled that the installation and use of pen registers was not a search under the Fourth Amendment. In a 5–4 decision, the court held that there was no constitutionally protected reasonable expectation of privacy in the numbers dialed into a telephone system and hence no search within the meaning of the Fourth Amendment. Congress adopted the reasoning in Smith when passing section 216 of the Act and analogized the routing of electronic communications on the Internet to the dialing of a telephone (Osher, 2002). This language now permits law enforcement officials to obtain information such as Web and e-mail addresses and session times based on a lower standard than the probable-cause necessary for a standard search warrant. By making the necessary certification that the information is relevant to an ongoing criminal investigation, an FBI agent can obtain the order because the Act obligates the court to issue the order. However, as critics have noted (Osher) the analogy to telephone records is flawed because the Internet is not like a telephone wire. It functions by employing packet switching. Data is broken down into small packets of information that are transmitted and reassembled in the correct order at the destination computer. The Smith opinion reasoned that pen-registered supplied information was not private because the device did not overhear the content of oral communications, and did not indicate whether calls were actually completed (Osher). However, information contained in e-mail messages is transmitted in packets and whoever intercepts the message must separate the address from the contents of the e-mail. The FBI responds to invasion of privacy concerns by asserting that it can be trusted to separate addresses from content and retain only the former. Smith has been criticized for its narrow and limiting view of privacy, but this criticism did not prevent the FBI from using the holding of this case in its application to the Internet when seeking warrants under the Act. One could argue that the Smith holding was employed by federal law enforcement to legitimize section 216. Available technology, it could be said, has led to a further erosion of Internet privacy rights (Osher).

As one commentator has noted, "[t]he Internet revolution has altered the calculus for what may be considered a reasonable expectation of privacy" (Corn-Revere, 2000). Privacy expectations have eroded with increased Internet use. Internet users, and this includes those engaged in virtual reference transactions, must realize that the very framework of the Internet poses serious security issues. If a person is willing to proceed with an Internet transaction even after he has been warned that he is using an unsecured connection, he has made an affirmative recognition of the privacy risks associated with online use (Dowley, 2002). Virtual reference patrons and librarians may not employ tracking software, but they should realize that such software is commercially obtainable. Some employers have installed software called "Superscout" on their networks, which enables them to track an employee's e-mail and Internet activities. Using this software, companies often fire employees for Web surfing on company time. Courts have often sided with employers on workplace privacy issues, holding that "office practices, procedures or regulations may reduce privacy expectations" (Horn, 2002).

Just as with private employers, federal law enforcement can employ tracking monitoring software. Since the USA Patriot Act now allows Internet-based communications to be intercepted using many of the same procedures as with pen/trap devices, it is increasingly likely that the FBI will employ its Carnivore, or now more benignly called DCS1000, system.

CARNIVORE

Carnivore (DCS1000) is an FBI program that can scan millions of e-mails per second. It is capable of intercepting information regarding instant messaging, Web-site access and chat groups. It can be used in two ways, as a content wiretap or as a pen/trap register. While it is more often used as a pen/trap, it has the capability, despite initial FBI denials, to capture the full content of e-mails, messages to and from a specific user's account, and all the network traffic to and from users or IP addresses (Horn, 2002). Carnivore can list all the servers (Web servers and FTP servers) that a suspect accesses. It can track everyone who accesses a specific Web page or FTP file. It can track all Web pages or FTP files a person accesses. Carnivore acts like a packet sniffer. It can eavesdrop on packets and then save copies. Since it is a passive system, it does not interfere with communications. It is in a box that consists of a commercial, off-the-shelf, Windows NT or Windows 2000, box. It has a two Gigabyte Jaz drive that can contain evidence. The box can not be hacked from the

Internet. FBI agents exchange the Jaz disk daily. The FBI maintains that it minimizes the data collected and configures the system in such a way so that it will not capture data from innocent people. Carnivore is not sophisticated new technology; there are numerous products that are more advanced (Graham, 2001).

The controversy about Carnivore centers on how it is used and whether it violates privacy rights. Privacy groups maintain that the system invades the privacy rights of innocent Internet users by allowing excessive monitoring of online communications. Critics argue that in order for Carnivore to intercept the targeted individual's electronic messages, the system must analyze and filter all e-mail transmitted over an ISP network (Horn, 2002).

The FBI asserts that Carnivore actually enhances privacy rights by allowing law enforcement to apprehend individuals who pose a threat to the security of all. They further maintain that the system only gives law enforcement the ability to intercept and collect electronic communications from individuals being investigated subject to a court order (Horn, 2002). One should remember however that when used as a trap/trace device, the FBI can implement the system under less restrictive rules and not through compliance with the more stringent Title III standards of probable cause.

One could argue that Carnivore should not be treated as a mere pen register or trap-and-trace. In contrast to a true pen register, Carnivore collects a wide range of information, including the e-mail addresses of both the sender and the recipient. Carnivore, some believe, is more analogous to a wiretap (Horn, 2002). Similar to a wiretap's ability to collect all information passing thorough a phone line, Carnivore can be programmed to collect all information passing through an ISP.

The FBI's characterization of Carnivore as a mere trap-and-trace device is an example of an agency construing a law enforcement tool in a way to justify its widespread use. By characterizing Carnivore as a pen register/trap/trace device, the FBI, as must be stressed again, can circumvent Fourth Amendment and Title III protections.

While it is very difficult to obtain any concrete evidence, some believe that Carnivore is being used extensively. In a *Wired*

News article of September 11, 2002 (Scheeres, 2002), Seattle telecommunications attorney Al Gidari claims that the FBI has attached Carnivore to many ISP systems in order to check for Web-site visits, terms entered into search engines, and e-mail headers. Privacy advocates claim there is a surge in the number of ISPs inviting the government to install Carnivore onto their systems to combat credit card fraud. But in so inviting the FBI, these internet service providers are trusting the government to filter sensitive data that is unrelated to the investigation, such as the e-mail data of *any* customer (Scheeres, 2002).

THE USA PATRIOT ACT, VIRTUAL REFERENCE, AND PRIVACY

As should be crystal clear at this juncture, the USA Patriot Act puts librarians engaged in virtual reference programs in a rather precarious position. Since librarians cannot guarantee the confidentiality of virtual reference transactions, proper evaluation of these services becomes problematic. Written transcripts of live reference sessions could be legally seized by law enforcement officials. This poses an interesting issue since a careful analysis of these transcripts is a great opportunity to become informed about patron needs and to improve service. Marc Meola and Sam Stormont (2002), in their excellent How-To-Do-It Manual *Starting and Operating Live Virtual Reference Services*, urge librarians to keep and analyze transaction records. However in view of the federal government's expanded powers, one must now think twice about this excellent advice. A library could keep records for a short period of time and attempt to evaluate the service as quickly as possible, and then destroy all the transcripts. However this would put an added burden on the librarians and would not make it possible to track trends and patterns over a long period of time. One could eliminate all identifying information in the virtual reference transaction, attempt to categorize the questions in some way, and then discard the transcripts. However one decides, evaluation now has become more problematic and proper administration of virtual reference programs may become more difficult.

While librarians are concerned about virtual reference privacy issues, one may ask if patrons are. This question depends on several factors, as Amy Van Scoy and Megan Oakleaf made clear in their ACRL Eleventh National Conference presentation in April, 2003 (Van Scoy and Oakleaf, 2003). One factor is age. Older patrons "seem more concerned with privacy issues than younger patrons" (Van Scoy and Oakleaf). College-aged students share information and consider reference transactions public. Older students and faculty view transactions with librarians as private. College-aged students, Van Scoy and Oakleaf report, seem resigned to the idea that anyone can get information about them off the Internet.

Patron confidence in the library increases if the library has a carefully articulated privacy policy (Van Scoy and Oakleaf, 2003). This may mean that the policy should be placed on the library's Web page with information about the USA Patriot Act. Libraries may now be forced to articulate what they do with the transcripts of transactions. Libraries must also work closely with vendors who supply and maintain the software used in the virtual reference program. In light of the Patriot Act, it behooves librarians to ascertain from the vendors the answers to such questions as: What patron and transaction information is archived? Can patron information be purged from the system? Who has administrative access to the information and when do they use it? As Van Scoy and Oakleaf make clear, some patrons, especially college-aged students, may not value privacy as much as librarians think, but this does not mean that librarians cannot concern themselves with trying to find the proper balance between online privacy and "enhanced virtual reference."

DOMESTIC SECURITY ENHANCEMENT ACT (PATRIOT ACT II)

This balance may become even more difficult to maintain if the Domestic Security Enhancement Act of 2003 should ever become law. Dubbed "Patriot Act II" by its critics, this draft legislation would greatly increase governmental surveillance powers. Given all the negative publicity about this draft—which is not even a bill before Congress—it is unlikely that it will become law. The Department of Justice was less than forthcoming about the details of Patriot Act II, even continually denying its very existence right up to the day when the Center for Public Integrity published a leaked version on the Internet (Lumpkin, 2003).

Both conservatives and liberals oppose Patriot Act II for a host of reasons, the main two being an unwarranted extension of federal executive power and a lack of judicial oversight. Some of its provisions include a possible revocation of citizenship for Americans who are found to have contributed "material" support to organizations deemed terrorist by the government. This provision would represent a drastic change in the law because traditionally Americans can only lose citizenship by declaring a clear intent to abandon it. However, under Patriot Act II, the intent to relinquish nationality need not be manifested in words; it can be inferred from conduct. Another provision would permit the government to build a database of citizen DNA information aimed at "detecting, investigating, prosecuting, preventing or responding to terrorist activities" (Hentoff, 2003). Samples of DNA could be collected without a court order. One need only be suspected of wrongdoing by a law enforcement officer. The term "suspected terrorists" would be defined broadly and could conceivably include political protestors or anyone else the government dislikes. Any person refusing to comply with the warrantless search could be charged with a Class A misdemeanor, punishable by up to one year in prison and a $100,000 fine (Ramasastry, 2003). Patriot Act II would explicitly collapse the distinction between domestic and international terrorism, treating wholly domestic criminal acts as subject to the same loose legal rule and standards that apply to foreign intelligence gathering (Ramasastry).

The proposed statute would also permit authorities to wiretap anyone for 15 days and monitor anyone's Internet usage (including chat and e-mail) without obtaining a warrant (Schabner, 2003). In addition, if an individual does discover that he was illegally spied upon in violation of the Fourth Amendment, he could not sue the federal government because Patriot Act II would provide immunity from liability to law enforcement officials engaging in spying on the American people (Ramasastry, 2003).

The original USA Patriot Act has sunset provisions. Several

sections, including 215, will expire in 2005 if not renewed by Congress. Patriot Act II, however, does not include such provisions; in fact, it would remove this language from the original act (Ramasastry, 2003).

THE VICTORY ACT

Patriot Act II received such negative publicity that it is unlikely even to reach the bill stage. However, this does not prevent the government from trying different tactics. In June 2003, a draft of a bill authored by Senator Hatch began circulating in Washington D.C. This draft bill, entitled the Vital Interdiction of Criminal Terrorist Organizations Act of 2003, or Victory Act, included significant portions of Patriot Act II. For example, it would allow the FBI to obtain a wiretap order for a wireless device, such as a cell phone, from any federal district court in the country. It would force defendants who are trying to exclude illegal wiretap evidence to prove that the police intentionally broke the rules. It would increase the ability of the FBI to issue administrative subpoenas for terrorist investigations without being forced to go before a judge (Singel, 2003).

Critics believe that these subpoenas simply give the FBI too much power and reduce judicial oversight to an alarming level. Patriot Act II and the Victory Act represent classic examples of one branch of government using a terrible tragedy and very legitimate fears to justify attacks on basic Constitutional liberties. One need only examine our history to see a pattern of such activity, going back to the Alien and Sedition Acts of 1798.

The other tactic the Executive Branch is navigating may also be cause for alarm. The additional invasion of individuals' rights proposed in Patriot Act II may now, at least in part, be legally undertaken. On December 13, 2003, President Bush signed the 2004 Intelligence Authorization Act, which gives the FBI the power, without judicial supervision, to obtain a wide range of personal records through the use of national security letters. These letters would be in the form of administrative subpoenas, thus not requiring judicial oversight, and according to one critic, allow the FBI to obtain business records from financial institutions, credit card companies, airlines, stockbrokers, and the United States Post Office (Hentoff, 2004). The enlarged scope of national security letters was enacted without public hearings. Furthermore, individuals receiving such letters are bound by law not to reveal that they received them. It thus appears that the United States Justice department is trying to "slip parts of Patriot Act II into law piecemeal" (Hentoff, 2004).

THE USA PATRIOT ACT OPPOSITION

Opposition to the USA Patriot Act is growing in Congress. For example, Bernie Sanders, an independent congressman from Vermont, introduced H.R. 1157 in March 2003. Titled "The Freedom to Read Protection Act," this bill would revise section 215 and return the government's capacity to search records of libraries and bookstores to pre-Patriot Act standards. The FBI would still have access to records, but only after a court issued a search warrant with probable cause, not the lower standard of the USA Patriot Act, which essentially rests on the personal belief of an FBI agent (Bradley, 2002). Currently this bill is being considered by the House Subcommittee on Crime, Terrorism and Homeland Security.

CONCLUSION

In the final analysis, one could agree that a balance must be struck between governmental surveillance powers and legitimate expectations of privacy. One can argue that certain provisions of the USA Patriot Act are necessary. For example, the sections dealing with international money laundering, bank security, currency crimes, and border protection are all important improvements to existing statutes. However these provisions do not apply to libraries. There is much in the Act that has the potential for abuse. Carnivore can be configured to capture full content. The wall between criminal and intelligence investigations is crumbling, and the executive branch of the federal government seems determined to expand its power. The recent provisions of the USA Patriot Act should remain in force, permitting Congress to review them in 2005. The Sanders bill exempting libraries and bookstores should be made law. One would be naïve to expect that the executive branch will voluntarily retrench and not push to increase its power to investigate Americans. Be that as it may, the USA Patriot Act is the law of the land, and although some call for its complete repeal, librarians engaged in virtual reference must not ignore the law, cannot ensure the confidentiality of transactions and must take the necessary steps to inform patrons of these unfortunate facts and write policies and design programs that will protect virtual reference patrons as much as possible.

REFERENCES

American Library Association. 2002. "Privacy: An Interpretation of the Library Bill of Rights."(June 19, 2002) Available: www.ala.orgTemplate.cfm?section =Interpretations&Template=/ContentManagement/ContentDisplay. cfm&ContentID=31883.

Bradley, Alison. 2002. "Extremism in the Defense of Liberty? The Foreign Intelligence Surveillance Act and the Significance of the USA Patriot Act." *Tulane Law Review* 77: 465.

Cooper, Henry. 2001. "The Electronic Communications Privacy Act: Does the Answer to the Internet Information Privacy Problem Lie in a Fifteen-Year-Old Federal Statue? A Detailed Analysis." *John Marshall Journal of Computer and Information Law* 20: 1.

Corn-Revere, Robert. (Sept. 6, 2000) "Electronic Privacy." Statement before the H.R. Comm. On the Judiciary, Subcomm. On the Constitution, 106th Cong 2.

Dowley, Michael. 2002. "Government Surveillance Powers under the USA Patriot Act: Is It Possible to Protect National Security and Privacy at the Same Time? A Constitutional Tug-of-War." *Suffolk University Law Review* 36: 165.

Graham, Robert. 2001. "Carnivore FAQ." (October 6, 2001) Available: www.robertgraham.com/pubs/carnivore-faq.html.

Haglund, Rich. 2003. "Applying Pen Register and Trap and Trace Devices to Internet Communications: As Technology Changes, Is Congress or the Supreme Court Best-Suited to Protect Fourth Amendment Expectations of Privacy?" *Vanderbilt Journal of Entertainment Law and Practice* 5: 137.

Hector, Matthew. 2003. "Privacy to be Patched in Later, An Examination of the Decline of Privacy Rights." *John Marshall Law Review* 36: 985.

Hentoff, Nat. 2003. "Ashcroft Out of Control." (February 28, 2003) Available: www.villagevoice.com/issues/0310/hentoff.php.

Hentoff, Nat. (February 9, 2004). "Rebellion against the Patriot Act; Ashcroft Moves Draw Skepticism." *The Washington Post*, A19.

Horn, Kimberly. 2002 "Privacy versus Protection: Exploring the Boundaries of Electronic Surveillance in the Internet Age." *Fordham Urban Law Journal* 29: 2233.

Ku, Raymond. 2002. "Modern Studies in Privacy Law: Searching for Meaning of Fourth Amendment Privacy after Kyllo v. United States: The Founders' Privacy, the Fourth Amendment and the Power of Technological Surveillance." *Minnesota Law Review* 86: 1325.

Lichtblau, Eric. September 28, 2003. "U.S. Uses Terror Law to Pursue Crimes from Drugs to Swindling." *The New York Times*, sec. 1, p. 1, col. 1.

Lumpkin, Beverly. 2003. "Patriot Act Redux." (February 21, 2003) Available: http://abcnews.go.com/section/us/HallsOf Justice/hallsofjustice.html.

Meola, Marc, and Sam Stormont. 2002. *Starting and Operating Live Virtual Reference Services*. New York: Neal-Schuman.

Mitrano, Tracy. 2002. "Taking the Mystique out of the USA-Patriot Act: Information, Process and Protocol." (May 14, 2002). Available: www.cit.cornell.edu/oit/PatriotAct/article.html.

Osher, Stevon. 2002. "Privacy, Computers and the Internet." *Florida Law Review* 54: 521.

Rackow, Sharon. 2002. "How the USA Patriot Act Will Permit Governmental Infringement upon the Privacy of Americans in the Name of Intelligence Investigations." *University of Pennsylvania Law Review* 150: 1651.

Ramasastry, Anita. 2003. "Patriot Act II: The Sequel: Why It's Even Scarier Than the First Patriot Act." (February 17, 2003). Available: http://writ.news.findlaw.com/ramasastry/20030217.html.

Safeguarding Our Patrons' Privacy: What Every Librarian Needs to Know about the USA Patriot Act and Related Anti-terrorism Measures. 2002. Produced by Lynda Santangelo-Broderson 120 min. Association of Research Libraries. Videocassette.

Safier, Seth. 2000. "Between Big Brother and the Bottom Line: Privacy in Cyberspace." *Virginia Journal of Law and Technology* 5: 6.

Schabner, Dean. 2003. "Conservative Backlash: Provisions of Patriot Act II Draft Worry Those on Right." (March 12, 2003) Available: http://abcnews.go.com/sections/us/2020/conservatives_patriot030312.html.

Scheeres, Julia. 2002. "Where We Stand One Year Later." (September 11, 2002). Available: www.wired.com/news/print/0,1294,55056,00.html.

Singel, Ryan. "Patriot Act II Resurrected?" (August 21, 2003). Available: www.wired.com/news/politics/0,1283,60129,00.html.

United States Foreign Intelligence Surveillance Court of Review. 2002. "In re: Sealed Case No 02–001" (Decided November 18, 2002). Opinion for the Court filed Per Curiam. Available at: www.epic.org/privacy/terrorism/fisa/FISCR_opinion.pdf.

Van Scoy, Amy, and Megan Oakleaf. 2003. "Online Privacy vs. Enhanced Virtual Reference." Presentation at the ACRL Eleventh National Conference, Charlotte, North Carolina, April 10–13, 2003. Available at: www.ala.org/Content/NavigationMenu/ACRL/Events_and_Conferences/vanscoy.PDF.

Chapter 13

The Digital Reference Research Agenda[1]

R. David Lankes

INTRODUCTION

A research agenda is defined as a reference document that seeks to indicate

- The scope and scale of a phenomenon
- What is known about a given phenomenon under investigation
- What gaps are recognized in the understanding of a phenomenon
- A common understanding of the priorities in filling the gaps in understanding

The digital reference research agenda consists of three elements, each of which will be discussed below:

- A definition of digital reference
- A central driving question
- A series of lenses, or approaches to the central question

DEFINITION OF DIGITAL REFERENCE

For the purposes of this agenda, digital reference is defined as **the use of human intermediation to answer questions in a digital environment**. A definition is necessary, but insufficient, to create a research agenda. It is sufficient to identify a field or practice, but it lacks the analytical ability necessary to define the shape and direction of the field. Any domain of inquiry is predicated on a central question.

CENTRAL DRIVING QUESTION

The central driving question provides boundaries for the unique nature of a discipline and situates the domain in the realm of other streams of exploration. In the specific case of digital reference, the central question must address why digital reference is different from traditional library-based reference research and digital library research. It must also, of course, define how digital reference is related to these domains (as well as to information retrieval and computer-mediated communication). The digital reference research agenda poses the following central question in digital reference: **How can human expertise be incorporated effectively and efficiently into information systems to answer information seekers' questions?**

This central question has several components and assumptions that form the basic framework of the research agenda.

Question Components

Question components are defined as the key areas of understanding needed to explore digital reference and those areas from which deeper understanding can be drawn and studies conducted to further the understanding of the central question. They are the atomic units of inquiry that may be shared by many disciplines, but which in combination are unique to the study of digital reference. This agenda defines five question components:

1. **Human expertise**: What is the nature of human expertise in a system? It is proposed, for further exploration, that expertise exists in a continuum from subject knowledge to process knowledge. Subject knowledge is the understanding of a core collection of facts and their interrelations, such as in the field of chemistry, in which the facts

range from natural laws to molecular structures. Process knowledge is defined as the ability to manipulate a system to achieve a desired result and does not require core understanding of the system's content.

2. **Efficiency and effectiveness**: How can the costs and benefits of digital reference be measured and assessed? In this context, efficiency and effectiveness are defined in economic terms, where an ideal state — the most effective service — may be defined as the most parsimonious use of available resources (e.g., time, money, staff).

3. **Information systems**: What is the proper configuration of technologies and resources needed to produce a required output? The concept of "information system" used in the digital reference definition can be characterized as a special case of a general system in which the input to the system is a user question, the process is the involvement of human expertise, and the output is an answer.

4. **Questions**: What is the nature of user input to a digital reference system? The concept of "questions" as expressions of a user's need or a user's cognitive gap introduces a rich area for exploration. The question component refers specifically to the identification, classification, and use of questions.

5. **Answers**: What sets of information, and in what form, can be bundled to satisfy an information need? Like questions, answers are imperfect media used to transfer knowledge from a recognized source of expertise to a recognized point of information need

Underlying these explicit question components are the implicit assumptions described below.

Assumptions

Assumptions are necessary conditions for asking the question or, at the very least, to see the question itself as significant. Like question components, assumptions should be both testable and provocative. That is, they should be susceptible to theoretical and empirical scrutiny as well as able to provide a departure

point for further research and examination. The agenda identifies two significant assumptions:

1. **Human expertise is useful to incorporate into information systems**: If human expertise is not necessary in the
   ongoing functions of an information system, then there
   is no need for the exploration of digital reference.
2. **The digital nature of digital reference systems provides
   a significant differentiating context**: There is a close relationship between the domain of digital reference and
   other allied domains, such as information retrieval, digital libraries, and reference theory. In many ways digital
   reference was born out of the marriage of several lines of
   investigation and practice, but this assumption implies
   that digital reference provides a unique set of questions,
   components, and approaches. In essence, the whole of
   digital reference is greater than (or in this case different
   from) its component progenitors.

The agenda adopts the metaphor of conceptual lenses to discuss how different researchers and different communities might
reflect and build upon the core framework of question components and assumptions.

A SERIES OF LENSES, OR APPROACHES TO THE CENTRAL QUESTION

A "lens" embodies a given community's values and concerns
through which they act. The action may be in research, systems
building, or simply in discussion. The lenses presented are
meant to be significant, but they are by no means complete.
There are unlimited lenses defined by the nature of concern or
preoccupation of a community—and the community may well
be a single person. Among the many lenses are geographical
lenses ("How does this question component work in Canada?");
institutional lenses ("What is the relationship of these assumptions to the work of Syracuse University?"); and personal lenses
("How can I incorporate these research questions in my
study?").

Significant lenses described in this article represent a set of clear and pressing issues (and values) in digital reference as expressed by researchers and the practice community. The lenses also represent broad concerns encompassing a large potential audience of scholars, funding institutions, and practitioners. The agenda incorporates four lenses:

1. **Policy**: The policy lens is concerned with both the process and effect of organizational decision making and the actual products of digital reference.
2. **Systems**: The systems lens focuses on the means by which technologies can be used to improve both the efficiency and effectiveness of digital reference. One should note that this lens differs from the evaluation lens in that measures of efficiency and effectiveness are often seen as secondary to the actual implementation of systems, standards, and procedures.
3. **Evaluation**: The evaluation lens is the means of determining success in digital reference. Evaluations are assumed to be (a) behavioral as they attempt to assess the impact of human behavior and change in both user and expert abilities; (b) technical as they assess the ability of a system to perform as designed and expected; and (c) economic as they assess digital reference systems' ability to account for and be effective stewards of the resources used in delivering service.
4. **Behavior**: The behavioral lens focuses on human attitudes and interactions with and within a digital reference system.

Representing the Agenda

There are a number of ways the framework of question components, assumptions, and lenses can be presented. Examples of two representations are shown here. The first is graphical as seen in Figure 13–1.

In Figure 13–1, digital reference is shown as question components and assumptions (on the bottom) and lenses (on the top). Each lens is also linked to differing fields of inquiry, which

Figure 13–1
The Digital Reference Research Assumptions and Lenses

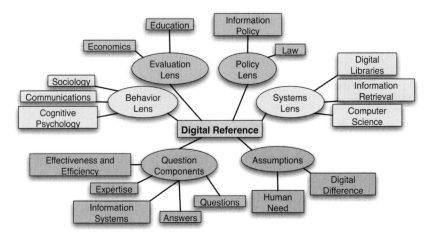

are situated around the periphery of the upper part of the graphic. Perhaps more usefully, the framework can be presented as a matrix, where the horizontal axis represents lenses and the vertical axis represents question components (see Table 13–1). The research questions are organized into a matrix drawn from the framework outlined previously. While domain interconnections are not explicitly stated, the author assumes that these domains will aid in the determination of methodology, reporting, and potentially theory development.

This matrix is far from complete. It represents an opportunistic view. Empty cells do not represent a lack of research potential, but rather a lack of immediately identifiable research projects. The agenda assumes that this matrix will change over time as some research questions are answered and new questions are identified.

Table 13–1
The Digital Reference Research Lenses and Questions

	Policy	Systems	Evaluation	Behavior
Human Expertise				
The value of human expertise What does a user and/or system gain by the inclusion of human expertise and mediation?	What level of staff expertise and training is required to provide high-quality digital reference services?	How can the output of digital reference be incorporated into digital collections?	What are the perceived values of human expertise by the users (e.g., familiarity of a human voice, content expertise, process expertise, instruction)?	Do users phrase questions differently when they know a human intermediary is involved?
The functions of human expertise What is the scale and scope of human involvement in digital reference services?		What is the relationship of question answering to other roles, such as knowledge base construction?	How are non-question-answering functions of human expertise measured and evaluated?	
Efficiency and Effectiveness				
Cost What is the cost of human expertise in the digital reference system?	What are the limits to service provided to the users (e.g., providing answers versus citations)? What are the methods for determining these limits (e.g., are these limits context dependent or universal to digital reference services)?		What are the metrics and standards needed to evaluate costs in digital reference? What factors must be considered in a cost equation (e.g., staff time, resource expense)?[2] Do these measures change with the digital reference setting (e.g., library, AskA) or the scale of the service (e.g., local settings versus consortium services)?	Does knowledge of the costs affect use of the system (e.g., are users willing to pay for digital reference services)? How can a digital reference market or service assign cost to a question a priori (i.e., before a question is answered)?
Benefits What are the benefits of human involvement in digital reference systems?			What are the metrics and standards needed to evaluate benefits in digital reference (e.g., return use, satisfaction)?	
Value What is the necessary level of value demanded by users in digital reference systems?		What level of automation can be brought to bear in digital reference services?		Can users make value judgments in digital reference services?

Table 13–1 *(Continued)*
The Digital Reference Research Lenses and Questions

	Policy	Systems	Evaluation	Behavior
Information Systems				
System Components What is the proper configuration of technologies and resources to produce a required output?	What policies are needed to ensure the appropriate use of digital reference systems? How can digital reference systems be constructed to protect individual privacy and licensing while achieving maximum benefit for an intended community?	What are the required components of a digital reference system?	What are appropriate performance metrics for system evaluation?	How do experts and users interact in a digital reference system? What are the needed skills and training for acquiring a digital reference system?
System models and architectures How can digital reference systems be represented and conceptualized?		Is there a single high-level architecture that represents both real-time and asynchronous systems? What is the value of inductive versus deductive system construction?		
Interoperability How can digital reference services find and ensure proper levels of interoperability?	What policies and policy instruments are needed for service collaboration?	What technical standards are needed to ensure service interoperability (e.g., NISO Networked Reference Committee[3])?		
Questions				
Questions as input What is the nature of user input to a digital reference system?		Are there identifiable taxonomies of questions? Do these taxonomies provide functional and computational power in digital reference systems (e.g., for automatic question routing)?	Do questions to a digital reference service qualitatively change in nature over time (e.g., become harder or more synthesis oriented)?	What digital aids can be provided to users so that they can better phrase their information needs?

Table 13–1 *(Continued)*
The Digital Reference Research Lenses and Questions

	Policy	Systems	Evaluation	Behavior
The reference interview[4] What is the role of the reference interview in digital reference?		How do digital reference systems best elicit the information needs of users (e.g., through human-to-human reference interviews, Web forms, or serial e-mail)? Does the method change based on information need?	What is the current state of practice in digital reference question negotiation? What are the best indicators and measures of success of the reference interview?	
Answers				
Satisfaction What set of information and in what form can that information be bundled to satisfy an information need?	What policies are needed to bind answer types to a service (e.g., copyright)?	How can systems automatically match user questions to appropriate answer types?	What measures are needed to evaluate "right" and "wrong" answers in digital reference?	What components of an answer are needed to meet a user's information need?

NOTES

1. This document is the result of wide-scale input from the symposium participants and from the co-editors of the *Digital Reference Research Agenda* book, Scott Nicholson and Abby Goodrum. Special thanks also to Jeffrey Pomerantz for his contributions.
2. See McClure et al. (2002) for an example.
3. See www.niso.org for more information.
4. It has been a longstanding practice of librarians to conduct an interview constituted of a series of open- and closed-ended questions to identify the compromised information need (Taylor, 1968). In a digital environment, some services have attempted to replicate this human-to-human exchange in so-called real-time systems. Other services, primarily asynchronous services, have sought to replicate this process through the use of Web forms or iterative e-mails.

REFERENCES

McClure, Charles R., R. David Lankes, Melissa Gross, and Beverly Choltco-Devlin, eds. 2002. *Statistics, Measures and Quality Standards for Assessing Digital Reference Library Services: Guidelines and Procedures.* Available: http://quartz.syr.edu/quality/quality.pdf.

Taylor, Robert S. 1968. "Question-Negotiation and Information Seeking in Libraries." *College & Research Libraries* 29: 178–194

Index

About the Editors

CHRISTINA M. FINNERAN

A Ph.D. student at the School of Information Studies at Syracuse University, Christina M. Finneran's primary research interest is digital libraries. She is currently working on a project funded by the National Science Digital Library to evaluate metadata using metrics from both the user and the system perspective. Finneran holds a B.S. from Cornell University, an M.A. in Geographic Information Systems from the State University of New York at Buffalo, and an M.S.L.I.S. from Syracuse University. Her professional experience includes working as a research and instruction specialist at Wellesley College Science Library as well as conducting needs assessments and designing user interfaces for Geographic Information Systems.

JOSEPH JANES

Joseph Janes is associate professor and associate dean for academics at the Information School of the University of Washington and founding director of the Internet Public Library. A frequent guest speaker in the U.S. and abroad, he is the co-author of eight books on librarianship, technology, and their relationship, including *Introduction to Reference Work in the Digital Age*. He writes the "Internet Librarian" column for *American Libraries* magazine. He holds an M.L.S. and Ph.D. from Syracuse University, and has taught at the University of Michigan, the University of North Carolina at Chapel Hill, the State University of New York at Albany, as well as at Syracuse and Washington.

R. DAVID LANKES

R. David Lankes, Ph.D., is executive director of the Information Institute of Syracuse (IIS) and an assistant professor at Syracuse University's School of Information Studies. The IIS houses the Gateway to Educational Materials (GEM), the Virtual Reference Desk (VRD), the Educator's Reference Desk, and several projects related to the NSF's National Science Digital Library (NSDL). Lankes received his B.F.A. (multimedia design), M.S. in telecommunications, and Ph.D. from Syracuse University. Lankes' research is in education information and digital reference services. He has authored, co-authored, or edited eight books, and written numerous book chapters and journal articles on the Internet and digital reference. He was a visiting scholar to Harvard's Graduate School of Education and is currently a visiting fellow at the National Library of Canada.

LINDA C. SMITH

Linda C. Smith is professor and associate dean in the Graduate School of Library and Information Science at the University of Illinois at Urbana-Champaign (UIUC) where she joined the faculty in 1977. Dr. Smith holds a Ph.D. from the School of Information Studies, Syracuse University. Her research interests include information system design, education for library and information science, and the impact of new technologies on reference and information services. She is currently investigating models for online pedagogy and implications for faculty development. Her major teaching responsibilities are reference; scientific, technical, and medical information; and online information systems. She is a co-editor of the textbook *Reference and Information Services: An Introduction* (Libraries Unlimited, 3rd edition, 2001) and has authored several journal articles and conference papers. She received the Isadore Gilbert Mudge-R. R. Bowker Award for Distinguished Contribution to Reference Librarianship in 2000.

About the Contributors

LEELA E. BALRAJ

Leela Balraj received her M.L.S. from Kent State University in 1994. She has been an information services librarian at Kent State's Main Library since 1994 and is currently Liaison Librarian for the College of Education. She was involved with the library's implementation of their Ask-a-Librarian e-mail service in 1998. She was also involved with Kent State's first synchronous virtual reference initiative using H323 software and Web cams in 2001. Since August 2002 she has been staffing and coordinating Kent State's participation with their statewide library consortium's chat service.

HENRY BANKHEAD

Henry Bankhead is a recent graduate from the Masters program in Library and Information Science at San Jose State University. He studied anthropology as an undergraduate at Stanford University, and went on to obtain an MFA in painting from the San Francisco Art Institute. He is currently a librarian at the Gilroy Library, part of the Santa Clara County Library System. He is a member of the Special Libraries Association and the American Bamboo Society.

JESSICA G. BELL

Jessica Bell is a reference and instruction librarian at Lesley University in Cambridge, Massachusetts. She provides services to both on- and off-campus students and manages the instruction schedule and the freshman library-instruction program. She received her M.S. in library science from Simmons College and her B.A. from Tufts University.

GLEN BENCIVENGO

A graduate of Rutgers, Cornell, and Columbia Universities, Glen Bencivengo has worked as an academic, law, public, and special librarian. After graduating from law school in 1989 and being admitted to the New Jersey Bar, Bencivengo worked as a law clerk to a New Jersey Superior Court judge and practiced law. Since 1998 he has been an associate professor at the Pratt Institute School of Information and Library Science, where he teaches courses in law librarianship and legal research, database searching, and a general introduction to the information and library science professions. He has presented papers on knowledge management, virtual reference, and legal research techniques and has written about how the Internet has affected the legal profession. In addition to his law degree, he holds degrees in American history and library science. His current research interests center around the USA Patriot Act, Internet privacy and virtual reference, e-discovery, the lawyer as counselor, and the law for the learning disabled. He is a member of the American Association of Law Libraries and the New Jersey Bar Association.

JOEL CUMMINGS

Joel Cummings is the Electronic Resources Librarian for the Owen Science and Engineering Library and the Fischer Agricultural Sciences Library of Washington State University, Pullman, Washington. His research interests include SFX and library technology for public services.

LINDA FREDERIKSEN

Linda Frederiksen is the Access Services Librarian at Washington State University Vancouver. Current research projects include virtual reference, electronic document delivery, and distance library services. Linda graduated from Emporia State University in 1997.

ESTHER GILLIE

Esther Gillie serves as the User Services Coordinator and Assistant Professor of Library Administration for the Music Library of the University of Illinois, Urbana Champaign. Her duties include reference services, collection development, and user instruction. Previously, Esther was the Digital Services Coordinator at UIUC, a position where she developed and maintained digital resources and services including online reserves (both print and audio), the Web page for the Music Library, online instruction, the creation of online access tools, and digital preservation projects. Esther has a Bachelor's degree in Music from Skidmore College, and an M.S. degree in Library and Information Science from the University of Illinois, Urbana Champaign. She also serves as Secretary for the Association of Recorded Sound Collections (ARSC) and is a member of the Music Library Association (MLA), and the American Choral Director's Association (ACDA).

LYDIA EATO HARRIS

Lydia Eato Harris is currently a doctoral student at The Information School, University of Washington. Her research areas include digital reference, reference education in library and information science programs, information-seeking in context, and the application of activity theory to user studies. Her contributed chapter is a summary of her presentations to the Virtual Reference Desk Conferences from 2001, 2002, and 2003. Lydia is a Project Athena Fellow — a fellowship program funded by the Institute of Museum and Library Services focusing on recruiting and educating the next generation of library and information science faculty. She has a B.A. in psychology from Wesleyan University (CT), an M.S. in Human Development and Family Studies from The Pennsylvania State University, and an M.L.I.S. from the University of Illinois Urbana-Champaign. Previously, Lydia was an assistant professor of psychology at Bloomsburg State [College] University (PA), a research analyst for a private firm, and worked for the U.S. Bureau of the Census in Alaska.

M. KATHLEEN KERN

M. Kathleen Kern is an Assistant Reference Librarian at the Central Reference Library of the University of Illinois at Urbana-Champaign. She co-manages the library's three and a half year old chat reference service and supervises the graduate assistants who staff the Information Desk. She is active in the Reference and User Services Division of ALA and co-chairs the committee which is developing guidelines for the implementation and evaluation of virtual reference services. Kathleen has an M.S.L.I.S. from the University of Illinois at Urbana-Champaign and a B.A. in Religious Studies from Grinnell College. Her primary areas of research are management of chat reference and evaluation of reference services.

APRIL P. LEVY

April Levy is a Reference and Instruction Librarian at Lesley University in Cambridge, Massachusetts. She coordinates the scheduling and training for in-person and digital reference services to on- and off-campus students. Previously, April served as off-campus services librarian at Austin Peay State University. She received her M.L.S. from Indiana University and her B.A. from Oberlin College.

ERICA B. LILLY

Erica Lilly received her M.L.S. from University of Maryland in 1987. She has served as both Coordinator, Electronic Information Services and Reference Librarian at Kent State's Main Library from 1995–2003, where she coordinated the development of the first two versions of the Libraries' Web site and is currently Liaison Librarian for Biological Sciences, Biomedical Sciences, Geology, and the School of Exercise, Leisure and Sport. She has participated in the OhioLINK consortium's statewide chat service since Fall 2002. Her prior positions include science librarian at Miami University (Ohio) and reference and cataloging librarian at the National Institutes of Health Division of Computer Research and Technology.

ROBERT S. MARTIN

Robert S. Martin, Ph.D., Director of the Institute of Museum and Library Services, is a distinguished library professional, author, and educator. He was nominated to be Director of the Institute of Museum and Library Services by President George W. Bush, and confirmed by the U.S. Senate, in July 2001. Prior to his appointment to IMLS, Dr. Martin was Professor and Interim Director of the School of Library and Information Studies at Texas Woman's University, and Associate Dean of Libraries for Special Collections at Louisiana State University. He has also worked in the archives and special collections at the University of Texas at Arlington and the University of Texas at Austin, and taught at the University of Wisconsin at Madison. He has authored, co-authored, or edited several publications, and has served on editorial and advisory boards for scholarly library journals and other publications.

ALISON C. MORIN

Alison C. Morin, Digital Reference Specialist, has been a member of the CDRS/QuestionPoint/Ask a Librarian team at the Library of Congress since 2001, primarily focusing on the development and implementation of digital reference services. She is a member of the Library of Congress' Advisory Group for Digital Reference and has been added to the National Information Standards Organization (NISO), Networked Reference Services, Standards Committee AZ. In addition, Mrs. Morin is the coordinator of the Library of Congress' Luminary Lectures @ Your Library, instituted by the Public Service Collections Directorate at the Library of Congress. She is an M.L.S. graduate from San Jose State University in San Jose, California, and is a member of the Beta Phi Mu Omega Chapter. The views expressed in this paper are her personal views and do not represent those of the Library of Congress.

JEFFREY POMERANTZ

Jeffrey Pomerantz is Assistant Professor in the School of Information and Library Science at the University of North Carolina–Chapel Hill. He earned his Ph.D. in Information Transfer from the School of Information Studies at Syracuse University in 2003. He is currently working with the State Library of North Carolina as the program evaluator of NCknows, the State Library's new chat-based reference service. He is a Research Scientist for the Information Institute of Syracuse, and has been closely involved in the Institute's work on developing user services for the National Science Digital Library. Pomerantz's research seeks the appropriate balance between automation and human-intermediated services in the various contexts of traditional and digital library environments. Much of his work has been in the arena of virtual reference services, and the integration of virtual reference services into digital library collections.

JOSEPH A. SALEM, JR.

Joseph Salem received his M.L.S. from Kent State University in 1999. He has worked as a Government Documents Librarian at the Kent State University Main Library since January 2000 and assumed his current position as Coordinator of Government Documents and Head of the Map Library in 2002. As a member of the Main Library's Reference Services Team, Professor Salem staffs Kent State's online chat hours as part of the University's involvement in OhioLINK's statewide "Chat with a Librarian" service.

JOSEPH E. STRAW

Joseph Straw, Associate Professor of Library Administration at the University of Illinois at Urbana-Champaign, received his M.L.S. degree at Kent State University in Ohio in 1993 and his M.A. degree in history from Kent State University in 1994. Currently he is the Instructional Coordinator for the Reference Library at the University of Illinois

BETH THOMSETT-SCOTT

Beth Thomsett-Scott has been a librarian for eight years and is active in reference, Web, user needs, and information literacy activities. She has given several talks on focus groups and presented a variety of sessions on Web site usability. Her professional goal is to ensure that her patrons are able to access and retrieve the information they need in the most efficient and effective manner. Beth has a B.Sc. (Agriculture), M.Sc. (Agriculture) and received her M.L.I.S. in 1995 from the University of Western Ontario. After working for a year in the former Engineering Library, she worked for several years at the University of Guelph. Beth currently works in the Science and Technology Library at the University of North Texas where she is the Biology and Chemistry Librarian.

LARA URSIN

Lara Ursin is the Instruction Librarian at Washington State University–Pullman. Her current research interests include library services for distance education students, digital reference issues and the first year experience. She earned her M.L.I.S from the College of Library and Information Sciences at the University of South Carolina in 2001.